Also available from Camphor Press and Eastbridge Books

FORMOSA BETRAYED, BY GEORGE H. KERR
A TASTE OF FREEDOM, BY PENG MING-MIN

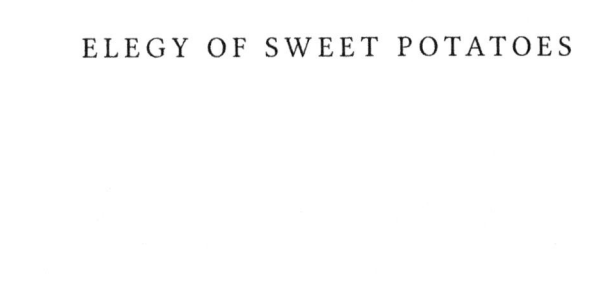

ELEGY OF SWEET POTATOES

Elegy of Sweet Potatoes
Stories of Taiwan's White Terror
Tehpen Tsai

A Camphor Press book

Published by Camphor Press Ltd
83 Ducie Street, Manchester, M1 2JQ United Kingdom
www.camphorpress.com
Copyright © 2002 Taiwan Publishing Co.
Republished with the kind permission of the Taiwan Publishing Co.
All rights reserved. This edition 2021.
This edition has been reset.
ISBN   978-1-78869-243-4 (paperback)
           978-1-78869-244-1 (hardcover)
The moral right of the author has been asserted.
Set in 10 pt Linux Libertine
Except in the United States of America, this book is sold subject to the condition that it shall not, by way of trade or otherwise, be lent, re-sold, hired out, or otherwise circulated without the publisher's prior consent in any form if binding or cover other than that in which it is published and without a similar condition including this condition being imposed on the subsequent purchaser.

The author shortly before his arrest in October, 1954

The author as he began this book, 1993

The author with Huang Chi-nan in 1995

The author with Mosula (Ye Chin-kuei) in 1996

The author with Wu Che-fu in 1997

The author with translator Grace Hatch in 1999

*The author with George Chang, mayor of Tainan,
at the Fu-Cheng Literature Awards in 2000*

The author with his wife, enjoying life outdoors in 1998

Contents

	Translator's Note	xv
	Author's Preface	xvi
	Peng Ming-min's Preface to the Mandarin Edition	xvii
1.	Under the Pomelo Tree	1
2.	Chi-lin! Chi-lin!	7
3.	Arrest	9
4.	Heading East on Tropic of Cancer Highway	13
5.	Self-Renewal Policy	17
6.	Choose One of the Two	19
7.	The Mouse That Supped with the Cat	21
8.	Now, Write!	25
9.	What to Write	27
10.	This Friend, That Friend	29
11.	Tough Guy — Yu-kun	33
12.	Restoration — A Moving Experience	35
13.	Ah! Blue Sky, White Sun (*Ch'ing-t'ien, pai-jih*)	39
14.	Drama Society and Friendship Association	43
15.	A Kind Secret Police	47
16.	A Ray of Hope Vanished	51
17.	Li Shui-ching — A Man from the Same Hometown	53
18.	A Crazy Fellow	59
19.	About Books	63
20.	Wires Around His Neck	67
21.	A Childhood Chum	69
22.	Undershirt	73
23.	Big Shantung	77
24.	Ho's Complaints	79
25.	A Friend Named Francesco	81
26.	Su's Violence	87
27.	Compromise	89
28.	Long Whiskers	93
29.	Ho's True Nature	95

30.	Toward an Unknown World	99
31.	A Lad in the Same Cell	103
32.	A Killer	107
33.	Scream of Self Recrimination	111
34.	Inventory Clearance	113
35.	Political Prisoners Who Were Left Behind	115
36.	The Sobbing New Inmate	119
37.	Shouts of Wan-sui	123
38.	On the Night Train to Taipei	127
39.	New Cellmates	131
40.	Dragon-Head Peng	135
41.	The Sundry Criminals	139
42.	Long-Denied Enjoyment	143
43.	A Feast	145
44.	Re-interrogation	149
45.	Statue of Liberty	153
46.	The Doctor Who Was Not Immunized	157
47.	Regrets	161
48.	To the Military Court	163
49.	Unexpected Welcome	167
50.	New Brothers	173
51.	Open-air Bath	177
52.	Lovable Little Lu	181
53.	Five-Star Flag on the Window	185
54.	The Village of Luku	187
55.	Flimflam Loo	191
56.	The Permanently Un-sentenced	195
57.	Letters	201
58.	Reward for a Favor	205
59.	A Mistake of One Character	209
60.	A Puzzling Message	213
61.	A Spy-Judge	215
62.	Talk of Divorce	219
63.	A Momentary Reunion	223
64.	Questioning in Court	227
65.	Petacos (White Helmets) Are Here	233

66.	The True Meaning of *Zaijian* (Meet Again)	239
67.	Sending Chin-huo Off	243
68.	Brother Lung	247
69.	New Year's Day	251
70.	Sent to the Investigation Bureau	255
71.	Little Devils	259
72.	People at the Crypt	261
73.	The Bull's Final Struggle	265
74.	Picture	269
75.	Anti-Communist Freedom Fighters	273
76.	It's Wiser to Let the Matter Drop	277
77.	Life-Extending Tactic	279
78.	A Helplessly Nice Guy	283
79.	Favorite Songs	287
80.	A Forerunner of the Independence Movement	291
81.	A Middle-of-the-Night Happening	295
82.	A Request to Confront the Accuser	299
83.	Return to the Old Nest	301
84.	Message from the Next Cell	305
85.	Prison Divorce	307
86.	Chou Shui's Mother	309
87.	A Friend of the Bull	313
88.	Lin the Bull, Covered in Blood	317
89.	Shen's Verdict	321
90.	An Old Taiwanese Communist	325
91.	Implicated by a Big Fish	331
92.	Cousin Tien	335
93.	A Common-Law Wife	337
94.	Two Documents	341
95.	The Decision on Ex-policeman Wu	345
96.	Loo Spoke of Mosula	349
97.	Leaving the Military Court Prison	353
98.	Beginning Re-education	357
99.	A Rain Shower	363
100.	Two Section Leaders	367
101.	Unexpected Reunion	371

102.	Study Session	377
103.	Visitation	381
104.	America Amid the Bitter Sea	385
105.	Walk with Mosula	387
106.	A Parting Note	393
107.	A Phantom	397
108.	On the Train	401
109.	To Repay Enmity with Virtue	405
110.	A Father's Heartbreak	409
111.	Individual Conversation	413
112.	Parting with Mosula	419
113.	Release from Prison	423
114.	Going Home	429
	Postscript	433
	Historical Chronology	435

Translator's Note

I am profoundly grateful and honored to have been entrusted with the English translation of this fictionalized memoir.

I was thirteen in 1953 when my uncle, the author, was arrested. I remember vividly the family trauma of his imprisonment and the subsequent years of fear all through my school years in Taiwan. The arrest, imprisonment, and execution did not happen to most of us. Nevertheless, my generation suffered the long shadow of the White Terror, which imprisoned our souls and turned us into the "silenced majority" for decades.

This translation is based on the Japanese original, with some minor modifications supplied by the author. The romanization of the names of people and places are based on Chinese Mandarin pronunciations, with some exceptions when minor fictional characters are involved and a Japanese pronunciation seemed more readable and memorable. The names of the many, actual historical persons are done in Wade-Giles, while liberty was taken for fictional characters to increase familiarity. For "Chinese savvy" readers, the unorthodox romanization may seem off-putting; but the reality is that English names for Taiwanese people — be they government officials, well-known literati, or students on U.S. campuses — are truly "free form." In fact, to be true to the language of the time, most names in this book should be either in Japanese or Taiwanese, not Mandarin.

I am indebted to my husband, George Hatch, for counsel and encouragement, and to Ellie Yuska, my daughter, for a valiant editing effort. I am also grateful to the many friends and family who have offered practical advice as well as abundant moral support. Lastly, I am grateful to the author for his diligent proofreading, patience, and unfailing faith in this project.

Grace Tsai Hatch
August 31, 2000

Author's Preface

Since time immemorial, Taiwanese people called themselves "sweet potatoes." This is because the island uncannily resembles a sweet potato and also because sweet potatoes are the chief crop of its immigrant pioneers and remains a mainstay of the Taiwanese diet. Sadly there were times when many farmers toiled tirelessly in their rice paddies, only to fill their stomachs with sweet potato sticks, unable to afford a grain of rice. Indeed, the relationship between sweet potatoes and Taiwan is truly intimate and the affection that the Taiwanese hold for sweet potatoes is literally deep-rooted.

Taiwan's history of the recent centuries may be termed a history of successive foreign domination. The sweet potatoes on this island were ruled, oppressed and abused. While the rulers walked away with their golden eggs, the people were left to eat the humble sweet potatoes. Unavoidably, many memorable rebellions and heroic sacrifices occurred throughout this time and the elegies never ceased. However, the most heart wrenching and at once most enduring are the elegies from all over Taiwan after the end of the Second World War. The sorrowful tunes persisted for forty years.

Perhaps out of oversight or maybe out of helplessness, the modern mass media has neglected its duty by burying this sorrowful past. As a result, people are ignorant of the reality of political terror, even to the degree of regarding victims as evil doers.

But regardless of one's political outlook, it is undeniable that a terrifying reign of political terror existed.

In this book, based on my personal experience, I merely sketched a small portion of it in fictional form. It is like a yellowed photograph from that terrifying period.

As we congratulate ourselves on the passing of the reign of terror (maybe not entirely over), we need to strive to establish a genuine, democratic nation. We must refuse to ever again live in the shadow of terror. I hope all the peoples on this island will get along in peace and redouble their efforts to prevent the reappearance of another regime of terror.

February 1995

Peng Ming-min's Preface to the Mandarin Edition

A despotic nation must necessarily produce political prisoners, and they in turn will create a unique genre of literature: prison literature. The Soviet Union had it, the Eastern bloc nations had it, likewise Cuba and China. Taiwan is no exception.

Taiwan was ruled as a Japanese colony for fifty years. Then, in 1945, it again fell to the hands of the feudal, backward, and barbaric Chinese tyranny. To this day, its existence and its future are still seriously threatened by the same kind of Chinese.

In the several decades since the massacre of February 28, 1947, countless Taiwanese people of idealism, of conviction, who believed in democratic principles, have been persecuted, arrested, imprisoned, tortured, and killed. It is an unbearable history.

Mr. Tsai Tehpen wrote about his experience in Japanese, exposing most graphically the vileness, cruelty, and ugliness of the Chinese regime. At the same time, he fully expressed the courage, the harrowing sorrow, and the utter helplessness of the victims of political persecution. His writing is penetrating yet true to the facts, humble without being self-debasing, plain speaking and devoid of self-aggrandizement. It is without qualification an outstanding work of "prison literature." Now with the publication of this story in Chinese, a broad readership will be able to appreciate this special genre of literature. I think this is quite significant. To a former political prisoner like myself, the book elicits empathic memories of the past, the bottomless lament. To a general reader, it will enhance his understanding of Taiwan's past history of political terror. Especially when the bells of democratic reform are ringing loud and clear in the air as they are now, this book will cause thoughtful people to reflect on the painful sacrifices and the enormous price paid by the previous generations of democrats. In this way, it is also valuable material for Taiwan's socio-political history.

Lastly, as a Taiwanese, I want to say that I sympathize with the sense of injustice born by Mr. Tsai, as well as to express my deepest respect for his writing effort. At the same time, I would like to recommend this book to all who are concerned with Taiwan's political and social development.

February 1995

ELEGY OF SWEET POTATOES

1

Under the Pomelo Tree

It was Saturday, October 2, 1954. The sky was clear, the sun brilliant, the southerly breeze gentle and pleasant. It looked to be another peaceful day. But to Youde, this day was the beginning of the nightmare that he would not forget for the rest of his life.

That afternoon, under the pomelo tree in his backyard, Youde was playing *go* (black-and-white chess) with his grade school classmate Yung-chuan. The spot was cool, amply shaded by luxuriant, overlapping leaves. Youde was in the habit of leaving the *go* table out there, where he would sometimes study the manuals by himself or play a game or two with his *go* cronies, Yung-chuan among them. They were comparable in skill. This afternoon, as always, they started alternately with black stones.

"Hey, you haven't lost any of it, not only that, your game has gotten better, even though you haven't touched the thing for a whole year," Yung-chuan said. "I think maybe a stay in America did make you stronger in *go*. I wonder if it helps *go* when one broadens his horizons."

Youde had just returned from a year in America. He was granted a leave of absence from his teaching job to study abroad with an all expenses paid government scholarship. During the year abroad, his horizons had indeed broadened greatly.

At that time, America was at the height of its economic prosperity. Under the aegis of the Marshall Plan, America was spreading its wealth to assist the economic development of many poor countries. Even though the war effort ended eight years earlier, Taiwan had not yet recovered from extreme devastation and a shortage of goods. The country was barely sufficient in rice, its main staple. Electrical appliances such as refrigerators and televisions were literally unimaginable. Like any citizen from a war-ravaged country in Southeast Asia, Youde felt his trip to America was no less than a beggar's tour of heaven. To him, even tin cans and packing materials were too precious to be thrown away.

A year ago in Putzu, a town of thirty thousand people that borders the Tropic of Cancer, when the news arrived that Youde was selected to go to America to study, the town's people were surprised and delighted for him. He was the pride of the town.

Youde was an English teacher at the newly established Putzu High School. Having graduated from the Normal University of Taipei at a time when qualified English teachers were in short supply, he had chosen to return to his hometown in spite of more lucrative job offers in the city. Just at this juncture, the Marshall Plan passed the American Congress and the Republic of China in Taiwan became an aid recipient. The amount of 100 million dollars per annum was akin to rain during a drought for Taiwan, a country whose foreign currency reserve was practically nil at the time. U.S. aid dollars were used mostly for direct economic aid; but a portion of the amount was allocated to promote democracy in education as well. Among the programs, one was to send educators to America to observe firsthand democracy in action. Youde was very fortunate to be the only applicant selected, being only a lowly high school teacher. Three criteria were used to review the applicants: first, the person had to have graduated from an accredited college; second, the person had to be fluent in English; and third, the person must have taught for at least three years.

In addition, there was one essential pre-condition: the candidate must be a member of the Chinese Nationalist Party, the Kuomintang (KMT).

Youde had joined the Kuomintang soon after graduation. At the time, all college graduates were forced to go through a job orientation program to gain employment. However, the high-sounding, so called "job program" was in reality a mechanism for thought control. One on one, the counselor then urged the graduate to join the KMT.

"The Party needs able intellectuals like you," the counselor said. "Besides, it would be wise for you to join the Party. You should do it for the country, for the Party, but also for your own good. If you say yes, we can get the president of your college and the director of this program to be your sponsors, both are big names in the Party, you know. So you see, it is to your advantage to join now rather than later. In any case, there will be no path of advancement unless you join the Party. For example.... Now do the right thing and show us the spirit of the true patriotic youth that you are."

The counselor openly urged and pressured. As if destined, many Taiwanese joined the Party. Not a few, however, resolutely refused and chose to face a life of teaching with no advancement.

Youde had solicited advice from his uncle with regard to joining the Kuomintang. The uncle, a graduate of Tokyo's medical school and a general practitioner in town, was highly regarded for his knowledge and insight; a *kungming* (an ancient Chinese wise man), some called him.

"Go ahead and join the KMT," he had advised. "The way I see it, you would not be joining to gain advancement. The Kuomintang government is indeed corrupt, but at least it still propounds democracy — and that makes it better than the Communists. If good, righteous young Taiwanese join the Party in numbers, I think we Taiwanese will eventually gain a voice in the Party and some of our proposals will perhaps prevail."

Youde joined the Kuomintang and, along with three hundred others, was sworn in at KMT headquarters. Right before the swearing-in ceremony, Hsiao, a graduate of the department of Chinese literature, patted Youde's shoulder from behind. He said with a smirk, "So you too joined the muddied."

To join the muddied is a Chinese expression. It means a clear stream running into a muddied river and thus losing its own purity. Hsiao acted embarrassed, as if he was partaking in a Satanic rite and selling his soul. Youde chuckled and said, "If there are more clear streams joining the river, even the big muddy can eventually become clear."

Shoulder to shoulder, the two entered the hall. They raised their hands and were sworn in.

And, barely three years later, the reward arrived. Youde was allowed to go abroad to study, or to be exact, to become a trainee in the U.S. aid program. During his absence, his family in Taiwan was to receive his school salary in full while he himself was to receive a three-hundred-dollar monthly stipend from the U.S. government. At a time when the monthly salary of a college graduate was a mere thirty dollars, it was a sweet deal indeed! An additional stipend of US$150 was given out for travel preparation. On September 1, with US$150 in his pocket and a Northwest Airline travel bag swung over his shoulder, his chest swelling with hope, Youde boarded a propeller airplane for Tokyo's Haneda airport together with three other trainees. They were to stay overnight in Tokyo then continue their journey to Seattle in a larger propeller plane. In Tokyo, through the car window, Youde saw that the city had returned to peace yet was littered with remnants of wartime fire bombings. Here and there, people gathered in front of shops to watch television. In the entertainment district U.S. soldiers swaggered as if they owned the place.

To Youde, Tokyo was not new. He had attended this city's high school. For five years, he had lived the stoic wartime life of this city. Then in 1943, when Japan's defeat had become quite apparent, he gave up the hope of attending a university in Japan and returned to Taiwan by boat, taking considerable risks. The boat took thirteen days to reach Keelung — normally only a two-day journey. Upon his return, Youde took a job as a substitute teacher in his hometown of Putzu but was soon drafted into the Japanese military and greeted the end of the war eight months later. After the war, he again left home and entered the Normal University in Taipei.

Nevertheless, seeing Tokyo after eight years, Youde was filled with longing, stirred by sentiments from his youth. That evening, he purchased a suit, a suitcase, and other things from a department store — spending all of fifty dollars (U.S. dollars were worth a lot then). The next morning the traveling trainees once more boarded the late-model propeller plane and flew toward America.

The America that Youde found was full of confidence; its mainland received not a scratch of damage during the war. It remained the only number one, wealthy, big power in the world. That year Youde met numerous trainees from the four corners of the world, and they shared their lives in America together. These fortunate people were able not only to live comfortably during their stay but also to take home with them rare and novel goods. Youde, too, lugged home a can opener, an electric shaver, a record player, and an electric fan, among other things, to the envy of many onlookers.

Presently, the melody of "The Tennessee Waltz" from that 33-1/3 LP player wafted through the courtyard and onto the shade underneath the pomelo tree. The music ended after thirty minutes of play.

"Hey, it's finished," Yung-chuan reminded Youde.

"It's OK. The turner will stop automatically," Youde replied without lifting his head from the *go* board.

"So it does! It stops automatically!" Yung-chuan was impressed.

"Sorry, I am taking these." Youde advanced.

*The author and his classmates of George Peabody College,
Nashville, Tennessee*

At a good breaking point in the game, Youde stood up to go inside the house to put on a new record. But this turned out to be unnecessary, as his wife Panto beat him to it. This time a symphony was playing. Youde sat down once more and, with a resounding clack, took a stone.

"I give up." Yung-chuan threw in the towel. That was the third game in a row Youde had beaten him.

"Let's have one more. Boy, you sure did get stronger," Yung-chuan said, combing his fingers through his hair.

Grinning with satisfaction, Youde leaned back in his chair, picked up the glass and drank the iced juice that Panto had set down beside him. The breeze stirred once more. The pomelo leaves trembled.

2

Chi-lin! Chi-lin!

Alerted by the clicking sound of the *go* stones, Youde's only daughter Ah-jing rushed into the courtyard. When Youde left for America, she was eight months old and barely crawling. But now, a year later, she was able to run, was quite a talker, and had quickly become attached to her daddy since his return. Ah-jing had already bathed and had on a nylon dress that Youde had brought home from America. Panto, Youde's wife, had picked out the dress for Ah-jing — her way of hinting that it was time to quit *go* and to take Ah-jing out for a while.

"Papa, chi-lin, chi-lin."

Ah-jing tugged at Youde's hand which was sweeping the *go* stones into the bowls. "Chi-lin, chi-lin," the sound of bicycle bells, was Ah-jing's verb for riding bicycle.

These days, a daily routine for Youde was to perch Ah-jing in a rattan basket seat mounted on the front handle bar of the bicycle and ride around to different places. The bicycle ride was Ah-jing's "chi-lin chi-lin" and her greatest joy. She liked most to ride to the riverbank. In modern times Putzu River skirts the town, then meanders to the fishing port of Tongshih, where it empties into the Taiwan Strait. But in the old days the river was deep enough for ships from China to sail up to Putzu, whereby Putzu prospered into a center of commerce with southern coastal China. After Taiwan became part of Japanese territory, the trade gradually slackened off and the riverbed rose with sand accumulation, so that ships were no longer able to enter the town and Putzu's economy quickly shriveled.

Fortunately or not, Putzu possessed one important characteristic: the town's folk were unusually devoted to their children's education. As a result, its rank of high school and college students had always outnumbered other places. In a steadily deteriorating economy, the investment in education was no doubt quite a burden to many. How sad, it turned out, that many whose parents had exhausted the family savings for their schooling were imprisoned or executed before graduation, bringing not glory and wealth but only tears to their families. Town of Sorrow, its name was Putzu.

"Chi-lin, chi-lin," Ah-jing again tugged at Youde's hand.

"It's about time that somebody else shows up." Youde glanced toward the house. If another person would show up then Yung-chuan could play with the new arrival, freeing Youde to take Ah-jing out for her ride.

Youde's home had been a gathering place for friends and their friends. People came to listen to music, to take part in lively conversations and would often borrow books to take home with them. Whenever he watched their faces immersed in music, Youde was glad that he had lugged the LP player home from America. But today, for some reason, nobody appeared at the house other than Yung-chuan.

Yung-chuan, ignoring Ah-jing's fussing, placed the first black stone on the front star position.

Youde's mother came to the rescue. In her hand she was holding a bowl and a spoon.

"Ah-jing, have some green bean soup," she said and gestured for Ah-jing to come to her. Ah-jing left Youde and ran toward her grandmother. The effortless, harmonious life of this family, four people of three generations, was happiness itself. It would not have been extraordinary for it to go on forever.

But at that very moment the town's police department had already received from the Taipei Garrison Command the order to arrest Tsai Youde and had completed the arrangement to execute the order.

3

Arrest

THE *go* game progressed smoothly. Soon they finished the stone placement and entered the mid-game.

"Anybody home?" a voice came.

In a typical Taiwanese house, it was the custom that gates were left open during the day; and since there were no doorbells, visitors customarily would call out at the door, "Is there anybody home?" while close friends and relatives would often just walk right in.

"Anybody home?" the voice asked again.

"Somebody is finally here," Youde said without lifting his eyes from the board. He assumed the voice belonged to a friend, a late Saturday visitor. The footsteps approached.

Suddenly, Yung-chuan shot up. His sudden motion jiggled the stones violently as his knees were touching the board. His face paled.

Youde looked back toward the house. He saw three large men approaching in a line side by side. One was a policeman in uniform with a gun tucked in the holder. One was detective Hsu, a schoolmate a year ahead of Youde. Hsu was a well-built kid and was on the judo team. Youde had heard that Hsu entered the police-training program upon discharge from the Japanese army. Between the policeman and Hsu was a third man, smaller than the other two, and wearing a Sun Yat-sen suit. From his apparel, it was apparent that he was a mainlander, a *waishengjen*.

The Sun Yat-sen suit, or Chung-shan-fu, originated in China, reportedly designed and favored by Sun Yat-sen, the father of the Chinese republican revolution. The suit has a buttoned-up collar and four gigantic pockets on the outside. When Taiwan was restored to Chinese rule after the war, people had at first saved up their meager income to acquire a Sun Yat-sen suit, as a show of respect for Sun Yat-sen. But as they learned about the true nature of *waishengjen*, Taiwanese stopped donning the suits lest they be taken for *waishengjen*. Cynics joked that the gigantic pockets were better for stuffing the "Sun Yat-sen's," the Taiwan paper bills that carried Sun's likeness.

The man in the Sun Yat-sen suit faced Youde and said, "Are you Tsai Youde?"

"Yes," Youde nodded slightly.

"We would like you to come to headquarters with us."

"Well?"

"It's not a big deal, but we have some things to ask you about, so we decided to ask you to come with us."

His words were polite. Nevertheless, they carried a tone that foreclosed any arguing. Youde noticed also that both Hsu and Sun Yat-sen suit carried pistols on their waists.

"I understand. I will change my clothes presently."

Youde put down his *go* bowl and stood up, "Yung-chuan, I guess this game will just have to wait."

Yung-chuan was stone still, not uttering a sound.

Youde thought himself pretty calm. He had anticipated this day in his imaginings and even dreamed it in his dreams. Even after learning the visitors' intention, Youde did not experience the terror that he had in his dreams.

At the house entrance Youde almost bumped into Panto, who was just hurrying out.

"What's going on?"

"Well, they said that they wanted to question me and would like me to go to headquarters."

Maybe to prevent an escape attempt, the policeman moved to stand by Youde and Panto while Hsu and the Sun Yat-sen suit followed closely behind. Youde went into his bedroom, put on a dress shirt, dropped a pack of cigarettes in the breast pocket, and changed into a pair of slacks.

"Are you all right?" Panto inquired.

The Sun Yat-sen suit, who had followed right into the bedroom, replied for Youde, "Mrs. Tsai, it's nothing. He will probably be back by tonight."

Stepping out of the gate, Youde saw the images of his mother and Ah-jing but had no time to speak to them. In the front, a large jeep was waiting with the engine running. Hsu jumped in first, then pulled Youde up and seated him in the back between himself and the uniformed policeman. The Sun Yat-sen suit rode in the front passenger seat and whispered something to the driver.

Youde turned his head and met Panto's eyes. She had just comprehended the situation. Youde smiled self-consciously and waved. The jeep sounded its horn, jerked, and started out.

Suddenly, from behind Panto, Ah-jing's cry exploded.

"Papa — chi-lin chi-lin. Papa!"

4

Heading East on Tropic of Cancer Highway

The jeep quickly passed through the town and entered the Tropic of Cancer Highway, a well-paved road that runs east–west alongside the Tropic of Cancer demarcation. Tall green trees framed the highway on both sides, creating a scenic vista. Although it was already past four o'clock, the sun's rays were still harsh. Youde, sandwiched between detective Hsu and the policeman, could hardly move his body. It was clear that the jeep was heading for the city of Chiayi, where there were at least three intelligence organizations: the security division of the Taiwan Garrison Command, the Investigation Bureau of the Interior Ministry, and a security office that directly reported to the Defense Ministry. The three organizations were said to outdo one another at arresting suspects in order to court favors.

The jeep swayed and Youde's side touched a hard object — it was the handcuffs hidden under Hsu's coat. "Hsu was considerate not to use the handcuffs on me," Youde thought, and studied Hsu's profile, silent and expressionless, like a lead statue. Youde was not friendly with Hsu but was acquainted with him because they were only a year apart in school. Growing up, Hsu was an energetic athlete and a popular youngster. Because he was the town's police officer, he was always asked to lend his presence whenever the intelligence organization wanted to arrest a young man from Putzu. Youde had heard that Hsu was present at Chang Yu-kun's arrest. Now, all of a sudden, Youde remembered the time in grade school, when Yu-kun and Hsu represented their school and competed in the county-wide athletic meet. Hsu had received the baton from Yu-kun for the last leg of the relay race and had sailed past other runners to crash the goal line. How Youde himself had clapped with frenzy. "Is this some kind of fate?" he wondered.

* * *

Perhaps sensing Youde's glare, Hsu touched his breast pocket and pulled out a pack of cigarettes and silently offered to Youde. Youde thanked him and took a cigarette. Hsu lit the cigarette for Youde.

Puffing on the cigarette, Youde turned his eyes to the sugarcane fields on the sides of the highway. He was unsure about what was to happen next. He knew one was not to be released easily once he was summoned, and he was certain that interrogation, if not torture, awaited him. The important thing to figure out, though, was on whose implication was he being arrested and what he was suspected of having done. He also knew that something, maybe quite trivial to him, could come out differently in the questioning and later cause him to be put to death. There were many cases of people executed for no good reason except having put their thumbprint on the fabricated confessions at the end of long interrogations. He also knew of many who returned from interrogation crippled. It was common knowledge that the intelligence organizations had a special order: "Never miss one true criminal, even if a hundred are killed mistakenly."

But Youde had one strong suit: they had let him go to America only a year ago. At the time, they had conducted a thorough investigation of his "thoughts" before issuing his exit papers, in reality clearing him of his conduct and activities during Youde's college years — the most questionable period. "There shouldn't be any questions about that," Youde thought to himself.

On the highway, there were no other vehicles but for occasional ox-pulled carts on the roadside. Ahead lay the green ranges, standing in sharp relief against the autumnal blue sky. The jeep continued to speed east toward Chiayi. They passed the marker for the Tropic of Cancer and entered the city of Chiayi. The jeep passed through the city's busy marketplace and stopped in front of the Chiayi police headquarters. A plaque in front read "Security Command — Detective Battalion — Chiayi Home Division." To the general public, the various intelligence organizations were very confusing. They were alike yet distinct, and one often found multiple signs hanging in front of a single building.

Chiayi Police Headquarters

Youde, held by each wrist by Hsu and the uniformed police, got off the jeep and was quickly led through the front door. Following the Sun Yat-sen suit, they climbed a flight of stairs. Awaiting them in front of a room were two large men, also clad in Sun Yat-sen suits. Youde was handed over to these two and led into the room. The drapes were drawn despite the daylight. Instead, the room was lit by four or five naked light bulbs. To one side of the room, there were six desks arranged in three facing pairs. Opposite the desks was a sofa set. Youde thought it was a fairly common office — not much for atmosphere, but it did not look like a venue for interrogation either.

One of the large men sat Youde down at the middle desk by the wall while the other set a cup of tea in front of him. The desk was clear save for the cup and an ashtray. The two large men sat down and waited, their work seemingly finished. "What's to follow?" Youde had no idea. Youde took out a cigarette and lit it. He could feel his hand trembling.

5

Self-Renewal Policy

THE door opened. Five or six men entered, a Sun Yat-sen suit in the lead. The man in the Sun Yat-sen suit was different from the previous one in that he appeared more worldly and his suit was of obviously more expensive material.

"This is Captain Tao," the man in the blue shirt said and pulled out the chair opposite Youde. Captain Tao gestured Youde to sit down as Youde stood up to greet him across the desk. The man in the blue shirt leaned on the desk and said to Youde, "Captain Tao thinks rather well of you. Do listen to him carefully. Really, you can't do better than doing as he says."

Other men all took seats around Youde. Three packs of cigarettes were put on the desks. Tao pulled out a cigarette, which was instantly lit by the blue shirt. Captain Tao drew a long one on his cigarette, then said, "So, Mr. Tsai, How was America? Did you have an interesting time?"

"Yes...," Youde hesitated, as the question was quite unexpected.

"You are a lucky man, being selected from among many to go abroad. Our country has spent a lot of money on you and can surely use your service. You have an enviable future awaiting you, Mr. Tsai. You would probably become the principle of the high school in a short time and then advance rapidly from there."

"......"

"But something has happened that only you, yourself, can solve."

Captain Tao's eyes turned menacing.

"All right? It all depends on you. Your brilliant future can vanish in an instant. Are you understanding what I am saying to you?"

"Yes," Youde nodded.

"As you know, we investigated your past before you left for America. To be truthful, at the time, we had different opinions as to whether to let you leave."

The blue shirt weighed in, "It was Captain Tao who made the final favorable decision."

"Thank you." Youde bowed shallowly and uttered his heartfelt gratitude.

"But during your tour abroad, we discovered a blind spot in our investigation."

"……"

"While you were enjoying the good life of America, back here, we were sitting on needles."

Nevertheless, the intelligence organization did not arrest Youde at the airport upon his return. Instead, they had put him under observation and had let him stay home for a whole month.

Captain Tao took a sip of tea and continued, "Are you aware of the Self-Renewal Policy?"

"Yes."

The "Self-Renewal Policy" was a law announced in May 1950, a year after the "Laws on Rebellion" was enacted in June of 1949. Its thrust was that a person, even a Communist Party member, would be rendered not guilty if he came forward voluntarily and supplied all relevant information. It appeared to be a rather lenient law, on the surface, but because tens and even hundreds of arrests could result from one single "Self-Renewal," and also because a slight untruth or a minor omission in the confession could incur the maximum penalty instead, it was also exceedingly cruel.

Captain Tao said," Now, if you lay out all the facts, I will make an effort to apply the Self-Renewal Rule in your case. No, I can even promise you that we will."

"……"

"You wouldn't know, of course, but I have always thought well of you." Tao continued, as the blue shirt was about to interrupt. "I can't stand sending a young man of your bright future to the military court. I hope you understand my feelings."

Captain Tao leaned back and started to drink his tea, fixing a steady gaze into Youde's eyes. Youde, wanting to look away, gingerly picked up his teacup.

6

Choose One of the Two

Finally, Captain Tao stood up and asked, "You know Chen Ming-chih, don't you?"

"Yes, I do."

Ming-chih was a younger brother of Youde's classmate and a childhood friend. A doctor's son, lacking nothing, he was also bright, energetic, and outgoing, and was always bringing new toys to school. He went to Tainan Second High School, then entered National Taiwan University. But then, he abruptly quit school, an act that confounded his friends until this day. He was a strong *go* player who had snatched a title as a freshman. Even with a two-stone advantage, Youde was rarely able to beat him.

Captain Tao said, "Ming-chih came forward and confessed, you know. The Self-Renewal Rule was applied in his case and he is now leading a pleasant life. Isn't it so?"

Youde knew of Ming-chih's affair, that he had turned himself in about three years ago. That night, almost simultaneously, three college students from Putzu who had been home on vacation, were arrested. Huang Lieh-tang got the death penalty. Wu Che-fu and Tu Ping-lang were sentenced to fifteen and twelve years, respectively. They were serving their sentences on Green Island at the moment. As for Ming-chih, he had remodeled his deceased father's clinic and opened a pharmacy — a pleasant life, no doubt, compared to the three others.

"You know Huang Lieh-tang, too, don't you?"

"Yes, I know him."

"He lost his life because he did not think it through. Look at the father he left behind: an old man overnight."

The sight of the white-haired father of Lieh-tang, mindlessly lumbering around town, after losing his only son had brought tears to all, Youde remembered.

"Well, the preliminary has kind of gotten long, but, in any case, the important point is that a person's fate can be as different as heaven and hell, all by just one thought. Right now, you are in a position to choose one or the other."

"But —"

"Speak truthfully. You should tell us all, without covering up anything."

"But I don't have anything special to tell."

"Listen. We have in our possession certain information about you. I can't tell you just now what it is all about, because if we tell you first, the Self-Renewal Rule could not be applied. Believe me, we are trying very hard to minimize the matter and find you not guilty."

Mystified, Youde could not bring himself to say thanks.

"So," Tao leaned forward, "the most important thing to tell us is when, by who and at what place you were recruited into the Communist Party, what you did, and who you recruited. Tell us truthfully. We will then fix the matter up properly and let you go home as soon as possible."

"I did not join the Communist Party. I did not participate in any of their activities. Therefore, I did not recruit anybody," Youde quickly replied, pouring out what had been bottled up for a while.

"Be serious!" the blue shirt barked. "We have firm evidence. You don't seem to appreciate Captain Tao's good intentions."

Youde said firmly, "I am grateful for your good will. But it is the truth that I did not join the Communist Party."

Tao appeared disappointed and said, "Coming so suddenly, maybe you have not been able to weigh the matter carefully. Perhaps, you need some time. All right. Take some time to think it over and decide."

Captain Tao glanced at his watch and said matter-of-factly, "Let's eat."

7

The Mouse That Supped with the Cat

When Captain Tao rose, everybody followed. Uncertain, Youde remained seated hesitantly. For the first time, it hit him that he had lost his freedom. When he looked around, he discovered a folding table had already been set up on the other side of the room and many dishes of food were being laid on top of it. As if attending an ordinary dinner gathering, one by one, the men took their seats. Youde knew only one of them, General Hu, because he was stationed in Putzu and was much feared by the townspeople. The general's full name was Hu Han-chang and was actually just a lieutenant general in the army. But because he always wore his uniform with the gold shoulder bars, he was addressed as General. For an overseas Chinese from Indonesia, he spoke Taiwanese well. According to the general himself, he had answered Chiang Kai-shek's call to duty and had returned to China to serve in the Intelligence Bureau and had eliminated more than one high-ranking official in the puppet government of Wang Ching-wei.

Youde turned to General Hu with a beseeching look on his face.

"Mr. Tsai, come here. We are to have dinner together."

Hearing General Hu's unexpectedly gentle language, Youde felt relieved and sat down next to the general. The dinner was rather sumptuous. There were eight dishes and even soup. Including Youde, there were ten people around the table. A man who was dressed in an old Japanese Navy pea coat put a bowl of rice in front of Youde. Youde thanked him timidly.

"Well, let's start." General Hu said.

Like a mouse invited to the cat's dinner party, Youde moved his chopsticks tentatively. A half-bald officer joked, "Don't stand on ceremony now. It is like we are being treated by you."

During dinner, the men talked among themselves, ignoring Youde's presence. Youde felt that he should say something to General Hu but could not find a topic, so he merely moved his mouth. Perhaps General Hu was in the same bind, because the only common topic they had between them was about mahjong. Mahjong playing was prohibited by law, even though many people played semi-openly. It did not seem appropriate to talk about mahjong on this occasion. Halfway through the dinner, General Hu finally opened his mouth.

"How is your mahjong luck lately?"

Youde had not touched mahjong since his return from America a month ago.

"I haven't played for a long time."

Youde had played mahjong with General Hu maybe ten times. When Hu would drop by Ming-chih's pharmacy while Youde and Ming-chih's were in the middle of their *go* game, Ming-chih would quietly put away *go* and switch to mahjong. This was no problem if Hu had brought along a partner, as they were able to make a foursome. But when Hu showed up alone, Ming-chih would hop on his bicycle to round up the fourth hand, which was not always easy. Several times Youde also had been asked to be the fourth hand at Ming-chih's. Especially hard for Ming-chih was the fact that many people despised playing mahjong with General Hu. After drawing several bad tiles in a row, he would often swear and even curse "fuck!" and slam down the tiles on the table so hard that they would sometimes fall off the table and roll around the floor like jumping squirrels. Always it was Ming-chih's job to pick up the tiles from the floor. But so long as General Hu was in the game, they did not have to worry about a raid by the police.

Around the dinner table, casual conversation continued. They talked about movies, about food, about the new drug penicillin, about bicycles, their children, the new kindergarten, fabric for men's suits, and about shoes. Youde thought it was reasonable to talk about where to buy cheap shoes, as a pair of shoes could cost a man's monthly salary. But they were not completely oblivious to Youde either. When the conversation turned to women, about "hostesses" and prostitutes, the talk would halt and the sentences left unfinished. At these times, Youde felt he was being watched by others.

Even though the conversation was rather frivolous, Youde was able to take in some points. Since they addressed each other as "old" so and so (Mr. so and so), Youde was able to learn the names of the ones he had not been introduced to. He was also able to guess at the home provinces of some of them, from the accent of their speech. Old Ho, who set the rice in front of Youde, was the only Taiwanese among the bunch. The half-balding man was "Old Su" and was from Fukien Province. The man in the blue shirt was "Old Wang," who, like Captain Tao, was a native of Chechiang Province. Captain Tao apparently had interrupted his college education to join the Youth Army. He also seemed like a rather devoted father to his children.

The dinner was over at around nine o'clock. Youde had inconveniently forgotten his watch. He knew that the dinner started late, but had no idea what time it was, being unwilling to ask the others about it. "They must be worried about me at home," he thought. He saw the faces of his mother and his wife in his mind.

"Do you need to go to the toilet?" Ho, a seemingly nice person, invited Youde to go along.

The men's room was across the hall from their room. Three or four of them entered the men's room together. Ho stood behind Youde and waited. Youde pulled out his shrunken penis but was unable to urinate even though it had been hours since he last went. Youde felt bad about keeping Ho waiting, yet the more anxious he became the less able he was to urinate. The others had finished their business and gone out, but Youde's muscles were too tense to function properly.

"Don't be so tense, take your time," Ho said to Youde and stepped up to another urinal himself. Urinating, Ho said softly, "You have been treated rather well. You really don't need to worry so much." Then, Ho said something perhaps he shouldn't have said to a suspect, "To your good fortune, recently, they have changed their policy to not rough up intellectuals unless there is firm evidence."

"Might Ho be hinting they had decided not to torture me? So don't say irresponsible things! What a considerate gesture from a fellow Taiwanese!" Finally, the muscles relaxed and Youde urinated copiously. When he came out to the hallway he found the others were waiting. Youde was taken back to the room and seated once again in the same spot.

8

Now, Write!

There were papers on the desk.

Captain Tao again sat down at the opposite side of the desk and threw a cigarette across to Youde. But his attitude had become cold.

"Since you seem to have difficulty talking about it, we will have you write it down then. Write down everything, large and small, of all your associations and social activities, beginning from the time of the restoration of Taiwan to China in 1945 up to the time you left for America. If what you write agrees with our intelligence report, thus proving your truthfulness, we may be able to accept you as a "Self-Renewal" case and send you home right away. You will then be able to resume your teaching job. As you can imagine, by now, your family must be quite worried. You should ease their minds, the sooner the better!"

"But social activities — what sort of things should I write about?"

"I think you know quite well, better than we, what we meant. You were pretty active."

"……" Youde could not exactly ask, "for example?"

Captain Tao straightened up in his seat, looking hard at Youde through the corner of his eyes and said, "You have participated in a lot of things. In fact, before your return from abroad, we have reviewed your case and the more we looked into it, the more suspicious points we have turned up."

"……"

"Maybe they are mere friends or maybe they are your comrades, but, so far, more than thirty of them have been found guilty. Can you see how we just can't really leave you alone any longer? We did not invite you over just for dinner tonight, you know."

"……"

"But if you do not admit to what you have done and stubbornly stay mum, this matter can get a little sticky for all of us."

After flashing a brief sardonic grin, Tao looked long and sharply into Youde's eyes. Then he stood up, leaned over the desk, placing one hand on the desk to support himself, he gently patted Youde's shoulder with the other hand and said, "Do not forget. This is your last chance."

Tao turned and headed toward the exit. He appeared angry. Five or six others followed Tao out of the room. At the door, Tao whispered something to Wang who nodded his head several times. The door closed. Left in the room were Wang, of the blue shirt, and another man in a loud floral Hong-Kong shirt. The latter, addressed as Old Tien by others, did not talk much during dinner. The two locked the door from inside and pulled up chairs opposite Youde and sat down.

Wang took out a ballpoint pen from his breast pocket and placed it in front of Youde.

"Now, write! Truthfully."

9

What to Write

Picking up the pen, Youde had no idea how to start.

Had he actually joined the Communist Party, he would have no problem following Tao's instructions. But since he never joined the Party, that was out. In fact, Youde was not knowledgeable about Communism. He read a few books but did not find them particularly useful, nor did he find the ideology sympathetic. To him, proletarian literature was just another genre, neither superior nor poisonous. Turning over Captain Tao's words — phrases such as "re-investigation," "blind spots," "friends who were found guilty," "reliable intelligence" (Wang used "reliable evidence") — Youde contemplated: Why is it necessary to re-investigate? It is hard to believe that the investigation before the granting of his exit-permit was nothing but thorough. Some new circumstances must have developed during my absence.

The friends who had been found guilty were roughly of two camps: those who were from his hometown, Putzu, and those who were college friends. Most of them had already been arrested and convicted prior to Youde's trip abroad and his associations with them were part of the original investigation. Thus, Youde had been already absolved of the matter. Otherwise, Youde would never have been able to leave the country.

However, there was one exception: Chang Yu-kun, who was arrested during his absence. Youde had learned soon after his return, that there had been over twenty people arrested from Putzu and its vicinity alone, all implicated by Yu-kun. "Something injurious to me must have turned up in Yu-kun's investigation," Youde pondered. "It's true that I've had a long and deep association with Yu-kun, yet there shouldn't be anything that could be construed as criminal evidence. And, Yu-kun would never invent things, would he? If I were to write about Yu-kun, five or six pages would never do. Besides, since they did not openly say that I am here on account of Yu-kun, it would be odd to single out Yu-kun among many friends. Can't have them think that I am acting guilty."

Youde was in even more of a quandary as to how to start. "Come on. Start writing!" Wang urged, his up-slanting triangular eyes looking definitely unfriendly. "No point asking him for help," Youde thought to himself!

Youde finally decided to write it in the autobiographical style. He outlined in his head, in chronological order, the details of his introductions and subsequent associations with his convicted friends, taking care to clarify what might be deemed suspicious or what Tao might have referred to as "blind spots." He started with his own birth.

10

This Friend, That Friend

"I AM Tsai Youde. I was born in 1925 and entered Putzu Public School at age eight. In my class were Yeh Chin-kuei, Huang Shih-lien, and Chen Chin-tu. Chang Yu-kun was a class above me. Li Shui-ching was four years above me, and three years under me were Chen Ming-chih, Huang Lien-tang, and Tu Ping-lang. After graduating from grade school, I went to Japan and enrolled in a middle school there. The Pacific war broke out when I was in my third year of middle school. Subsequently, after graduation I returned to Taiwan and became a substitute teacher in the Putzu Boy's Public School. Soon after, I was drafted into the army. Eight months after that, the war ended and Taiwan was restored from a Japanese colony to a Chinese province. Like many others, I shed tears of joy at Taiwan's restoration to the motherland. Soon after, I enrolled in the newly founded Normal University in Taipei. I was twenty-two years old.

"In Taipei, I lived with my brother's family in the faculty housing of Chienkuo Middle School, where my brother became a teacher after his return from Japan. Li Shui-ching, who also taught at the same school, moved in with us, he being from the same hometown.

"In my freshman year, I started the Taiwan Drama Society and was elected its president. During the summer vacation, I returned to Putzu, where, together with Chang Yu-kun and Cheng Wen-bang, I organized the Putzu Student Friendship Association and was elected its president. During my college years, I translated and adapted several pieces of drama and staged them in Taipei, Chiayi, and Putzu.

"In 1947, the February 28 Incident erupted. The number of English majors in my class in the Normal University dropped by ten. After this incident, student movements became popular and the campus was thrown into tumult. The president of the Student Self Government, Chou Shen-yuan, appointed me to head up the recreation committee. On April 6, 1949, a general student crackdown was ordered. All student activities were banned, the Student Self Government and the Taiwan Drama Society were disbanded. My class drastically dropped to a little over twenty. Arrests continued. The last year and half of my college years we lived in fear. At graduation, my class of fifty had fewer than twenty left.

"After graduation, during my job-orientation sessions, I joined the Kuomintang Party. I then took up teaching at Putzu's new high school. A year later, at age twenty-seven, I got married.

"In 1953, I went to America on a U.S. aid program and returned after one year of study. One month after my return, I was taken in by the Garrison Command."

Youde knew that the most problematical were the four years during college. First of all, Youde lived with Li Shui-ching for almost a year under the same roof. Li was a committed, bona-fide, pro-mainland Communist Party member and also was the chief officer of the National Alliance of Student Members. Li was the first to be arrested in the April 6 student incident and was executed in September of 1950 by a firing squad at the bank of the Machangting River, along with ten other students and one elementary school teacher. Li's body was displayed in public as a warning to others.

The elementary school teacher whose body was also publicly displayed was Huang Shih-lien, Youde's childhood friend. When Huang's name appeared in the newspaper, people who knew him were incredulous, "A gentle person like him!" One of the ten students was also from Putzu, Cheng Wen-bang, who was a student at the College of Law and Commerce. Cheng's father was a doctor and an influential person in town. Consequently, Cheng attended the elementary school reserved for Japanese children. He was the treasurer at the Putzu Student Friendship Association. Despite being born into the town's foremost capitalist family, Cheng became a believer of Marx; and now his life disappeared like the fleeting dew of Machangting.

Four of the remaining nine students were members of the Taiwan Drama Society. Youde remembered that he was quite startled when he learned about their involvement from the newspaper. He knew he couldn't escape the suspicion of having played a role in bringing them together. Perhaps this is what Captain Tao had referred to as a "blind spot."

Youde could not skip over Chou Shen-yuan, the president of the Student Self Government. Chou was from Shuishang, a neighboring town of Putzu, and was a graduate of Chiayi Middle School. Because his brother lived in Putzu, he visited often as a middle school student. Chou had a strong build and also a keen sense of justice. He and Yu-kun were fast friends. Later on, he was elected president of the Student Self Government at Normal University and became the ringleader of the student movement there.

Many stories of derring-do surrounded him. One month prior to the April 6 incident, the secret police showed up at the university dormitory. Handcuffed and sitting between two secret police, Chou was taken away in a pedicab. As they passed in front of the student dormitories of the National Taiwan University, Chou threw himself off the pedicab and yelled for help. The students there rushed to his rescue and the secret police made a hasty retreat. His next bravado took place on the eve of the April 6 crackdown. He again miraculously broke through the ring of military police and escaped. But two years later, the goddess of luck finally deserted him. Lured into Taoyuan by an informer, Chou was again surrounded. This time he resisted to no avail. His body riddled by bullets like a honeycomb, his fresh, crimson blood spilled across the road, his young life ended.

Youde wrote about meeting Chou, about becoming an officer in the Student Self Government, about his reasons for organizing the Taiwan Drama Society, about its goings on, and about various activities. He also explained his relationships with the student demonstrations.

11

Tough Guy — Yu-kun

Having used up his own pack, Youde reached for the cigarettes on the desk.

"May I?"

"Ya."

Wang nodded. Wang had been silent ever since Youde started writing. He did not press, but whenever a page was filled, he would pick it up, scan it and set it back with a dismissive gesture. "Is he being contemptuous? Is the writing not meeting his expectations?" Youde wondered.

Finally Youde had to turn to Yu-kun.

Yu-kun was a year ahead of Youde in school from kindergarten on, through elementary school. There was so much to write about him, as he was such a standout. Putzu's only kindergarten was shared by Taiwanese and Japanese kids. Whenever a Taiwanese kid was picked on by the Japanese, big, strong Yu-kun was at the ready to take on the fight, sometimes taking on two or three opponents at a time. On the athletic field, he was on the relay team, often winning much applause from his schoolmates. And later on while a student at Tainan Second High School, he was said to cut quite a figure on campus, being a black belt in judo. In a word, he was nothing less than a heroic character to his friends.

Earlier during the February 28 Incident, Yu-kun, like other college students, did not participate much. Most victims of the February 28 Incident and its aftermath were either Taiwan's cultural elite or from the small-town gentry class. In contrast, college students who had neither positions nor means were relatively unharmed. Nevertheless, the incident was a turning point. The fact was that the college students, in their despair, quickly turned against the Kuomintang government and looked toward the Communists in search of hope. Yu-kun probably joined the Communist Party at this time. Within a year, left-wing fever spread like a prairie fire, practically getting out of control. The students marched and shouted anti-government slogans. Needless to say, Yu-kun stood at the head of the crowd.

The government finally decided on a crackdown on intellectuals and persons with "thought problems" and began mass arrests of university students. This is the so-called April 6 student incident of 1949, two years after the February 28 Incident. The ranks of college students were badly decimated. In Youde's English department, the number of students dropped from forty to twenty. In the mathematics department where Chou Shen-yuan was a student, only one student remained.

Of course, not all disappearances resulted from arrests. Perhaps more than half either escaped or gave up on college altogether.

Naturally, Yu-kun was a target for arrest. Sensing the impending arrest, he went home to hide. The secret police, after missing him in the school dormitory, traveled southward at once and surrounded his home. Yu-kun, in dark clothing, roped himself up to the roof from the second floor window, then leapt from roof to roof and escaped, leaving the secret police pounding at the front gate. That was Yu-kun's first escape. For a year afterward, he was sheltered by the village of Hsia-chi-tze, a remote seaside place about ten kilometers from Putzu. When the secret police eventually got wind of it and mobilized a large number of police for his capture, he had slipped out of the village just the day before. This was his second escape. He then entered the mountains and joined the other political fugitives in a camp where they led a minimally self-sufficient existence. In this manner, Yu-kun and his friends stayed leisurely for two years in the mountains, oblivious to the bloodhound-like secret police. Then, one day, for some reason, Yu-kun came into Chiayi dressed like a farmer, and when he was eating a bowl of noodles in the marketplace, he was overtaken by several large men, his schoolmate officer Hsu among them. They handcuffed him and tied his body around and around with a heavy rope and took him to the intelligence agency. The secret police must have received rewards and congratulated themselves for catching such a big fish.

This all happened while Youde was in America. Panto had informed Youde of Yu-kun's capture in her letter, just one line, very casually: "Gandhi," which was the nickname of Yu-kun, "has been arrested."

12

Restoration — A Moving Experience

Setting aside their shared childhoods, Youde started his association with Yu-kun after the Restoration. "Restoration" — *kuangfu* — refers to Taiwan's return to Chinese rule. It became customary to use "before Restoration" and "after Restoration" when one talked about Taiwan's history.

In August 1945, when Japan surrendered, the dream of many Taiwanese suddenly became a reality; a dream shared by many past generations whom had struggled vainly in search of the motherland. People wept with deep gratitude. It is not too much to assert that those who do not know firsthand the outpouring of feelings of the Taiwanese people at the time of Restoration are not qualified to talk about Taiwan's history. Old and young, farmers, merchants, day laborers, civil servants, housewives and children, even the underworld figures were all drunk with the fine wine that was the Restoration! One did not forget to carry a small national flag even if just out for a stroll. The underworld figures and common thieves voluntarily organized themselves into Loyalty Tong to keep order after the Japanese police had left town. It seemed that overnight the crime rate had dropped to zero.

The town's young people returned one by one from their military service: Youde from the Japanese Air Force; Yu-kun from the Japanese Army; and Wen-bang, Che-fu, and Ming-chih from the Student Corps. They immediately formed the Three People's Principles Youth Corps so they might be the foundation of the new government, this time, their own. They spontaneously assisted in matters of all things. The first order of things was to learn the national anthem then teach it to the others. But since they were not able to pronounce the words in Mandarin Chinese, they had to annotate the characters with Japanese kana. The pronunciation was atrocious, the butt of many jokes in later years, but there couldn't have been many national anthems sung with as much tearful passion. They gathered what they could in the way of musical instruments and taught the townsfolk how to sing the national anthem, in the temple courtyard, in assembly halls, or in empty lots — always with a large national flag hanging in the background. Men's voices, women's voices, children's voices, old people's voices; the sound of the national anthem echoed in every corner, in every port. At this same period of time, the song "Righteous Army March" also entered the airwaves. The townspeople sang it too because it was a song about the courageous Chinese Army, with no inkling that the song would later become the national anthem of the Chinese Communist regime, the People's Republic of China. The words of the march moved many people to tears:

> Rise! Do not remain enslaved.
> Let's build a new Great Wall with our own blood!

Then, there were new songs written in Taiwan:

> Today Taiwan celebrates a great day.
> Above is the blue sky and white sun.
> Six million people share in the joy
> Food and drink to show welcome.

The tousle-haired, young men on the podium cut heroic and manly figures as they stood and waved their batons. To the people present, they symbolized the brilliant future of Taiwan.

The young people also helped with the town's cleanup, which had become unkempt during the war years: weeds on the no longer needed air shelters, long neglected potholes filled with festering water. Youde and his friends divided areas among themselves and gathered townspeople, even grade school children to tackle the cleanup. Every morning, with bamboo brooms and hoes in their hands, they persevered. In just a few weeks, the town was spruced up, nearly unrecognizable from its old self. Also, the young men and women started a class to study the Three People's Principles and to study Mandarin Chinese. They happily studied the language of their motherland along with its political ideas.

To a Taiwanese youth like Youde, the sky was truly blue with the white sun, *ch'ing-t'ien, pai-jih*, just like the symbol of the national flag, and the whole world was filled to the brim with beautiful hope.

They were totally unaware that a fate, more cruel than that of "before Restoration," was waiting for them in the wings.

13

Ah! Blue Sky, White Sun
(*Ch'ing-t'ien, pai-jih*)

Youde finished writing about their activities during the exhilarating months following the Restoration. He hesitated at the mention of one certain event. Although it had no relevance to his case, it was just the example to show how the Taiwanese "sweet potatoes" had loved their motherland at the time. Nothing bad can possibly come of it anyway, Youde thought and decided to write about it. The event was that amid the joyous frenzy following the Restoration, three anti-Japanese heroes returned to Putzu from the Tainan prison. All three were Youde's older schoolmates. In May 1939, two years after the onset of the Sino-Japanese war, the three were arrested by the Japanese secret police for sedition and were later sentenced to long prison terms: the leader, Huang K'un, to fifteen years, Li Chin-min, also to fifteen years, and Huang Chia-tsung to twelve years.

At this time, the three had spent six years of their youthful lives in prison. When they were arrested, Huang K'un was a sophomore at Tainan Second High School, while both Li Chin-min and Huang Chia-tsung were students at Tainan Teachers School. All three were eighteen years old. The three had taken blood vows and sworn their allegiance to the motherland of China and had taken to meeting in the deserted public cemetery, where they sang the Nationalist national anthem and studied the Three People's Principles. This went on at a time when the Japanese Imperial Army was striking advance after advance on the Chinese mainland and the town was staging a "victory parade" of lanterns. To most people, it was inconceivable that the Chinese army would one day set foot on Taiwanese soil, yet supposedly the three had sworn to respond from behind Japanese lines once the Chinese army landed. No wonder they were branded "non-citizens" and subjected to repeated beatings and long prison sentences. If the war had lasted a little longer, they likely would have died in prison of physical abuse and malnutrition.

Learning of the return of the three men, Youde and his friends, each with flags in their hands, hurried over to the train station. The train station was located in the southern outskirts of town, a free-standing, white structure that belonged to the sugar company.

This place must have been a memorable place for the three men. Back then, when the time came to return to school after the semester recess, the town's boys and girls, wicker trunks in tow, in their school uniforms and school hats, would arrive at the station one or even two hours ahead of the train's departure time, as this was conceivably the only place where boys and girls were able to smile at each other and exchange a few words. And all through the semester, the boys would be sustained by remembering the few words "she" had spoken.

Now, on this day, several of the girls from the old days were also at the station, among them a lady with a little girl who was holding a carefully arranged spray of flowers. The members of the Loyalty Tong arrived with huge drums and gongs loaded in a pushcart.

The narrow-gage railroad car slid into the platform with a high-pitched whistle. Immediately the sounds of firecrackers, drums, and gongs assaulted the ears of those present. Everybody was shouting "Banzai! Banzai!" as they wildly waved the flags.

Amid the thunderous welcome, the three men descended onto the platform. Huang K'un, who used to be on the school tennis team, walked with a limp. His pale face and hands and bony body told of the six years of suffering. But his moistened eyes were clear and shone with brilliance. The three men also could not stop waving their flags as they exchanged handshakes and said thanks to the people there. Shouts of "banzai" continued. The little girl ran up and presented the flowers. Applause. Huang K'un picked up the little girl; large teardrops burst from his eyes.

Finally Huang K'un put the little girl down. He took off the tennis cap he had on, threw it into the air and shouted at the top of his lungs, "It's a blue sky and a white sun! *Ch'ing-t'ien, pai-jih.*"

Without a second thought, Youde and his friends also threw their hats into the air and screamed, "*Ch'ing-t'ien, pai-jih!* It's a blue sky and a white sun!"

Their voices reached heaven and earth. Their faces were wet with tears.

Then the world was undoubtedly filled with blue sky and white sun.

Japan surrendered on August 15, 1945. Between the surrender and October 25 the same year, when the Nationalist Chinese government arrived to take over Taiwan, Taiwan had no government. It was a time of anarchy. Yet it truly was a time of blue sky and white sun.

14

Drama Society and Friendship Association

There was a knock at the door. T'ien went to open the door. Two men stepped in, a chubby man answered to the name of Su and another to Hung who wore wire-rim glasses.

"Ah —" Wang stood up with a big, loud yawn.

"What? Still writing?" Fat Su muttered.

At the door, Wang whispered something to Fat Su then left the room with T'ien. The door was again locked from inside. The two replacements sat down across from Youde. Hung with the wire-rim glasses threw a pack of cigarettes on the desk. A favorite treatment, it seemed.

"Write only the truth. Lies would soon be found out anyway." Fat Su said somewhat menacingly.

Youde nodded and continued to write. There was not a sentence of falsehood in what he had written. Now, he proceeded cautiously to write about his motives in forming the Taiwan Drama Society and about its various activities. Youde realized that if the Drama Society were taken to be a Communist front organization, he would probably not escape the death sentence. Most of the campus organizations at the time were in fact Communist fronts, and that is the reason that only very few of the leaders are still living today.

During the latter part of the Japanese colonial rule of Taiwan, the use of the Taiwanese language was prohibited in all levels of schools and, as the "Japanization Program" raged, there were even people who proudly acknowledged the fact that they were not able to speak Taiwanese. After the Restoration, the Taiwanese language was used in schools for a very short period but was soon again banned in the name of "national language advancement." Through neglect and mistreatment over the years, the language lacked written words for many expressions and had also become vulgar. The Drama Society's stated intent was to advance Taiwanese language and culture — it engaged in the research of lost words and strived to elevate its literary expressions. Youde was the founder. He drafted the bylaws, assembled the members and was elected its president unanimously.

By then the communist students had gradually infiltrated various campus groups. Before long they took over the leadership roles and showed their true colors. Because the Taiwan Drama Society was clearly associated with the Taiwanese language, its members were all Taiwanese — there was no room for the mainland students with questionable backgrounds.

Before the February 28 Incident of 1947, the students were mostly calm, dissatisfied though they might be. However, angered by the massacre during the incident and the ever-worsening corruption in the government, they became active in anti-government activities. Already, the fervent hope raised by the Restoration had gradually turned to disappointment. After the incident, despairing students looked to the new regime on the mainland for hope. What the Taiwanese had wished for was a strong regime, regardless of ideology, that was able to topple the utterly corrupt government. Perhaps that was exactly what happened on the mainland; otherwise, how did one explain the rapid advance of the Communists?

One by one, the innocent Taiwanese students were absorbed into the Communist cells, each consisting of only three or four people, so that only members of the same cell know about each other's involvement. At every campus assembly, anti-government speeches were made. Plays that satirized the government were performed. The Communist songs were openly sung. The campus was buried in anti-government handbills and large-character wall posters. Thus it was not surprising that the Taiwan Drama Society had in its ranks more than ten members of the Communist Party.

On the other hand, there were the Kuomintang's professional students, who secretly informed on the activities of the fellow students. Some two-faced creatures would bad-mouth the government like Communists while in fact working for the Kuomintang.

The Taiwan Drama Society, for its debut, staged the mainland playwright Ts'ao Yu's *The Sunrise* in Taiwanese. It was a great success. The tragic story, a piece of proletarian literature, depicted the gulf separating the rich from the poor. The Communist students especially clapped in a loud ovation. As it turned out, the playwright Ts'ao Yu turned Communist a year later; after that the play was banned. Youde explained that his intention to perform the play was to introduce well-known literature from the motherland to Taiwan. The next production of the group was Takeo Arishima's *Death of the Stutterer* (*Domomata no shi*), a play whose tenor was rather incongruent with the tumultuous campus. Youde translated and acted in this play. Aside from the content of the play, Youde had wanted to demonstrate that the Taiwanese language, just like other languages, could be used in refined literary works.

In the same year that the Drama Society was founded, the Student Friendship Association was formed in Putzu. Youde was elected its president also. About sixty college students and over one hundred high school students joined the association. Huang Lieh-tang was the only college holdout. It was surmised later that he had already joined the Communist Party at the time. During the election of the president, Yu-kun had highly praised Youde for the organizational skills and acting talents he had shown leading the Taiwan Drama Society and had strongly recommended Youde's election. Wen-bang became the treasurer; Che-fu the activity director and Bin-lang the set designer. Yu-kun, Wen-bang, Che-fu, and Bin-lang all joined the Communist Party soon after this time.

Judging from what had happened, it was fortunate that Youde, instead of Yu-kun, was elected the association's president. If it had been the other way around, the Friendship Association probably would have been marked as a Communist front organization and its entire student membership jailed.

The Friendship Association put on performances in rented theaters when the members were home for summer vacation: choral singing, dances, also plays like Ts'ao Yu's *The Sunrise* and *Return Southward* by T'ien Han, another Chinese playwright. In the days before the advent of television, the townsfolk gladly paid to see the shows. As a result the ticket sales exceeded expenses, creating a surplus which they donated to the missions for poor children.

Pleased with himself, Youde further adapted the hit movie *King's Row* into a three-part drama with five scenes in Taiwanese and produced it. He had some doubt that small-town folk could comprehend a play of considerable psychological subtlety, but the result was a resounding success. In this drama, Youde played the hero Parris; Yu-kun played the father of Parris's lover. They showed perfect timing. The success proved that it was not necessary to pander to the popular taste, rather that the public was able to enjoy programs of high quality. Youde and his friends were elated and emboldened. Just as they were raring to go, the April 6 student crackdown occurred, and both the Taiwan Drama Society and the Student Friendship Association met their demise. Wen-bang, Che-fu, Bin-lang, and others were arrested, and Yu-kun began his life as a fugitive. Youde had not seen Yu-kun since then.

Luckily, Youde's name was not among the ones given to the authorities. He had taken care to send the scripts to be reviewed by the student counselor or the police. Even the billboards or advertisements were submitted, by Youde in person, for permission. At the time, some complained that these were acts of cowardice. But in hindsight, the extra caution turned out to be the most important reason that Youde's name was excluded from the list.

When the storm of the April 6 incident was over, all student activities ceased. There was nothing more to write about. Youde briefly touched upon his graduation, his subsequent teaching job, his marriage, trip abroad and return, then ended the statement.

The statement had exceeded fifty pages.

15

A Kind Secret Police

"So, you finally finished! The first time I've seen such a long confession." Fat Su, without paying any attention to the content, gathered up the papers, straightened the stack by tapping the sides on the desk then shoved them into a Manila envelope. He swiped a cigarette from the desk as he hurried out of the room.

Two other men arrived for their shift — a man called Ho and the other "Big Shantung." Ho said as he locked the door from inside, "Do you want to use the toilet?"

Youde felt no urge at all so he declined politely.

"Come here." Ho sat down on the sofa and gestured Youde to come. Youde stood up and dragged his numbed legs over to the sofa. Big Shantung said something to Ho in a tiny voice, unbecoming such a big man.

Youde picked up a few words: "... documents ... meetings ... fried dough (*youtiao*)...."

Ho nodded. Big Shantung left the room.

Ho sat Youde down opposite himself in a sofa and said, "Relax a bit. You must be tired. You had better rest a little."

Such considerate, gentle words! Youde felt that he could probably ask Ho a few things. When Ho returned from locking the door, Youde asked, "Is it going to be all right?"

"Probably, if your statements are true. You've written quite a bit, haven't you?"

"What I've put down is all true."

"Now, I am also a fellow 'sweet potato,' and I know how you feel. It's really been painful for me to see Taiwanese people being brought into here one by one and handed over to the military court, especially because they are all intelligent young people with a sense of justice. If it were not for getting tangled up with the 'thought problem,' they'd all be very capable people with great futures."

Youde was startled by the unexpected words.

"Particularly, there have been many young men from Putzu. Already, there were Li Shui-ching, Cheng Wen-bang, Huang Lieh-tang, Huang Shih-lian; all had been executed by the firing squad. Why? Why are there so many from Putzu?"

"……"

Youde did not know the answer either. Perhaps the only possible explanation was that it was the town's tradition. Without waiting for an answer, Ho changed the subject. "During the war, you were in the Japanese Air Force, right?"

"Yes. I was in the Makoto Battalion. Makoto belonged to the Air Force, but it served only ground duty."

"I myself was in the Navy, assigned to a destroyer. Our chief mission was to escort the supply ships."

Ho told Youde to go ahead and sleep if he felt like it, then started on his own Navy adventures. Ho talked about Hainan Island, Hong Kong, Singapore, even about the "comfort women" and prostitutes he had procured in various ports. Youde was not in the frame of mind to listen to this kind of talk with any interest; nevertheless, he felt a closeness to Ho, who talked on sentimentally. Ho might not be a Buddha in hell, but a friend nevertheless. Still, Youde was not able to fall asleep. He closed his eyes and listened as Ho continued on.

Catching a break, Youde opened his eyes and said to Ho, "My family is probably worried about me by now."

"Ya, I should think so."

"They probably don't know that I am here."

"I don't think they do."

Youde had reasons to be concerned. There had been many cases where people were taken in for questioning about the February 28 Incident and while their whereabouts were still unknown to their families, turned up several days later as dead bodies floating in the river, or corpses abandoned under a bridge. "My family, no doubt, is worried about me turning up the same way," Youde thought.

"Could you possibly let them know? Just that I am here and that I am all right? If you could just do that, to relieve them of the worry...."

"I've never done anything like that, so I can't make any promises. But if this is going to go on any longer, I gather they should be told somehow."

"Taking longer?" Youde said.

"Ha ha. I don't know about that. It's up to you, you know. Some people go home in two or three days, but then some take a few years."

"......"

"If what you wrote checks out with our investigation's findings, it would be meaningless to keep you here any longer. Besides, you yourself had just returned from abroad. You must have reports to make as well. But if your statement is considered to be untrue, then we will have to re-investigate and the matter can get troublesome."

"What I wrote is all true."

"I don't know about the others, but as I am a 'sweet potato' too, I will do my best to help you."

"Thank you." Then Youde added a rather brazen, embarrassing saying — a wisdom learned from the Chinese — "If I get to go home soon, I would never forget your favor for as long as I live."

"Ha ha." Ho stood up, tapped gently on Youde's shoulder and said, "Rest your mind, even just a little. You can go to sleep if you wish. I'll wake you when somebody else shows up."

Youde thanked his lucky stars for running into such a kind secret police.

16

A Ray of Hope Vanished

Big Shantung returned with a paper bag from which he took out soy milk, fried dough, and flat bread, all typical Chinese breakfast fare. This must mean that the night was over, although with the heavy drapes still drawn tight, Youde could see no sign of daybreak in the room. Big Shantung urged Youde to eat, while he himself also took to the food. When he was finished eating, Ho sat Youde back at the desk and went out of the room, leaving only Big Shantung.

Big Shantung sat down across the desk from Youde and began talking about how cruel the Communists were back in his home village in Shantung Province, China. Landlords strung up on a tall post were dropped to the ground then pulled up repeatedly until they died their bloody deaths. His stories were all about cruelty. Big Shantung urged kindly, "I'm saying this for your own sake; leave the Communist Party as quickly as you can."

It seemed that he had worked his way up from a foot soldier. Youde felt that Big Shantung was quite sincere.

Maybe an hour had passed when the door opened and Captain Tao with five other men swaggered into the room. As before, they sat down circling Youde, all looking angry. Captain Tao slammed down Youde's statement, by now stapled into a booklet, and said.

"Let me state the conclusion first. Our unanimous opinion of your statement is that you avoid the serious and touch upon the insignificant. You did not mention one single important thing. Instead, you wrote down a whole lot of nonsense. You just stepped on and crushed my good will toward you. We gave you plenty of time to write, not about matters like these. We wanted you to take time to think and write down accurately about true facts."

"What I wrote is all true." Youde said hastily, his lips quivering.

"That is so. But the problem lies in what you left out."

Suddenly, Fat Su stood up and yelled, "This one isn't going to talk unless he knows some pain."

"But I think I did write down everything significant."

"A sly one," Wang spit out angrily.

No one would accept Youde's word for it. From the hostile atmosphere in the room, Youde knew that a ray of hope born of the captain's words, "Tell the truth and you'll be let go," had completely disappeared.

Captain Tao continued, "You totally abused my good will toward you. You have made a bad judgment. Also, you are taking us too lightly. You should know that you cannot hide the facts, even if you wanted to."

Captain Tao vacated his seat. There's no relying on his goodwill now," Youde realized. Wang moved into Tao's seat as T'ien took away the ashtray from in front of Youde. It seemed that the favored treatment was no more. Leaving only Wang and T'ien, the rest of them quickly withdrew from the room. T'ien sat down next to Wang and placed the investigation forms on the desk.

This was the beginning of the "fatigue investigation" that lasted for four or five days, a number of which Youde himself was not certain afterward.

17

Li Shui-ching — A Man from the Same Hometown

WANG asked questions while T'ien recorded the answers.

"Since when have you known Li Shui-ching?"

"Since he returned to Putzu from the mainland after the Restoration."

Li's return occurred about two weeks after the passionate welcome for the three anti-Japanese heroes. Although Li did not receive the same welcome, he was perhaps the genuine anti-Japanese hero. That is because he had traveled to far-away Chungking and actually participated in the fighting against the Japanese. Huang K'un's threesome also showed up at the train station to greet Li's return. As it turned out, Li was one of the blood brothers. Just his luck, Li successfully evaded the Japanese secret police and escaped via Japan, then Korea and Manchuria to throw his lot with the Nationalist government in Nanking. Finally he went all the way to Chungking when the war situation necessitated. His life was an adventure to fill a book. When the war ended, he came home by way of Shanghai within half a month's time.

At the time, as nobody else in town could speak even passable Mandarin Chinese, Li was in great demand to help out in language classes. Eventually, he became an instructor at the Education Council. It was a precarious system at best in which Li taught the teachers one day, after which the teachers turned around to teach the students the next day. But it worked rather well proving the point that dedication can beat all odds. Not long after, he became a journalist and left for Taipei, much to Putzu's regret.

Once in Taipei, he was hired as a teacher of Chinese by Chienkuo Middle School, the top-ranked school in Taiwan.

Flipping through Youde's written statement, Wang inquired, "Did you live in the same room with Li Shui-ching?"

"Not the same room, just under the same roof."

"That's like the same thing. Why?"

"Because my elder brother was also a teacher at the same school and was given faculty housing, and since Li was a fellow townsman from Putzu, he was assigned to share the housing."

Housing was in extreme short supply then and therefore, it was not uncommon to house two families in the same unit, especially since Li was single and from the same town. All this had been included in the written statement, but Wang now picked a point from here and there while T'ien recorded the answers in the forms.

"How long did you live together?"

"About a year."

"Exactly from when to when?"

"From about six months before the February 28 Incident, that is, August 1946 to August of the next year."

"When did he recruit you into the Party?"

"No. I was never absorbed into the Party."

"Living together for a whole year as you did! Nobody is going to believe that he did not absorb you into the Party."

"It's the absolute truth that I was not."

"It's odd that you are so emphatic. You see, he joined the Communist Party back when he was on the mainland. He returned to Taiwan with the mission to absorb as many students as he could into the Party. He wouldn't have left a person like you alone."

In Youde's case, if he was thought to have joined the Party, because he had also engaged in various activities, he could be found guilty under Article 2.1 of the Law on Sedition — applied to the person who has joined the bandit Party and attempted to overthrow the government by illegal means. A death penalty would have been a certainty.

Youde denied the accusation vehemently.

After uttering some negative comments, Wang began to ask about books.

"He showed you books, didn't he? What kind of books did he show you?"

If one had read banned books, he would be guilty of Article 9 — Received Bandit Propaganda Material — and sent to the thought reform camp to be brainwashed. Or worse. Because it was the accepted practice of the Communists to lure their intended targets with the banned books as the first step in recruitment, the question is loaded, not merely about having or not having shown certain books. But the fact was that Li Shui-ching did not show any banned books to Youde.

Youde was still pondering when Wang said, "How about *Mao Wenchi?*"

While Youde was still turning over in his head *Mao Wenchi*, the unfamiliar Mandarin-pronounced name of Mao's collected works, T'ien already efficiently entered it in the investigation form. As soon as he realized what *Mao Wenchi* meant Youde hurriedly denied it, but T'ien was not willing to erase the book title from the investigation form easily. In chorus, the two accused Youde of lying and argued that a high school teacher must have owned books other than school textbooks. Tired of the continuous badgering, Youde offered some book titles of no significance: *History of Eastern Chou*, a fiction of Maupassant, a translation of poetry by Tagore. Several times, Wang stood up and pounded on the desk, narrowed his eyes and bellowed, "Don't take us for fools!"

Youde was desperate, but luckily not yet so confused that he would admit to banned books that he had not seen.

Next, Wang moved onto what Youde had seen in Li Shui-ching's room, everything he had seen in a year's time. Then the questions turned to their conversations. Youde was asked to elaborate them with examples. Wang asked, "What kind of bad-mouthing of the government did you do?"

At the time, there was not a single Taiwanese who did not criticize the government. At every gathering people always ended up criticizing the government.

Youde could not blatantly answer "We did not criticize the government at all," as it would be too far-fetched to be credible, like admitting to be fools. On the other hand, the most frequent and widespread criticism was that the government had used the secret police and arrested many people arbitrarily — hardly a suitable answer under the circumstances.

At his wit's end, Youde, searching through memory, cited some examples of criticisms and attributed them to Li Shui-ching.

Example I: Not long after the Restoration, Assemblyman Wang T'ien-ting questioned the government about the large quantity of surplus goods left over from the war: "Where did the sugar, rice, and camphor in the warehouse disappear to?" It was common knowledge that the goods had been sent to the mainland and the profit pocketed by private individuals, but the official answered shamelessly, "The goods were all stolen." "Then, what happened to the seventy kilos of opium in the custody of the Tobacco Monopoly Bureau?" "Termites got it all," the bureau chief answered with a straight face, whereupon the irate Assemblyman Wang pressed for the official's dismissal. The incident resulted instead in the promotion of the officials by the government. Furthermore, during the February 28 Incident, the government got its revenge and killed Assemblyman Wang.

Example II: Prosecutor Wang Yu-lin of Hsinchu indicted the mayor of Hsinchu with solid evidence of corruption. When Prosecutor Wang accompanied by the police arrived at the mayor's office for the mayor's arrest, they found the police chief waiting. The police chief, who was in league with the mayor, ordered the accompanying policemen to surround Prosecutor Wang. He then snatched away the arrest warrant and chased the prosecutor out of the building. When the angry prosecutor returned to the courthouse and reported what had happened to his superior, he was reprimanded instead. Thus Prosecutor Wang resigned in anger and took up teaching in a high school in Taipei. Prosecutor Wang too was murdered during the February 28 Incident, a revenge killing exacted by the mayor. Wang's body was thrown into the Tamsui River. This was the story of three corrupt government officials from the mainland killing a Taiwanese "sweet potato," one with an extraordinary concern for justice.

Example III: A military man's wife (all military men were mainlanders at the time) entered the hospital to give birth but unfortunately died at the operating table. The military man demanded a huge sum of compensation, a sum that was beyond the hospital's means. Taiwan had never seen this kind of extortion before. Eventually, the case was taken to the court with Judge Wu Chi-lin presiding. Judge Wu investigated the case and found the doctor not culpable. Alas, the military man took his private revenge. Judge Wu's body was found in a ditch.

When Youde was finished, Wang said glumly, "So you have some discontent toward the government. From what you say, I can see that some is justified, although the facts are not so simple. You only see things from Taiwan's point of view, while you should be viewing things from the standpoint of all of

China. What's wrong with sending Taiwan's goods to the mainland? Wasn't it to help save China? I guess that it's understandable, you not thinking of China, given the fact that Taiwanese had been enslaved by the Japanese for a long period of time. But it is not right to bad-mouth the government at will."

"......"

"So, Li Shui-ching, knowing your unhappiness with the government, lent you books to read, then around June or July urged you to join the Party, right?"

Youde was taken aback. In fact, in early July Li Shui-ching had casually mentioned something akin to recruiting. He did not clearly refer to the Communist Party, but he mentioned that there was a study group of patriotic youth, that they studied not only politics but also literature and theater. He asked Youde if he would be interested in joining the group.

At the time Youde had his hands full with the Taiwan Drama Society, so he gave an ambiguous reply and the matter was never raised again. Then, the following month, namely August, Li Shui-ching disappeared from the faculty housing without a goodbye and never returned.

Youde learned of Li Shui-ching's execution in the newspaper on November 30, 1950. Eleven were executed that day, with Li Shui-ching heading the list. Among the eleven were Cheng Wen-bang and Huang Shih-lian. According to Wen-bang's mother, who went to retrieve her son's body, Shui-ching was the only one who was shot through the head and died a gruesome death. It was said that Shui-ching had kept up his harangue of the government up to the end. Neither of Shui-ching's parents was living, so there were no kin to retrieve his body. Wen-bang's mother took it upon herself to retrieve the body and sent it to the mortuary to have it made up. "An impossible job," the mortician took a look and declined. So Shui-ching was thrust into the crematory kiln still in his blood-soaked prison garb — a sad ending of this free spirit.

Obviously, Shui-ching did not mention anything about Youde.

If he had, even in the slightest, Youde would have been snatched at the same time and the American trip three years later would have been totally unthinkable.

Wang persisted on tracing Youde's relationship with Shui-ching. Over and over, Youde denied and denied. It was a contest of wills with no ending in sight, requiring immense patience.

18

A Crazy Fellow

THE two inquisitors took turns to go to the toilet but did not bother to invite Youde to go along. They appeared angry. Youde did not need to go, in any case; it was as if all his waste matter had been wrung out like body oil. The two also took out cigarettes and smoked without offering Youde any. On his part, Youde did not beg for one either, not out of stubbornness but because he sensed that by begging for a single cigarette, a corner of his psychological defense levee could start to crumble.

Switching directions, Wang said, "OK, let's hear about Cheng Wen-bang."

Anybody who had known Wen-bang could not possibly speak of him without shedding tears. It was no overstatement to say that Wen-bang was the most honorable and most innocent soul who had ever lived, who seemed to not realize that evil exists in this world.

He was born the first son of the wealthiest family of Putzu. Unlike Youde and the others, he went to the school reserved for the Japanese children. His parents showered him with everything under the sun. They subscribed for him directly from Japan the pictorials *Children's Club, Youth Club,* etc. He also wore leather shoes even when he was just a young child, quite different from the public-school kids, who attended school barefoot. The image of Wen-bang riding around on his own child-sized bicycle was no less than a symbol of royalty. Yet he never prided himself on being a rich kid even when he was little. His books were lent out to whoever wanted to read them and his bicycle shared with whoever who wished to ride. As he grew older, Wen-bang resembled a royal even more, what with a great build and fine facial features classier than a movie star's. And such a person perished at the execution yard at just age twenty! All because he was introduced to Marxism in the economics class at the university.

Flipping through Youde's statement, Wang remarked, "You did not write very much about Wen-bang."

It was true that Youde only wrote about Wen-bang in connection with the Student Friendship Association.

"What do you think of Wen-bang?"

"It's a pity." Youde let his true feelings slip.

"Why is that so?"

"......"

"The fellow was an utterly despicable Communist. What's there to be sorry about?"

"......"

"He was a rebel, you know. He was our enemy, everybody's enemy. Why are you sympathetic?"

The two inquisitors pressed on.

How Youde wanted to scream: "I don't think so! The truth is he was a pristine flower amid the muddy field!" But this would be suicidal. On the other hand, for him to concur with "You are right about him" was absolutely out of the question. It would have been blasphemy.

Youde replied, "I meant it's a pity that he did not join the Kuomintang Party instead. He would have gone far."

T'ien put down his pen and offered, "I witnessed the fellow's interrogation in Taipei. It was crazy. Imagine! He sang the praise of Communism right in front of us and tried to enlighten us on Communism. Not only did he show no remorse, he acted like he felt sorry for our ignorance. I felt like slapping him."

"But he did admit to everything, didn't he?" Wang asked.

"He did. He admitted to all, straightforwardly. His interrogation was the shortest."

T'ien faced Youde anew and said sarcastically, "How about it? How about being a man like Wen-bang and admitting what you have done."

Maybe Wen-bang was but a "crazy guy" to them, but they couldn't help but recognize his manliness!

T'ien cut in sharply, "Seeing that he even tried to sell Communism to us, he must have tried to persuade his friends. Now, let's have the place, the time and what transpired."

To a certain degree T'ien was right. Wen-bang talked about Marx and Engels constantly, but he never forced it on anybody. The Wen-bang Youde knew was a serious young man who got along well with others, who was a sympathizer of Communist ideology but was not a Party member. It was likely that he remained so until Shui-ching got to him. He was the one person who should have been left alone in this turbulent world.

Youde allowed that he knew Wen-bang was sympathetic to Communism and that they had talked about it from time to time but insisted that Youde himself had always argued against it.

Alas. The answer only invited further trouble. Now Wang wanted to know when and what was discussed and how Youde had refuted the Communist ideology. Even if time and place could be fixed in some degree, to recreate the conversation was not so easy. First of all, "refutation" was not exactly the accurate term to describe Youde's role because most of the time he just listened.

"I can't remember too well."

The answer did not fare well. Youde almost wished that he had studied more about Marx.

Finding no other way out, Youde had to make up his own Marxism and then offered its refutation in a one-man show.

If Marx were listening he would surely have rolled his eyes.

19

About Books

GENERAL Hu and GI-cut Chen entered the room. Wang glanced at his watch and rose from his seat.

T'ien said, "Is everything you have said so far all true?"

"Yes, all true."

T'ien penned in the last two lines and pushed the investigation report over to Youde. T'ien took out the ink paste and instructed Youde to sign his name then press his thumbprint at the side of the last line of the report.

The report numbered about ten pages. There was no time to even scan through it. Youde picked out the part about Mao's collective work and insisted that Li Shui-ching never showed him the book. After a brief argument, T'ien reluctantly added small circles over the three characters for *Mao Wenchi*. Youde felt some unease at this as he himself would have drawn two vertical lines over the words instead. But in any event Youde was relieved that the words were scratched. He signed his name and put his thumbprint on the document.

General Hu signaled GI-cut Chen with his eyes to take Youde out to the toilet. Youde sat on the toilet seat unable to move his bowels. Constipation perhaps. Only a pitiful trickle of urine came out which turned the water in the toilet bowl the color of reddish brown. This was Youde's last memory of using the facility there.

For this round General Hu did the questioning and GI-cut Chen took notes. General Hu had a cold expression on his face, quite different from the General Hu around the mahjong table. He started off with *Mao Wenchi*. It seemed that instead of deleting the words, those small circles had the opposite effect of attracting attention.

"It seems that you first mentioned *Mao Wenchi* then later recanted."

"No, that's not what I remember. My answer was slow in coming because I was not sure what *Mao Wenchi* was."

"I don't think so. You were hesitating between admitting and denying, weren't you?"

"The truth is that because the book title *Mao Wenchi* was said in unfamiliar Mandarin Chinese that I did not comprehend it at first."

"Unfamiliar? Not a likely story. Everybody knows the book."

"Must be because I had nothing to do with it that I just did not get it right away."

"But you had the book in your house." General Hu said with confidence.

Youde immediately denied it.

"Think carefully. You need to remember who gave you the book or who lent you the book as the case may be."

As hard as he searched his memory Youde did not come up with the image of the book in his house.

"Listen. It's karma that you and I were acquainted. Isn't there a saying, 'To be acquainted imparts sympathy'? I will not be unreasonable with you. But if you keep denying it, it's a different matter."

GI-cut Chen interjected, "General Hu is listening to you with a lot of courtesy since he has known you for a while. He is trying to make it as favorable to you as he can. I won't give you bad advice, but you should admit your doing quickly and go home sooner rather than later. Save us both some trouble!"

"I don't remember anything about the book."

Hu stood up and said, "All right. In that case, tell us about the books you had at home at the time."

What an awkward turn of events! But Youde had no choice but to comply. Just when Youde opened his mouth Hu gestured irritatingly, "Write. Write them down," then added, "Write down the authors too."

Youde started with Natsume Soseki's *Young Boy*, followed by the books by Japanese authors he could remember, and ended the Japanese section with the poetry by Takuboku. It was easier to categorize them by nationality. Next, he listed the Russian works, from Dostoevsky to Chekhov. General Hu, who had been pacing the room, approached the desk and scanned the list. It appeared he did not know any of the titles. Youde sensed General Hu's mounting irritation.

"Enough of those. It's no use to keep writing about books of no consequences. List the Chinese books first."

Youde listed: *History of Eastern Chou, General History of China, The Story of Ah Q, New Treatise on the Three People's Principles....*

GI-cut who had been quiet sputtered, "Doing it again! Avoiding the serious and touching upon the insignificant. Do you take us for fools?"

General Hu walked over and patted Youde's shoulders from behind and said, "You are to write down the leftist books, Chinese or Japanese. It's not that any given book is of particular importance but that we just want to test your truthfulness."

Youde included Fujiwara Korehito's *Treatise on Art* even though it wasn't a leftist book. He included several books by Chinese authors that he had burned — all read before they were banned. They were banned not necessarily because the contents were left wing but rather because the authors had later turned Communists. These were innocent books. Nevertheless, out of caution, Youde burned them.

General Hu returned to his seat then asked, "You are forgetting an important book, are you not?"

"......"

"A plainly Communist book, not one easily forgotten."

"Was there such a book?" Youde pondered to no avail. General Hu prompted again with irritation. Youde was not able to say anything.

"It's obvious, he is not going to lay it all out," GI-cut muttered.

Hu said, "All right. Let me give you a hint. Its title starts with the character 'wei' and ends with the character 'pen.'"

"Oh, yes. I remember now. It's *A Reader in Materialist Dialectics* in Japanese."

"That's right. Why didn't you say so honestly in the first place?"

"That was not my book. It was borrowed from the library. I thought I was to list the books I own so I was concentrating on my bookcase."

Youde fumed: One can't possibly remember all the books he had borrowed from the library. Besides, how can one be criminally liable by reading books from the library! The book in question was but a basic reader and was not pertinent to Communism, but they seemed to equate Communism with materialism.

With a cynical grin, General Hu said, "The fact was the book was in your bookcase, together with the rest of the Communist books. Now, come clean with the rest of them."

Now Youde had to list the books he had checked out from the library that were considered left wing. The Normal University had inherited the former Taipei High School including its library, which had fortunately escaped war damage. The books in the library were 80 percent Japanese. Since the Japanese authorities also exercised rather strict thought control, there were no outright leftist books in the library — Kawakami Hajime's *The Story of Poverty* was about the limit. Youde included *The Story of Poverty* and a few proletarian books then put down his pen. Hu and GI-cut knew about Kobayashi Takiji's *Crab Boat*; maybe there was a Chinese translation of it. GI-cut was pleased to find the title and promptly entered it into the record.

They dwelled on *A Reader in Materialist Dialectics*: about whether it belonged to Youde or was it a library book, a fact that can no longer be verified by checking with the library, as the book was already gotten rid of when it was banned. Finally, they settled on the scenario that the book belonged to the library but Youde had it on his bookshelf for a time. A small relief.

A new anxiety soon developed. In front of Youde's very eyes, General Hu noisily tore up the sheets of papers filled with book titles Youde had written down. This left only four book titles in the investigative report, giving the impression that Youde had read just the four books, while in fact the four did not constitute 1 percent, not even 0.5 percent, of what he had read. Youde politely pointed out this fact to General Hu but was ignored entirely.

Mere commonplace books they may be to people today, but reading them was a serious offense — punishable by "thought reform" in accordance with Article 9 of the Law on Sedition — the sad truth of life under the regime of the so-called White Terror. A term of three years of "thought reform" may be repeated with no limit, perchance turning into a life sentence. It appeared that Youde was not going to be let go scot-free.

In any event the questioning about the books ended. One question remained in Youde's mind. How did they know that *A Reader in Materialist Dialectics* was among the books in Youde's bookcase?

20

Wires Around His Neck

THE two inquisitors walked around the sofa as they quietly whispered to each other. Maybe they intended to take a rest with a cup of tea. Youde leaned back against the chair and closed his eyes. His eyes were tired after days and nights of continuous questioning. Fortunately, he was still in complete control of his faculties. He reasoned.

How did they learn about the existence of the book? Of course, somebody who frequented my home had informed on me, and that person could be no other than Yu-kun. How did Yu-kun tell them about me? And when did he do that?

At the time of Yu-kun's arrest in February, there couldn't be any need for him to inform about books in somebody else's bookcase. He had a lot of people to talk about: the person who recruited him into the Party, the ones he in turn recruited, his fellow fugitives, people who hid him and aided him, about twenty in all. Enough material to fill a fat, impressive investigative report. Therefore, the most likely time that Yu-kun informed on me, a word I reluctantly used here, was after he had been sent to the detention facility of the Military Court. In that case, Yu-kun was no doubt seeking help through the Self-Renewal Policy, the rationale of which was to redeem one's wrong doings through the "merit" of uncovering others' criminal activities. If a so-far-unknown Communist cell was uncovered as a result, the informer was granted additional reduction in sentencing. Did Yu-kun inform on me because he was afraid of death?

Let's assume Yu-kun had said, "Tsai Youde had joined a different branch of the Communist organization." The intelligence agency would probably panic, because they had given the big fish a passport to go abroad. They would have recalled Yu-kun and pressed for more details.

"How are you so sure that Tsai Youde is a Communist? On what evidence? Or was there something for you to suspect so?"

Whereupon Yu-kun must have offered, as evidence or rationale, "I have seen the book *A Reader in Materialist Dialectics* on his bookcase." But just one book would not suffice. Suppose Yu-kun had added, "I also saw *Mao Wenchi*." Then, the accusation would be hard to ignore and a thorough investigation would be called for, for *Mao Wenchi* had been a favorite tool of recruitment.

If Yu-kun had further volunteered, "Li Shui-ching said Tsai Youde was a comrade," the consequences were obvious — Youde would have no chance of getting out alive since he played leadership roles in many student activities. Yu-kun's every word, every sentence, hung around Youde's neck like rings of wire. Youde must now untie the wires, one by one, with his own strength.

But this reasoning contained a big question mark, "Is Yu-kun such a base man?"

21

A Childhood Chum

The two inquisitors returned. A cup of water was placed on the desk.

"You wrote a lot about Chang Yu-kun." General Hu said while flipping through the written statement. "But what do you think of Yu-kun?"

"Well, he is a strong person, in both body and mind," Youde answered carefully.

"You've known him since kindergarten days, right?"

"Yes."

"That's a long time. So you are childhood chums."

"Yes."

"At the Putzu Student Friendship Association, you were the president and he was your vice president?"

"Yes."

"That's odd. He is a year ahead of you in school."

"Yes. I nominated and recommended him and he recommended me, but his idea prevailed."

General Hu smirked, "So you respect each other."

"......"

"I wonder in what way do you respect him, not merely about his strong body and mind, I think."

"He has a strong sense of justice."

"Is that so? On what basis?"

Youde gave a few more examples that were not included in his written statement, of Yu-kun's habit of "standing up for the meek" when he was a child. As a grown-up he also was unable to keep silent in the face of any unfairness. Youde cited a few of these examples.

"When did you know that he was a Communist?"

"After the April 6 incident, when I heard that he had gone into hiding."

Article 9 of the Statutes for Denunciation and Punishment of Bandit Spies states: One is guilty if he knowingly conceals the whereabouts of a Communist and fails to report it to the authorities.

"He persuaded you to join the Party, did he not?"

"No. Not even once."

"I can't believe that. He has no reason not to recruit a childhood friend who reads Communist books."

But the truth was that Yu-kun had never tried to absorb Youde into the Communist Party. Maybe he assumed Youde was already a Party member since Youde lived with Li Shui-ching under the same roof.

Over and over. General Hu and GI-cut continued to press Youde on whether Youde had known that Yu-kun was a Communist and if Yu-kun had recruited him. Youde defended himself desperately, not giving in an inch. The battle ended in a draw, both sides in utter exhaustion.

After a brief pause, General Hu inquired light-headedly, "You both entered National Taiwan University, didn't you?"

"Yes." Youde did not include this fact in his statement. Their background check was thorough all right.

"Why did you switch to the Normal University?"

"Because of the huge inflation, we used up our funds in no time and had nowhere to turn."

It was a sad day when they quit school and returned to Putzu. But, fortunately, the founding of the Normal University was soon announced. Youde passed the difficult examination and again left Putzu to study in Taipei. Six months later, Youde's elder brother returned from Japan to teach at Taipei Chienkuo Middle School and secured faculty housing. Youde's livelihood was thus solved.

"I see. You went there because the Normal University is a government-funded school. But Yu-kun stayed on with National Taiwan University. I didn't think his family was well off to that extent."

"He is the eldest son. His parents had said that they would send him to college even if they had to live on grass."

Momentarily, Youde saw in his mind's eye, the faces of Yu-kun's parents, ever honest and industrious, who had untiringly sacrificed for their son. They must be washing their faces with tears nowadays. Youde's heart ached.

"Did you see each other much during college years?"

"Yes."

"Did he visit you often in your house?"

"Yes."

"For what business did he visit you?"

"Nothing special."

"For instance."

"To go to the movies or to borrow or exchange books."

"What books did you lend each other?"

"I can't remember exactly."

"It's strange that you want to evade these things. There were some unmentionable books, weren't there?"

"No. There weren't books like that."

"Then, why don't you tell us about them?"

It was hard to remember. Youde gave four or five book titles.

"There were a lot of Communist books at his place. It wouldn't be unusual if he had lent you one or two of them."

"He did not lend me books of that nature, because he knew I was not interested in books like that."

Now back to books again, after all!

"Then what kind of books are you interested in?"

"Books on literature and theater. For example, Herman Hesse's books. Speaking of Hesse, I did borrow Hesse's collective works from the library and lent a couple of volumes to Yu-kun."

"Who? Hesse?"

"Yes. A German writer. He was called the 'conscience of the twentieth century.'"

"......"

"Contrary to materialism, his work depicts the world of idealism, such as young people agonizing over the search for truth."

"That's enough."

Youde wanted to impress upon them that a person with interest in Hesse could not possibly be sympathetic to materialism, but it was not possible. Not a single book of Hesse's had been translated into Chinese.

Still, judging from the line of questioning, Youde gathered that Yu-kun had only mentioned the books and nothing else in connection with his childhood chum, and felt somewhat relieved.

General Hu singled out Youde's friends one by one and questioned Youde for his thoughts about them and the nature of his association with them. He questioned about Shui-ching, Wen-bang and Shen-yuan repeatedly, going back and forth over the inconsistencies and sometimes, surreptitiously pop the question, "When did you join the Party?"

The tiresome questioning went on and on, endlessly.

GI-cut, who had stopped taking notes by now, couldn't stop yawning.

The only point they had was, "Admit it now. It's about time. We can all go home and rest."

22

Undershirt

Youde then noticed that Detective Ho was sitting on the sofa. Could it be that my head is getting muddled somewhat — not paying attention to people's movements anymore? When General Hu and GI-cut finished their questioning and left the room after acquiring Youde's pro-forma thumbprint, Ho invited Youde to the sofa, "Come here. It's more comfortable."

Youde stood up but couldn't lift his legs. Pain shot through his knees.

"Oh, that's right." Ho came over and led Youde by his wrist.

"I went to your house." Ho said as he helped Youde to the sofa. Ho's sidekick Big Shantung was nowhere in sight.

"How did it go?" Youde asked.

"They were worried. But after listening to me, they seemed somewhat relieved. I consoled them that you would be allowed to come home once the investigation is over."

"I don't know how to thank you. Thank you so much."

"Nah, we being both 'sweet potatoes,' this is nothing. So, how old is your child?"

"She is a year and nine months old."

"That's about the same age as mine. She sure talks well for her age. She was holding incense in her hands and was praying to the gods that her papa would come home soon."

Youde came dangerously close to tears. "I am weakening emotionally," he thought.

On the coffee table sat a bundle, wrapped in a scarf.

"Your family asked me to bring you a pillow and some underwear. They told me that you can't get to sleep on a strange pillow." Ho put his hand on the bundle.

"Why don't you have yourself a change of clothes?" Ho handed Youde a set of underwear.

Youde changed the top then the bottom. He had difficulty putting his feet through the leg openings. The pungent sweaty smell assaulted his nostrils.

Just as Youde finished changing, Big Shantung entered the room. He laid on the coffee table some steamed buns and soymilk contained in an aluminum carrying pot.

How long has it been since I was brought in here, how many hours? How many days? The drapes remained drawn. There was no clock in the room; rather, there were signs that a wall clock had been removed, a deliberate act to deny the detainee knowledge of time. Youde felt the urge to ask Ho for the time but refrained, for fear of putting this kind person in a difficult position. Knowing the time wasn't going to change things one way or the other.

Youde's mouth and throat were parched, his lips scaly dry. He would rather have water, but Ho picked up a steamed bun and pressed it on Youde to eat. Youde had no appetite.

"You must eat. It's been a long time since you last ate," Ho advised.

Youde put a piece of bread in his mouth. Instantly, his tongue was on fire. He spat it out reflexively.

"What's wrong?" Ho asked.

"It hurts terribly."

Youde felt like his tongue was covered with blisters. He gingerly stuck out his tongue. Ho peeked at Youde's tongue, "Ya, I see a lot of red blisters."

Youde pulled his tongue back. The back of his tongue was stiff.

"Well, drink this. It will help."

Ho poured a cup of soymilk. It was too hot to drink.

"Water please." Youde pleaded.

"OK. Water."

Big Shantung left the room to fetch water.

Youde closed his eyes and leaned back on the sofa. The blisters were a new phenomenon. It was not particularly unusual for Youde to stay up two straight days and nights. Before he was married, he was frequently quite reckless, staying up all night to do his writing, then playing *go* or mahjong through the next night. As a matter of fact, Youde had quite a reputation as an all-nighter. But never once had his tongue turned into a mess of blisters. This must mean that it had been more than two days.

Big Shantung came back with a water pitcher. A kind man. Youde poured himself a cup of water and sipped it gingerly. Luckily, his tongue received the water eagerly. He downed four or five in a row.

Sweat drenched his underwear, the ones he had just taken the trouble to change into.

23

Big Shantung

"I WILL be doing the questioning now. You can answer with your eyes closed." Ho laid out the investigation papers on the coffee table. Youde leaned back comfortably while Ho had to lean forward over the coffee table to do his writing. Doing his own recording, Ho asked, "In your student days, did you join any political party?"

"No."

"Were you invited to join the Communist Party?"

"No, I was not."

"There were many Communist believers around you."

"Yes, there were."

"Didn't you know that they were Communist Party members?"

"I did not know that any of them were."

Ho recorded the answers word by word. He did not refute or pressure.

"Among the plays you produced, were any of them banned?"

"Only Ts'ao Yu's *The Sunrise*. But it was banned after our production. At the time, we could have been commended for introducing well-known plays of the motherland."

"Where did you perform the plays?"

"In Taipei, Chiayi, and Putzu."

"Did you obtain permits?"

"Yes. In Taipei, from the school authorities; in Chiayi and Putzu, from the police."

"And the scripts were submitted for review ahead of time, also?"

"Yes."

It was obvious that Ho was composing a favorable investigative report.

"Ah —." Youde gave out a big yawn uncontrollably, the first one since he entered this building — most likely from a sense of relief that it was all right to let his guard down in front of Ho. For the past three days and nights, Youde had been under such strain, not knowing what a wrong word could bring, that he had no time for a yawn.

"If you can fall asleep, go ahead." Ho said with understanding.

Youde thanked Ho and tried but couldn't fall asleep. When he tried to open his eyes, he felt faint pain, perhaps from the tobacco smoke, or the light or from sheer fatigue. "My eyes are probably bloodshot now," Youde imagined. Youde shut his eyes and catnapped, but he was aware that Ho stood up; he could also hear Ho and Big Shantung talking.

A thump. Something was set down on the table. Reflexively Youde opened his eyes. Big Shantung had refilled the water pitcher. Youde straightened up and said thanks.

"Would you like a drink of water?" Big Shantung kindly solicited.

Without waiting for the answer, Big Shantung filled the glass to the brim with water. Youde thanked him again and drank the water.

"The sooner you confess, the sooner you go home. It's the right thing to do," Big Shantung said with understanding. Ho put his hand on Youde's shoulder and said, "Mr. Fan here is a nice fellow, a totally kind person."

Yet when Big Shantung left the room, Ho put his mouth to Youde's ears and related, "Nobody can stand up to this big fella from Shantung Province as far as the number of people he has killed. You see, he was an executioner in his youth. They said he used to decapitate the criminals with blue dragon knives." Youde imagined a blood-splattered Big Shantung.

What a shame. Just when Big Shantung had seemed a kind man, now he turned into a creepy figure.

24

Ho's Complaints

"How long was I allowed to sleep? Maybe about ten minutes." Youde was not sure, as his sense of time was all screwed up. He was thankful for the ten minutes of sleep and the resupply of water to his body, a significant matter. He was able to regain his strength somewhat, thanks to Ho and Big Shantung.

Ho continued with the questioning. He asked some non-essential questions and finished up the three-page report.

The next shift had yet to arrive, so the three chatted, although Youde just listened. Big Shantung again brought up the subject of Communist cruelty on the mainland, much to Ho's impatience who had apparently heard the story many times already. Knowing Big Shantung was once an executioner, Youde found the stories of killings taking on more reality. Big Shantung, however, was not able to monopolize the conversation.

Ho asked casually, "What is the name of Wen-bang's sister?"

"It is Su-yun."

"Quite a beauty. I saw her once."

"……"

"I heard that she is not yet married."

"No, she is not."

"I understand that a lot of college students had chased after her."

"Yes."

The expression, chase after, was somewhat distasteful to Youde. But it was true that a lot of college students had admired her like a flower on a tall fence.

"I wonder why she is so late in marrying?"

"I don't know. I don't think it is so late." Youde replied.

If she was late in marrying, the reason was obvious. It was because almost all the idealistic, elite young men had been arrested. The ones remained were far from her fancy. They were all weak, materialistic, and lacking in a sense of justice.

"Did Yu-kun chase after her?"

"Well...."

"That's not enough. What's the story?"

For what started out as an informal chat, Ho was unexpectedly persistent.

"I don't know." Youde replied. But Youde knew for a fact that Yu-kun had loved her. Whether Yu-kun had confided his love to her Youde did not know. It was not an age that a young man confided lightly of love, even if he had expressed his love in some other way.

Ho glanced at his wristwatch and stood up. He also gestured Youde to return to his seat at the desk. Ho himself also returned to the desk and started to review the report. When he finished, Ho faced Youde and muttered, out of Big Shantung's earshot, "I too, have complaints about the government."

"Take government housing, for instance. They all got good housing, but I had a hard time getting one. It's because I am a 'sweet potato.' I applied for it again and again. Finally, I got this tiny apartment with a leaky roof, only recently too."

"It also bugs me that they change their birth dates to suit the occasions. Taking advantage of the lack of residency registration on the mainland, they can just gather three friends and testify for each other. Take the police chief. He is supposed to be in charge of residency registration and he changed his own first! Some of them even changed two or three times. The chief himself, an older man over fifty, changed his birthday to pass as forty-ish, then duped a thirty-ish woman to marry him."

Ho's complaints were run-of-the-mill, nothing new.

Nevertheless, they were a little out of place. Youde shrank from chiming in. Somehow, Ho's talks always ended up with women.

25

A Friend Named Francesco

The duo of Wang and T'ien came back into the room. Wang took Ho's place. Like a knife cutting through to the bone, Wang immediately started the questioning.

"When did you learn of Chang Yu-kun's capture?"

"When I was in America."

Wang's eyes showed incomprehension.

"You mean you didn't learn about it after your return?"

"No, I knew about it several months before I came home."

"How did you know?"

"My wife touched upon it in her letter."

"That's strange."

Wang and T'ien exchanged glances.

It was strange all right. Letters from Youde's wife were opened and read by the secret police from some time back. The letter that mentioned Yu-kun's capture was either sent before that date, or, the one-line sentence was overlooked by the examiner. On the other hand, Panto's letter had referred to Yu-kun as Gandhi, a nickname due to his dark skin.

"Why was there a need to let you know about such things?"

"Not that there was a need, but my wife wrote me once a week. She wrote about the smallest things, such as the old man next door falling and spraining his ankle, or that the pomelo tree was about to bear fruit, or the chicken had hatched...."

"Do you still have the letters?"

"Yes. I brought home all of my wife's letters. They are in my house."

Youde rejoiced, this may turn out to be a good defensive evidence. If Youde were a Communist Party member, he wouldn't have returned to Taiwan after learning about Yu-kun's capture, for fear of being exposed. Instead, he could have gone to the mainland or asked for political asylum in another country. Only a fool would jump into his own grave knowingly. It was common sense.

But Wang saw it differently.

"So you returned, even after learning about Yu-kun's capture."

"Yes, that is correct."

"I see. So you returned to Taiwan with the new directives from Communist Central."

Wang elaborated a farfetched theory, "The Communists' channel of communication to Taiwan has been terminated for some time now. They can't use the wireless transmission because it would be like providing us with intelligence directly. You see, you would be the most suitable conduit to transmit the directives from overseas. Besides, you speak both English and Japanese, quite convenient when it comes to contacting foreigners."

"That is —"

"Don't panic. Hear me out."

Youde's sometimes-groggy mind snapped to full attention.

"You were with a foreigner from Honolulu on. You arrived in Tokyo by the same plane, stayed in the same hotel for four days and hung around together the whole time. You parted from him at Haneda Airport. Am I wrong?"

Wang stared into Youde's bloodshot eyes.

"No, just as you said. But the foreigner was not a suspicious person."

"Where did you meet him?"

"In September 1953. I met him in Washington, D.C., at the orientation for the foreign trainees that the State Department sponsored. We spent about a week together."

"What's his name?"

"Carlos Francesco, a Filipino doctor. He is in the field of public health."

Wang turned the pages in his file to check on the name.

Indeed, they had done some investigation.

Youde ran into Dr. Francesco, that's how Youde addressed him, again on the Pan Am flight to Tokyo from Honolulu. The plane was a propeller plane and had only a few passengers.

Dr. Francesco was so glad to see the Japanese-speaking Youde that he changed his original itinerary, which was to leave for the Philippines the next day, and decided to tour Tokyo with Youde instead. Youde booked rooms in a Japanese-style hotel in Ueno and gave Dr. Francesco a guided tour: Ginza, Shinjuku, Yurakucho, Asakusa, Kanda, even Yoshiwara. Every day Dr. Francesco exclaimed, "I am a lucky man;" and he was one satisfied customer when he departed for home.

There was nothing of a suspicious nature in their activities. They were too busy sightseeing to talk politics. Their conversations were bright and happy, full of laughter and friendship, no room for boring political topics. Consequently, even though Youde knew Dr. Francesco was of good character, he did not know anything about Dr. Francesco's political beliefs. There was one worrisome incident, however. At one point, when the big Red-hunter Senator McCarthy appeared on the TV screen, Dr. Francesco said, "He is mistaken," and laughed loudly.

Suppose Dr. Francesco was a Communist? Then what? These intelligence people are suspicious about little or nothing to start with; it is probably of no use to try to explain it away.

Wang asked, "What did you do in Tokyo?"

"We saw sights."

"Where did you go and what did you see? Do you remember?"

"I think so."

"Write them all down for us."

T'ien pushed the paper over to Youde. Youde put down ten or so famous place names and gave it back.

Wang stood up and in a loud voice and berated unsparingly.

"Don't take us for fools. There are twenty-four hours to a day. Write down, in order, the places you went to. Begin from the time you arrived till you left Tokyo. And be truthful."

Youde started from noon of August 27, 1954, when the plane arrived at Haneda Airport. The arrival scene was rather dramatic. As soon as the plane touched down, a red carpet was rolled out from the plane toward the waiting room. At the other end stood several girls, dressed in Japanese kimonos and carrying flowers in their hands. Youde remembered spotting a "Santori" banner among a sea of flags and thinking that they must be welcoming some VIP.

But among the ten or so passengers, no VIP-like person existed. Later, Youde learned that the welcome was for the two professional wrestlers, one of them by the name of Newman whom Francesco had suspected of being a smuggler. Youde and Dr. Francesco had a good laugh at the waiting room about that. The wrestling champion Rikidosan was among the welcoming party also.

Youde had to detail, in sequence, the time they left the airport, when they arrived at the hotel in Ueno, when and where they took their dinners, where they took their walk and how they spent the evening, and what time they went to bed.

When a person is starting his fourth day without sleep, his brain intermittently falls into a gray world for a second or two at a time. Driving such a brain to its limits, Youde filled in the 24 × 4 hours with appropriate activities, though he had no confidence that they were all accurate. He was exhausted when he put down his pen.

Wang was perusing a document. A moment of silence prevailed. All of a sudden, Youde heard a voice from inside his head, "There are limits to my tolerance. Fight back."

When Wang raised his head from the reading, Youde, without missing a beat, said in a somewhat elevated voice, "Mr. Wang."

"Yes."

"I am not a member of the Communist Party. Therefore, I did not receive any directives from the Communist Party. If Francesco were the person to pass on to me the directives, he would have disappeared as soon as he did so. Why would he spend four days with me? Furthermore, suppose I did return with the directives, I should have gone into hiding right away. Why would I spend a leisurely month at home to await the arrest? Isn't it because I have nothing to be afraid of?"

Wang looked at Youde with a startled expression.

Youde's refutation was perhaps rather common in other countries, but under the reign of the White Terror, this kind of argument carried a high degree of risk. It also seldom paid off. If the refutation was not well argued, it could result in a heavier sentence, the act of refutation taken as a lack of remorse. If the argument was well reasoned, it could anger the opposing party. After all, "shame turning into anger" is a known personality trait of the Chinese people.

"That's for us to decide." Wang frowned.

Yet it might have been the success of the counterattack, or maybe that they decided to wait for investigations from Tokyo or the Philippines, but Wang cut short the talk about new directives.

26

Su's Violence

Tien went to open the door and returned leaving the door ajar. The room had been locked from inside the whole time since Youde was brought in. Could it be that they now realized that Youde was but a small fry and decided to relax the security? Or was it because they knew the suspect was too weak from days and nights of questioning to escape? Or, maybe, merely because they couldn't stand the tobacco smoke anymore and opened the door for fresh air? Whatever the reason, the open door rid the room of the appearance of a secret chamber and the atmosphere in the room lightened somewhat.

Alas, it was short-lived. Soon, five men swaggered into the room and again the door was closed.

Wang brought up *Mao Wenchi* again.

"About the book *Mao Wenchi* at your house, who brought it there? Can you remember now?"

"The book was never in my house." Youde denied it for the hundredth time.

"We are certain that it was there. A fact is a fact, no matter how much you deny it."

"If it were there, I am sure I would have noticed it. But I have no memory of it at all."

Suddenly a sharp voice sounded above Youde's head, "Bastard!"

Youde looked up. With his blurry eyes, he saw Fat Su's fleshy, red face.

"This one is not going to talk unless we show him some pain. Hey, Wang, no use asking him anymore. Leave it to me."

Fat Su grabbed Youde by his shirtfront and picked him up from the chair. Youde felt his body float like a balloon.

"All right, Tsai, since you seem to prefer penalty drinks to the celebratory ones, we will just have to take you downstairs and let you have plenty of that."

T'ien said, as if comforting a young child, "You will suffer a lot downstairs. It's going to end up the same anyway, you are better off telling us now."

Fat Su tightened his hold further and barked, "Who brought the book to you? Are you going to tell us?"

"On the subject of *Mao Wenchi*, I don't have any more to say."

"Bastard!" Cursing aloud, Fat Su pushed Youde away.

His numbed legs and feet already too weak to support his weight, the push propelled Youde's body to the floor, overturning the chair as he went down. Sparks shot up inside his bloodshot eyes.

Fat Su turned to give the order. "Take this one downstairs."

Two men in Sun Yet-sen suits immediately approached. They each took a wrist and pulled Youde up from the floor. Maybe the sudden jerk had injured the muscles, but Youde was not able to stand. The two men dragged Youde toward the door.

To believe Ho's words — there will be no torture — was to engage in wishful thinking, after all.

"Wait!"

Just as they were about to cross the threshold came General Hu's voice.

"Bring him back. I'll give it another try."

Even though he knew this could be just a temporary relief, Youde felt a sense of being rescued. The normally impatient voice of General Hu's sounded rather kind.

"No matter what, I don't want to be taken to the torture room," Youde wished.

27

Compromise

General Hu came over and whispered.

"Trust me. I would not make it bad for you."

Youde, hanging onto the two men in Sun Yat-sen suits, returned to his seat. Fat Su sat down a short distance away, propped his shoed feet on the desk and started to smoke. General Hu took Wang's place across from Youde. T'ien remained the scribe.

General Hu said, "All right. We have concrete evidence with regard to *Mao Wenchi*. It's no use for you to go on denying it."

What could it be, the so called concrete evidence?

"Like you forgot to mention *A Reader in Materialist Dialectics* we can treat the matter of *Mao Wenchi* the same way — we would not put down that you had evaded that on purpose."

General Hu seemed to be begging Youde to understand his good intentions. "Was General Hu friend or foe?" Youde could not be certain any more. The so-called concrete evidence must be Yu-kun's testament. Youde could no longer evade it. Yu-kun must have realized that the possession of *A Reader in Materialist Dialectics* alone was not enough to convince the authorities that Youde was a Communist, so he added *Mao Wenchi* to the story. The authorities take everything a Self-Renewal person says as evidence.

Whether with good will or malice, General Hu began the questioning.

"In your house, wasn't there a book with a missing cover?"

"Several."

In the era right after the war, many books were printed without covers. Youde himself had bound quite a few books with plain, thick paper for covers.

"Wasn't *Mao Wenchi* one of them?"

"I don't know."

"It's important. You must recall."

Alas, the mind which was instructed to recall kept falling into ever lengthening periods of gray with ever shortening intervals in between.

"I don't know.... I don't know...."

"So, you are not saying it wasn't one of them?"

"......"

"Maybe it was there. Is it possible that because you did not read it, you had little impression of it?"

"No, I absolutely did not read the book."

"Well, maybe somebody brought it over, already in white paper cover?"

"If I had it, it must have happened the way you described."

"Suppose somebody brought it to you. Who could he be?"

"Maybe Yu-kun."

"Not possible," General Hu asserted instantly.

Youde noted: Just as I reasoned, Yu-kun must have testified that he saw the book. If Yu-kun had said that he himself had brought the book to Youde, General Hu would not be pursuing the identity of the book bearer with such intensity.

Suppose at this juncture, in his groggy state of mind, Youde had irresponsibly offered somebody else's name. That person, suspected of attempting to recruit Youde, would no doubt be arrested and taken into investigation. Even if Youde had named a person already in jail, this could cause the person to be subjected to further investigation and face untold troubles for having covered up some facts.

"A dead person has no mouth," the proverb says.

"It could have been Chou Shen-yuan," Youde replied.

"OK. Other possibilities?"

"Can't think of anybody else."

"How about Yeh Chin-kuei?"

"Yeh never visited my place in Taipei. It had to be either Yu-kun or Shen-yuan."

"All right. But that's odd. You are a person who does a lot of reading. You had to be curious about what Chou Shen-yuan brought to you. Didn't you at least flip through it?"

"I don't have any memory about the book."

Back to the futile back-and-forth again.

"So, you mean, when Chou brought you a book, you did not even ask what it was or take a look at it?"

"No. I do not have any memory about it. Maybe he came when I was out."

"Hmm. He came when you were not home and left the book there. Is this your story?"

"......"

"But isn't it strange that he would leave such an important book without saying something to you?"

"I wouldn't know."

"When you saw him again at school, didn't he mention the book to you?"

"Maybe we didn't have an opportunity to see each other again after that, because he became a fugitive soon after."

"What happened to the book after that?"

"I don't know."

"Did it remain in your bookcase?"

"No. The book was not there."

"The book would not disappear by itself."

"Chou could have taken it back."

"So he took it back during his flight from the authorities?"

"I don't know. If it was after he was in flight, I think I would have remembered. It had to be before he went into hiding."

"Why did he take back the book?"

"Must be because I did not respond."

"So he just took it back without a word."

"Yes. He never mentioned the book. It's possible that he tried to put his possessions in order before taking flight."

"We are supposed to think that he gave up recruiting you because he was rushed into flight."

"Yes. I think that might be what happened."

General Hu gave a lot of affirmative "um's" today, quite different from the last round. In places, he even seemed to match Youde's steps. "Did he harbor good or ill will toward me?" Youde was not certain.

In any case, the endless questioning about *Mao Wenchi* seemed to have reached a point of compromise.

28

Long Whiskers

Out of Yu-kun's fabrication yet another fabrication was born — the investigative report was placed in front of Youde. Reluctant as he was, Youde had to put down his thumbprint.

Youde looked steadily into General Hu's eyes and said, "May I have a word?"

"What is it?"

"I had many associations with many Communists, so I don't blame you for suspecting me to be one. But taking a different angle, isn't it possible that because I was strongly anti-Communist in my thinking that I was not absorbed into the Communist clique, despite being surrounded by them? I should have been commended for it, but instead I am being punished. This is unexpected."

General Hu did not "um" this time, but he did not refute either.

"It's not that I don't understand your complaint, but I would be laughed at if I included that kind of argument in the report. We are not lawyers after all. Let's wrap it up. Put your thumbprint down."

With some reservation, Youde pressed his thumbprint down as told.

General Hu offered cigarettes to Youde and then left the room with T'ien in tow. The others had already left the room, except for the two men in Sun Yat-sen suits. The two helped Youde to the sofa. On the coffee table still sat the bundle from home that Ho had brought. Youde untied the bundle and found a hand towel. As he took out the towel and was about to wipe his brow, one of the Sun Yat-sen suits ordered him to hand over the towel. Youde handed over the towel and took out a set of underwear. His body was sticky with grease and sweat, more accurately, sweat mixed with body oil, not in a condition to get into a clean set of underwear without toweling off first. In a short time, the Sun Yat-sen suit returned with the towel, freshly wrung out in cold water.

Youde put the towel to his face immediately. It felt cool and pleasant. Great help in dissipating the body heat! His eyelids could use the wet towel the most because his eyeballs were on fire. For several minutes, Youde could not bear to remove the towel from his eyelids. He forgot all about toweling off his body. As he was pressing the towel down on his face, his hands brushed against his whiskers. Youde had only scant facial hair, save for the mustache and a stringy goatee. He could easily go without shaving for two or three days.

"How many days has it been?" Youde measured the whiskers with his fingertips. Longer than the three-day whiskers. "It must have been at least four days then. This means that for four or five days straight, I have tackled the marathon-like interrogation by seven or eight inquisitors, who worked in relay." Feeling the length of whiskers on his fingertips, Youde felt sorry for himself. "If my mother were to learn about this, she would be in such sorrow!"

Somebody opened the door and said, "Oops!" The Sun Yat-sen suit whispered something about meeting. "They must be holding a meeting to come to a conclusion about my investigation, just like they have done many times before to discuss the various strategies during the interrogation. There is nothing else to do but to leave it to fate and wait for the meeting to end. One more thing, I must quickly cool off my head and make it regain some normalcy before facing their next move."

The towel was the only thing he could depend on.

29

Ho's True Nature

Youde was awakened by somebody shaking him by the shoulders. He had fallen asleep. Hurriedly, he removed the towel from his eyes. Ho's face came into view. The moisture from the towel had mostly evaporated; the towel felt somewhat warm to the touch now. Ho took the towel from Youde, handed it over to the Sun Yat-sen suit. Seeing Ho, Youde felt at ease.

"I am impressed by your stamina," Ho said as he sat down next to Youde.

"You've got physical endurance. Moreover, you were clear headed from beginning to end. Quite remarkable."

"Is it over?"

Since it was Ho, Youde felt he could ask freely.

"Not entirely. They are in a meeting now. It should end soon."

"What's going to happen to me?"

Ho drew a long one on his cigarette and said matter-of-factly, "You will probably be sent to Taipei."

"What?"

"You will be sent to a higher-level intelligence agency and they will re-investigate you all over again."

One more fatigue-interrogation, an even harsher one!

"How did it turn out this way?"

"Because the investigation here is stuck in a rut."

The Sun Yat-sen suit brought back a freshly wrung damp towel. Youde had no time for damp towels now.

"Isn't the investigation detailed and thorough enough?"

"No. The important points are not matching up. Even the most crucial point was not nailed down."

"What's that?"

"The person who tried to recruit you. Without knowing this fact, the matter cannot end."

"Aside from the question of recruiting, the report should have said that I thought Chou Shen-yuan probably had brought the book *Mao Wenchi* to my house."

"But that's not very credible."

"……"

"Even General Hu does not have much confidence in that story."

Ho suddenly clammed up, as if regretting something he had said unnecessarily. He leaned over slightly and said, "The truth is, it's best for you to solve the whole matter right here. I can be of help somehow, and General Hu is rather sympathetic toward you. Rather rare, you know. I, for one, cannot bear to see you sent to Taipei."

"What should I do?"

"There is a way."

Ho slid close to Youde and whispered.

"I will take the responsibility to do something about it, so just tell me, tell me the truth about the book."

"What do you mean?"

"The name of the person who handed you the *Mao Wenchi*."

Youde couldn't believe his ears. He repeated Ho's words in his head.

"The name of the person who handed you the *Mao Wenchi*."

Ho was holding his breath waiting for the answer. All of a sudden, Youde understood it all.

Youde said decidedly, "The truth is that there wasn't such a person. You couldn't have found *Mao Wenchi* in my bookcase even if you had searched it."

Ho feigned surprise, "Is that true?"

"Yes. I can swear."

Ten seconds of hard-to-bear silence passed.

"Even to me, you will not give out the name. Too bad. I just wanted to help you."

Another long pause.

At last, Ho said, "Huh!" and stood up. Youde tried to get up too but his knees buckled and he fell back into the sofa.

Ho did not look back. His mission was now completed. It seemed that his assignment was to ask that last question.

Youde stole glances at Ho's profile; he was lighting a cigarette. There wasn't a speck of the kind "fellow sweet potato" to be found. Instead, his face was as cruel and unfeeling as that of Fat Su's when Su pushed Youde away with full force. No, Ho's face appeared even more fearsome than Su's.

Ho turned his back to Youde and walked out the room without a word, slamming the door behind him. He must be heading to the meeting to submit his latest report.

Youde leaned back on the sofa and closed his eyes. Tears flowed into his eyes, unstoppable tears, which he wiped with the towel vigorously.

The tears were not tears of lament for his fate to be sent to Taipei; rather, they were tears of human indignation. The indignant tears born of his rights trampled and his humanity further insulted.

30

Toward an Unknown World

YOUDE wiped his body with the tear-soaked hand towel, changed into a set of fresh underwear and sat back down in the sofa. He was rolling and exercising his stiffened neck when General Hu came into the room alone. Hu peered into Youde's eyes and said, "You still have strength left." These veterans of fatigue interrogation seemed to judge a person's condition by looking into the eyes.

"We lost to your tenacity." General Hu grinned sardonically. Youde looked up and saw an unshaven General Hu with swollen eyes. General Hu's tone of voice, accompanied by a thin smile, was unexpectedly gentle. In front of others, he spoke bluntly, but now, just between the two of them, his speech was calm and comforting. "Probably a more humane person than Ho," Youde for the first time felt something akin to friendliness toward General Hu.

"What is going to happen to me?" Youde made up his mind and asked.

"Well —" General Hu started, then interrupted himself.

In the corner of his eyes, Youde saw Captain Tao enter the room with a few of his men. Tao is here to check on his prisoner no doubt. Youde decided to close his eyes and ignore them. There's no more to say, even less reason to greet them. Captain Tao whispered in General Hu's ear and left the room.

General Hu ordered the two Sun Yat-sen suits, "Take this man downstairs."

Downstairs? The torture room? Youde shrank.

Perhaps sensing Youde's trepidation, General Hu again grinned sardonically and said, "Go downstairs and have a good rest."

The two Sun Yat-sen suits approached and lent their hands to Youde, who stood up warily and walked toward the door. Youde was capable of walking under his own power but, nevertheless, was held by the wrists by the two men. General Hu followed with Youde's bundle of clothes.

They walked along a long hallway before descending the steps. Here and there hung naked light bulbs. Nobody was in sight. The quietude of a deep night was broken only by the eerie echoes of the footsteps. They passed in front of a room marked by a plaque "Interrogation Room." Youde assumed: That must be the notorious torture room.

Walking returned Youde's feet to their normal condition. He no longer needed the help of the Sun Yat-sen suits.

Facing the end of the hallway, stood a ceiling-high, black-painted iron gate, outside of which a man working the graveyard shift was sitting at the desk. After completing the admissions procedures, the man at the desk unlocked the gate and let the party in. They walked some more, made a ninety-degree turn then stopped at another iron gate. This time, at one about a man's height. The guard who was expecting them pulled the gate open, which made a screeching sound.

Having completed their mission, the Sun Yat-sen suits turned their heels around and left.

General Hu handed the bundle to Youde and said, "You may be sent to Taipei." His answer to Youde's earlier question. "For now, just take it easy and have yourself a good rest."

"Thank you for your troubles," Youde bowed and thanked him.

"Um." General Hu nodded, gently patted Youde's shoulder, turned around, and left.

Watching General Hu's receding figure from the back, Youde, for a moment, felt dizzy and almost fell down.

"Come on, get in," the guard urged.

Youde held the bundle closer to his chest and passed through the iron gate, setting foot into a new, unknown world.

The guard took out a paper bag from the large desk and said, "Put everything you have in your pockets in this bag."

A wallet and a handkerchief were the only items. The wallet went into the bag while the handkerchief was handed back to Youde.

"Watch?"

"I don't have one."

"Take off your belt."

Into the bag went the belt. From this point on, whenever standing, Youde had to hold on to his pants with one hand. A realization that he was a prisoner hit him in the head.

On the wall behind the guard's station hung an electric clock, an item Youde hadn't seen for a while. The time was a little past twelve thirty. The place was dimly lit and smelled dank. Youde could hear snoring and rustling sounds. Some inmates got out of bed and were looking with curiosity. Youde was dizzy again, more severe than last time.

A different guard who carried a bunch of keys opened the middle prison cell and gestured Youde to enter. Youde stooped past the barely meter-high doorway into a room with wooden floors. The room was oddly shaped with narrow front and widening back. One prior guest was already there, sleeping, so soundly that he was not disturbed by Youde's presence. Next to the sleeping person, was spread a thin blanket. "A place for me," Youde gathered.

Without bothering to take out his pillow from the bundle, Youde dropped to the pallet. Right away a black curtain came down in front of his eyes. There was nothing, unknown world or not.

31

A Lad in the Same Cell

As he was coming out of deep slumber, voices of people talking started to intrude, but Youde continued to sleep while the voices streamed into his ears.

The pallet is hard. I am not sleeping on tatami but on a board floor. The board floor of a prison cell!" Youde was abruptly brought back to reality. He realized that the voices were from the inmates in the adjoining cells. He opened his eyes. The innocent face of a teenage boy hovered above.

Hurriedly, Youde tried to sit up. But his body, perhaps still craving repose, would not move with agility.

"Ojisan, so you are finally awake." The teenager smiled.

"So this young man is the early guest I noticed last night." Youde's legs felt extremely tired, his thighs and calves about to fall off the bones. Forsaking sitting up, Youde closed his eyes again, his hand unconsciously pounded his thighs.

"What time is it?"

"Half past two in the afternoon," the teenager answered and moved over to Youde's side then started to massage Youde's thighs.

"Thanks. It feels very good."

Again, Youde drifted off to sleep.

"Ojisan, are you going to eat your food?" The teenager's voice floated into Youde's dreamy consciousness. Too tired, Youde shook his head as a reply.

The teenager must have continued on with the massage, because when Youde woke up two hours later, his body felt much rested. Youde sat up and took the still massaging hands of the teenager and said his thanks. "Thank you. Thanks to you I am completely revived."

The teenager couldn't hide his joy, as if he had brought back an unconscious man.

"Ojisan, I am so glad that you are all right. You moaned a lot."

"I am sorry. But your massage really put me back in shape. Thank you again."

The clock was in plain view from Youde's cell. It said four thirty.

"What's your name?" Youde asked the teenager.

"Ah-fu. Li Ah-fu."

Youde stood up, stretched, and exercised a bit by swaying his upper body back and forth.

"How old are you?"

"Twenty."

That was a little surprising. The innocent, boyish face appeared to be no more than fifteen or sixteen years old. His frame was small too.

"I am Tsai Youde. I am ten years older than you."

Ordinarily, one does not address somebody reverentially who is only ten years older as *ojisan* (literally "uncle"). But maybe it was not so strange that the lad addressed the unshaven and longhaired Youde as ojisan.

Youde met the eyes of the guard who was sitting at the desk by the guard's station; a different guard from last night's. Youde nodded and the guard returned the nod.

This place was a temporary holding facility for unsentenced suspects. The fan-shaped space was divided into seven prison cells with the raised guard's station occupying the fan's pivot. From that vintage point, the guard was able to watch all seven cells simultaneously. Each cell measured about 1.5 meters in front and three times that deep. Because the cells fanned out, their entrances lay in an arc. Youde's cell was bright, had good ventilation, and one could see the sky through the window high up on the back wall. In one back corner, there was a flush toilet and a sink with a faucet. The cell was big enough for twelve or thirteen people, lying head to toe.

Youde paced around the cell. An untouched food tray was still by the barred entrance. Youde offered the food to Ah-fu, who shook his head. He turned on the faucet and guzzled thirstily. Not yet any sign of a bowel movement, a matter that bothered Youde.

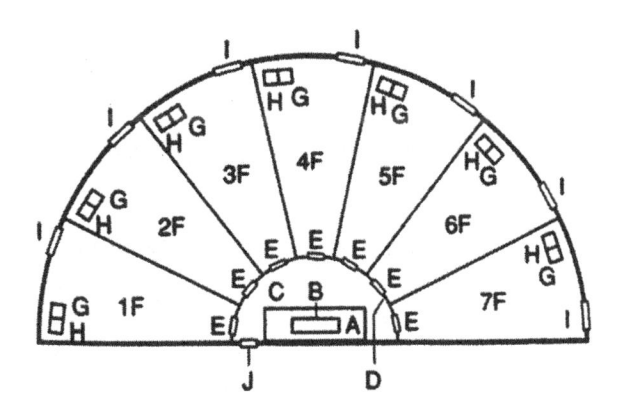

A. Guard station
B. Large desk
C. Hall
D. Iron-bar barrier
E. Cell door
F. Cell
G. Flush toilet
H. Sink with faucet
I. High window
J. Gate

Diagram of Chiayi Police Station holiding facility

This would make it five days without a bowel movement, a first in his entire life.

The people in the cell immediately to the right were talking loudly about gambling. "Keep it down," a guard admonished.

On the barred entrance of each cell hung a wooden frame in which the inmates' name plates were inserted. Because the entrances were in an arc, even when one could not read the names of the very next cell, he was able to read the names on the cells further down. The cell down further from the next cell had two name plates: "Gambling xxx" and "Burglary xxx." The name on the very end on the left caught Youde's attention — "Sedition Chuang Shui-ch'ing." A man accused of sedition, in other words, a political prisoner. Another unfortunate soul snared by the Sedition Law. His sentence would not compare with that of the gamblers and burglars. "What kind of person is he?" Youde wondered. Youde looked inside the cell but the inmate was not at the entrance to be seen.

Youde's cell also carried nameplates that faced outside. Youde imagined that one of them must say "Sedition Tsai Youde" but what about the other, Ah-fu's? Thinking it must be something trivial, Youde decided to inquire.

"Ah-fu, I am here as a political prisoner. What are you in for?"

"Killing."

"What?"

Ah-fu stuck out two fingers in front of a startled Youde.

"Two?" Youde was too dumbfounded to continue.

"Ya." Ah-fu nodded, unembarrassed. His face was so utterly guileless and otherworldly that Youde was not able to dislike him.

32

A Killer

Another guard entered, carrying in each hand a grass-woven bag. "Meal time!" somebody said, followed by noises of people getting up. The clock on the wall pointed at five. The sun was still shining high outside — an early supper. Cell by cell, the guard first checked the names then distributed the aluminum food boxes along with the disposable chopsticks. After fifteen or sixteen hours of continuous sleep, reinforced by the effect of Ah-fu's massage, Youde felt hungry.

Ah-fu right away opened the aluminum lid and started to eat. Youde too opened the lid. Atop the white rice there were some green vegetables, sun-dried turnip strips and a piece of braised fish. "How's my tongue?" Gingerly Youde put a lump of rice into his mouth. Nothing. The red blisters had gone away. First food in four days. Youde chewed each mouthful as much as possible, lest the enforced fast have weakened his digestive system. Frankly, milk would have been the food of choice, but he was not exactly in a position to order it. Next, he put some vegetables into his mouth. No taste at all. "Could I have lost the sense of taste due to drastic drop of salt in my body?" Youde wondered. The braised fish had some flavor. Youde ate the fish in little bites, chewing each mouthful methodically. The sun-dried turnip strips were too tough to chew. He finished half the food before his appetite disappeared.

Ah-fu had already cleaned up his plate. He said the food was better here than at home. At home the rice was usually cooked with strips of dried sweet potatoes mixed into it.

Youde found out about Ah-fu's personal background: His parents both died of malaria when he was eight. Since then he had lived with his grandmother, who brought him up working as a hired field hand. Ah-fu himself entered an apprenticeship at a bicycle shop at age thirteen and by now was sufficiently able to support himself in the bicycle-repair business. Unfortunately, his circle of friends was limited, and the few friends he had were all gamblers. Gambling was their only pastime, yet nobody nearby was available to provide guidance. Thus, sadly, the noose of crime was already prepared for him when he was merely thirteen, although his innocent face was far from that of a killer.

Youde asked, "Did you really kill somebody?"

"Kinky-haired Ah-pin and Big-head Chin-cheng."

"Why did you kill them?"

"They both swindled me and took my savings."

"What bad people. How much did they cheat you out of?"

"Eight hundred yuan."

The take home pay of a college educated government worker was barely one thousand yuan a month. So eight hundred yuan most likely represented six months to a year's savings to Ah-fu, perhaps a nest egg diligently put away to surprise his grandmother.

"Do you gamble a lot?"

"No. My friends were doing it all the time. But that was my first time. Before, I always just watched. That's how I saved as much as eight hundred yuan."

"Then why did you join in the gambling?"

"Kinky-haired Ah-pin enticed me. He urged me to take out my savings from the post office to go gambling." Ah-fu dropped his head, apparently too painful to recall.

"I was wrong to try to grow it into a thousand in a hurry. The bastard won four hundred and just ran away with the win. Then one sunny day, I ran into him having a nice snooze in the little duck-watching hut. I don't know, maybe the devil got the better of me, but I just picked up a two-by-four and hit him on the head. And he died."

Somebody laughed. It was the guard at the desk.

Conversation in the cells that may not be audible to the next-door neighbor could be heard by the guard, as he sat at the hub of the jailhouse.

"A person dies so very easily," Ah-fu said, looking at Youde with a half smile.

"What's going to happen to me?" Not minding at all being overheard, Ah-fu asked the guard with curiosity.

"Nothing. He died on his own, didn't he? Ha ha ha."

Ah-fu seemed relieved.

"But didn't the police call you in for questioning?"

"Ya. They came to the shop and asked about the fellow. I told them that I didn't know anything about it and the police just left."

"Ha ha. Then what happened to the other fellow, the Big-head somebody?" the guard asked with interest.

"Big-head Chin-sheng was the dealer at the gambling den, you see. I went back there to try to win back my four hundred yuan. But no matter where I placed my bet, the prize was always somewhere else. Hand after hand, it was always the same. He had to have it rigged against me."

"And then?" The guard seemed more interested in the way the killing took place than the motive.

"That night, I followed him out of the gambling den. When he squatted down to wash his face in an irrigation ditch, I grabbed his hair from behind and pushed his head into the water."

"And he died so easily?"

"Oh, no. He was much bigger than I was and he struggled like a crazed buffalo. I fell in the ditch with him, but I never let go until he became quiet."

"What did you do with the body?"

"I pulled him up on the bank, took out just eight hundred yuan from his pocket and left the rest there."

"What about the body?"

"Body? I thought he would come to, so I just left him there and went home."

Youde felt heavy hearted and lay down. His body still required more sleep. His limbs were still tired.

"What's going to happen to me?" Ah-fu asked the guard, as if beseeching a representative of the authorities.

"It's their karma. Both of them were fated to die on that day. Otherwise, how could they die so easily? You are not guilty. Go to sleep and don't worry about it now."

Ah-fu slid over to Youde's side, happiness on his face, he asked, "More massage?"

"Thanks. That's OK."

Youde meant to decline out of politeness, but Ah-fu must have taken it the other way because he started to massage Youde's feet. Regardless, the massage was much appreciated once it started.

Youde wanted to repay Ah-fu's kindness in some way, but there's nothing he could do. No possessions to give, save for kind words.

Youde pondered:

But what would I answer if Ah-fu asked me "What's going to happen to me," the same question I put to Detective Ho and General Hu the other day? It is the most pressing question. I can't tell an open-faced lie like the guard. Moreover, not a believer in heaven or the next life, I can't comfort others with religious platitudes.

Youde murmured to himself as he faded into dreams.

"This is going to be tougher than fending off General Hu's questioning."

33

Scream of Self Recrimination

YOUDE got up prompted by a stirring in his bowels, the first one in five days. Taking food must have gotten the digestive system going again, though constipation was to be expected. Straining hard, he produced five or six pea-sized feces and a large quantity of gas. Ah-fu handed Youde some cheap, coarse toilet paper that something one asked for from the guard.

After the bowel movement, Youde felt lighter both literally and mentally, a feeling of just finishing a difficult assignment that almost put him in a singing mood.

Somebody in the next cell started to sing. The time between dinner and the nine o'clock bedtime appeared to be the most enjoyable for the inmates. The guards, too, tended to be more indulgent with regard to talking and carryings on. Youde and Ah-fu found a song they both knew, a peasant's song.

Leaving the house at daybreak,
I go to the farm.
The sky gradually brightens,
None asks me how I toil.

Two of them harmonized and sang, walking around the room. For the time being, despite being amid misfortune, Youde was able to feel some pleasure — the atmosphere struck him as even family like. When the voices got too loud, the guard banged on the desk with a metal ruler and admonished them, "Too loud!" Even as he was enjoying the singing, Youde could not help but take frequent peeks at Cell 7, where Chuang was housed. Chuang didn't seem to be in. His cellmate, a burglar, was alone looking out at others through the iron bars. It turned nine o'clock.

"Bedtime," the guard shouted. The lights snapped out and the room darkened. Youde's body still demanded much more sleep. He lay down with Ah-fu by his side.

Youde did not know how much time had passed when Ah-fu awakened him. Somebody had entered the jailhouse. It has to be the political prisoner Chuang! Youde instantly rolled over to his stomach and peered. Helped by two guards, an extremely haggard man was slowly dragging his slippered feet toward Cell 7. No words were necessary as the man was obviously the political prisoner Chuang Shui-ch'ing. His overgrown hair was shaggy and his beard bushy; his face, glazed with grease, shined eerily under the naked light bulb. Ghostly. Slowly, Chuang passed by Youde's cell. It seemed that Chuang had been spending the nights in the cell but was taken to the investigation room during the day for grilling. "The authorities must possess some evidence against Chuang," Youde thought.

"Lately they don't rough you up unless they possess some evidence." Youde remembered what Ho had said, even though it was ridiculous to trust Ho's words now.

Youde crawled over to the iron barred entrance and stared at Chuang. The guard opened the barred door. Chuang let go of the guards and fell flat, face down, on his pallet. Heavy snoring could be heard. Chuang must have crawled further in because he disappeared from Youde's sight. The jailhouse was quiet once more.

Just when everybody fell back asleep, suddenly, in the midnight's stillness, sounds of a fist pounding fiercely on the wooden floor broke out from Cell 7. Two guards hurried over. Then, a thunderous scream, unimaginable to be from a man just returned from torture, echoed through the whole jailhouse.

"Damn, I sinned!"

It was a scream of self-recrimination, dripping with blood and tears, unforgettable to those who heard it.

What exactly happened to Chuang? Youde couldn't fall back to sleep for a long time.

34

Inventory Clearance

Youde woke up around six in the morning. It was October 8, a Saturday. His sleeping schedule seemed to be back to normal, he noted. He got out of bed and started to exercise with Ah-fu. It felt especially good to stretch. Youde glanced at Cell 7 from time to time but did not see Chuang. The guard began to distribute breakfast: two steamed buns and a bowl of soy milk. Youde ate them all. His appetite seemed normal again. But his physical strength had yet to recover completely; a sluggishness remained.

At a little past eight, there was commotion outside the iron gate of the jailhouse. The guard opened Cell 1 and ordered the inmates to take their possessions and come out. Four people came out empty handed. At the desk the guard handed back their money and watches then took out the handcuffs and chained the four together. Two uniformed police entered, to whom the guard handed over the chained four.

The policemen took the four inmates and left. Outside the gate there were signs of more policemen. When Youde turned around, he was confronted by Ah-fu's ashen face. Without putting it into words, his eyes were clearly asking, "What's going to happen to me?"

"Don't worry. Doesn't do you any good to worry." Youde invited Ah-fu to resume their exercise.

"You are honest and kind. I am sure that the gods will take good care of you."

Ah-fu flashed a smile. But it was short-lived. Now the guard started on Cell 2, Cell 3, Cell 5, and Cell 6, calling out the inmates.

This time eight of them lined up in front of the desk, handcuffed in pairs. Ah-fu tensed up. He's afraid of handcuffs perhaps. "Everybody is handcuffed when they leave from here."

"Will you, Ojisan, also be handcuffed?"

"Of course. Ka-chick, ka-chick." Youde imitated the handcuffing motion.

Youde and Ah-fu resumed their exercises, but Ah-fu's heart was not in it anymore.

"Li Ah-fu, get ready."

Finally, it was Ah-fu's turn. He was the only one in this round. Youde offered an undershirt to Ah-fu, who had started to pack. It was the only thing Youde had to give, but Ah-fu steadfastly declined.

"You are a very good person. I will not forget you as long as I live," Youde said.

Without a word, Ah-fu threw his arms around Youde. Reflexively, Youde clutched Ah-fu's small frame tightly.

"I am glad that I ran into you, sir," Ah-fu said, addressing Youde as sir for the first time. Youde couldn't speak except to squeeze Ah-fu even tighter in his arms. Yes, most of all, Ah-fu needed a person he could call sir, a "teacher." If he'd had a good teacher to guide him, his life wouldn't have taken this turn.

At last, Ah-fu was handcuffed and was led out. As he was about to leave Youde's sight, Ah-fu abruptly stopped, turned around and raised his cuffed hands high, a gesture of farewell to Youde. I probably will not see Ah-fu ever again, Youde thought.

Almost all the inmates were sent away to be charged. No wonder. Today was Saturday, October 8. The day after Sunday will be October 10, the National Founding Day of the Republic of China, a holiday. It dawned on Youde that this must have been the big inventory clearance before the holiday.

35

Political Prisoners Who Were Left Behind

Finally, only Chuang and Youde remained; the two political prisoners. Chuang appeared to still be sleeping as there was no sign of him, only occasional moaning. The guard distributed the food boxes, just two now. When he slipped the food into Cell 7, he shouted in a loud voice "Here's the food box," but got no response.

Youde uncovered his food box. Aside from rice, there were green vegetables, fried tofu, and scrambled eggs. Either he had gotten used to the prison food already, or due to sheer physiological craving, Youde finished almost all his food.

At last, there were signs of Chuang getting up. It was half past twelve. He appeared to be washing his face and using the toilet. It looked like he was able to get around without help.

Then Chuang entered Youde's sight. Chuang opened his food box, took a look and closed it again.

"Hurum," Youde cleared his throat to draw Chuang's attention. Their eyes met. Youde smiled at him, a gesture of friendship. Chuang got close to the barred entrance for a better look. He stared at Youde then moved his eyes to the nameplate in front of Youde's cell.

He must have read "Sedition Tsai Youde" because "Oh!" came out of his throat.

Fellow sufferers pity one another. Without exchanging a word, they understood each other.

"My name is Tsai," Youde introduced himself in a hushed voice.

The guard at the desk raised his eyes and gave Youde a dirty look yet did not interfere.

"You had better eat a little," Youde advised.

Chuang looked up again at Youde.

"I see. I am Chuang."

Chuang picked up his food box and ate a few mouthfuls, then again, closed the lid and shoved it into a corner; his manner was so quiet it was not at all reminiscent of last night's passionate person.

"I am from Hengchun."

"I am from Putzu. How do you do?"

"I run a charcoal business in Hengchun."

"I am a school teacher."

"It's nice to be a teacher. I was once a teacher. I went to Tainan Normal College."

At this point, the guard at the desk stood up and interrupted the exchange.

Youde lay down. Immediately, he was pained by the thought of Ah-fu who had laid beside him until so recently.

At around four in the afternoon, two new inmates entered the jailhouse. Since they were not handcuffed, Youde assumed that they must have come directly from the interrogation room in the same building. Following the rule, their possessions were detained and their belts pulled out from their pants.

Chuang of Cell 7 got up and clutched at the bars.

"Oh, Fu-lin! Sung-po!"

The new arrivals were startled and looked toward the voice.

"Ah! It's Chuang," one of them shrieked.

"So that's the story," the other one muttered.

At that point, Chuang dropped to the ground, put his hands on the floor and bowed.

"I am sorry. I am very sorry," Chuang apologized to the two with tears running down his cheeks.

The guard stopped the new inmates from talking further and led them to Cell 1, which was to the right of Youde's cell. But since Cell 1 and Cell 7 were at the opposite ends of the fan-shaped jailhouse, they could see each other well. Only talking was not allowed.

Chuang once more started to pound hysterically on the floor with his fist and wailed.

"I should have died. It would be better if I had died," he carried on, ignoring the guard's attempt to stop him.

The guard telephoned for help. Two uniformed policemen rushed in, handcuffed Chuang and took him out of Cell 7. Chuang cried to the two new inmates, "It's my fault. I am sorry. I should have died."

The two inmates in Cell 1 were silent.

Youde asked the returned guard, "Where did you take him?"

"To the infirmary," the guard replied brusquely.

Youde recalled passing by an infirmary the night he was brought in here, a room midway between the tall, iron gate and the jailhouse. The door to the infirmary had an opening for looking in and its four walls were padded with tatami mats. The so-called infirmary was but a solitary confinement cell to guard against suicides. It probably was also the place to lock up violent prisoners.

The two new inmates started to whisper to each other in worried voices. The fact that two people who were involved in the same case were put into the same cell meant that the interrogation was over and there was no need for further investigation.

The guard walked over to Cell 1 and added two names in the frame:

SEDITION, CHAO FU-LIN

SEDITION, LIU SUNG-PO

That's how the four political prisoners were left behind in this building to celebrate the glorious National Founding Day of this democratic country.

36

The Sobbing New Inmate

THAT night, except for cells 1 and 4, the rest of the jailhouse was empty. The guard, perhaps owing to the lightened workload, was in a good mood and did not interfere much when Youde and the new inmates talked.

Both men were arrested at dawn about five o'clock from Tung-kang and Tai-chung respectively, only a few hours after Chuang's interrogation. As in Youde's case, the authorities did not bother with the time-consuming warrants, but merely sent the jeep out to round them up. After eight hours of questioning, they were brought here at four in the afternoon. Chuang knew the two men would be arrested. "I sinned," Chuang had said, tortured by his self-recrimination. Yet meeting the two so soon barely after a night's sleep was more than Chuang could take. Was it more insufferable than physical torture for Chuang to face the two in the jailhouse? Youde could still painfully hear Chuang's words:" I should have died!"

Sung-po worked in a bank in Taichung, while Fu-lin had a job with Tung-kang's Marine Laboratory. They were both natives of Hengchun. While still in high school, they were recruited by Chuang and agreed to join the Communist Party. Yet they were not driven by ideology, but rather by a desire for an honest government. Thereafter, they did not engage in any political activities and had not seen nor corresponded with Chuang. Then, four years later, just when Chuang was about forgotten, out of the blue, a Sun Yat-sen suit and a plainclothes man showed up and handcuffed them in front of their wives and took them away.

"What crime would I be charged with?" one of them asked.

"Did you confess that you had joined the Party?"

"Yes, I did. But I was never given a membership card, nor was I sworn in."

Confession alone was evidence enough. Youde knew that a Party membership card or swearing-in were of no concern to the interrogator.

"You did not recruit anybody else, did you?"

The shorter one, Sung-po, answered, "I don't even know if I actually joined the Party or not. How could I think of recruiting others...?"

"In other countries, you would be guilty of nothing, but...."

"In our country?"

"Regrettably, in our country, there is the Sedition Law. You will be sent to the military court and be charged with Article 2.1."

"Hurum." The guard cleared his throat. No doubt, Article 2.1 caught his ear and induced anxiety. The guard ordered the conversation stopped. The saying "A ghost flees from talk of Article 2.1" was not an exaggeration.

But when the guard went back to dozing, the tall one, Fu-lin, inquired uneasily.

"Mr. Tsai, what happens after being charged?"

"You will be sentenced in the courtroom of the Military Court Building."

Sung-po interjected, "But those people told me that if I confess I would be allowed to go home."

Silence prevailed for a while. Fu-lin asked again, "How long would the sentence be?"

"In your case, since you did not engage in political activities, I think most likely you will be given ten years."

Only an old-timer by a couple of days, Youde felt funny talking like an old pro. The two seemed very startled by the talk of ten years, obviously ignorant of these matters. Youde regretted saying something unnecessary. Partly to give comfort, Youde added, "The sentences for Article 2.1 range from ten years to death. A ten-year sentence is the lightest."

Silence again set in.

Sung-po said, "But why did Chuang implicate us?" His voice suggested hatred, quite reasonable under the circumstances. Youde dropped his voice and replied, "Torture."

No response. Maybe Youde's voice was too low for them to hear, or maybe they could not immediately comprehend the meaning of the term "torture."

But the meaning was clear to the dozing guard, who stood up and gestured Youde to shut up.

THE SOBBING NEW INMATE

Youde stopped talking, whereupon the guard started to chat, from customs of various places to the duties of a guard. Guards probably occupied the lowest positions in the security organization and had no hope of advancement. Consequently, most of them were Taiwanese. These Taiwanese "sweet potato" guards were, if anything, sympathetic to political prisoners.

The guard let slip nonchalantly, "We all hope that you will be free to go home. In any case, we don't get any of the prize purse when you are found guilty."

Youde knew about the reward system but never imagined that he would be the object of it. The prize money, based on how much per arrest, was to be divided among the secret police. Most outrageous of all, the prize was awarded at the time of sentencing and the recipient was not required to give back the money even when the accused later turned out to be mistakenly arrested or wrongly executed. It was a setup that encouraged false arrests and arbitrary incrimination. While it's reasonable to praise a hunting dog for retrieving prey, one must not praise a dog that retrieves the wrong prey. Rather, punishment is in order lest crazed dogs become rampant.

The irrational reward system could not have passed any elected assembly. But here, the dictator's directive was of the highest order, the same as the law. Even if the directive were in fact proposed in the assembly, not a single assemblyman would have opposed it, knowing it came from the highest place. Still, if someone were to object, one could always arrest the assemblyman and receive the reward.

Youde lay on his side and reflected: The last two days, I've talked like I knew something. But what's going to happen to me, really? I am to be sent to Taipei and be subjected to an investigation from ground zero. It is possible that I'll be tortured. After observing Chuang, Youde had diminished confidence in his ability to withstand torture.

"But I can't wallow in sorrow. Better to leave my fate to heaven and take things easy," Youde told himself as he rolled over to sleep.

Listening intently, Youde could hear a man sobbing in Cell 1.

37

Shouts of Wan-sui

BAND music could be heard coming from beyond the prison building — the music from the Double Tenth celebration parade. Putzu was probably having a parade right now, and Youde wondered if his daughter Ah-jing was enjoying the parade. He thought of his wife and his mother too.

It's ironic that the most whole-heartedly celebrated Double Tenth Day took place during the first two years after Taiwan's restoration amid a dire shortage of material goods. Even in a small town like Putzu, people insisted on having not one but two parades: one parade of flags in the morning and a lantern parade at night. "We felt then the day was indeed the founding day of our nation," Youde reminisced. But now Youde could only consider this day the founding day of a conquering foreign regime. No matter, the day still must be an eagerly awaited holiday for children. Youde thought to himself: I wonder how my parents felt when I, as a youngster, celebrated Japan's founding day and the emperor's birthday? Is it the destiny of the Taiwanese people to forever celebrate the national day of a foreign regime? An Aggression Memorial Day was more like it!

As the parade came closer, human voices mixed with the music. Between musical pieces, somebody was leading the sloganeering. Gradually they came to the front of the police station.

"Wan-sui! Long live the Three People's Principles!" the leader shouted.

"Long live the Three People's Principles!" the crowd echoed.

"Oppose Communism and resist the Soviet Union!"

"Annihilate Chu and Mao!"

And the last slogan, as always, was "President Chiang wan-sui! Long live President Chiang!"

"Long live President Chiang!" Another band followed by another group. The same sloganeering, ending with "Long live President Chiang!"

Is President Chiang Kai-shek such a great man, a man worthy of such respect of the Taiwanese people? That's a question for future historians. But to the caged prison inmates, he was no other than the deranged killer, the person who bore the final responsibility for the February 28 massacre and the very person who gave the order "Do not let one criminal escape even if a hundred are killed mistakenly." In short, he was the instigator of Taiwan's White Terror.

Youde's wise uncle once said, "The United States dropped two atomic bombs on Japan. But on Taiwan it dropped the Chiang regime, an even more destructive, unlimited bomb."

Japanese died from enemy bombs, a fact more easily reconciled by the victims. But in Taiwan's case, Taiwanese people were slaughtered by their supposed "parents," whom they had welcomed with open arms. How can the victims rest in peace?

The scenes of frenzied welcome for Chiang were still fresh in Youde's memory.

On October 21, 1946, one year and two months after the restoration of Taiwan, when all Taiwan was still tipsy with the fine wine of returning to the motherland's embrace, President Chiang Kai-shek arrived at Taiwan from Nanking. The savior had arrived. The whole island was roiled in tumultuous welcome.

Representatives of Taiwan's elite class gathered at Taipei's Chung-shan Hall to bid him welcome. One gentleman, overwhelmed by the presidential charisma, said this to the reporters: "Today, I was able to see the greatest man, President Chiang Kai-shek, and also to shake his hand. I have never been happier in my life. I would have no regret if I were to die this moment." He meant his words then, but no sooner than February 28 of the next year, this very gentleman was killed with no reason, leaving us with no way to learn if he had any regrets after all.

People of all vocations, from all walks of life, came to Chung-shan Hall after the words of Chiang's presence spread. The campuses emptied out. Youde, then a freshman, also hurried over and secured standing room in the back.

The square in front of the building was jam-packed with people; the flowerbeds were trampled; every single tree around was overloaded with onlookers.

Someone shouted, "Don't climb up any more. The branch is about to break!"

The verandas of surrounding buildings, even the buildings' slate rooftops were loaded with people who waved the flags and shouted, "Long live President Chiang!"

At last Chiang Kai-shek and Madam Chiang Soong Mei-ling appeared in the balcony. The sound of "Long live Chiang Kai-shek" rose thunderously, shaking heaven and earth. The presidential couple raised their arms high and greeted the cheering multitude. What an untold number of anti-Japanese patriots could not accomplish with bloodshed was at last fulfilled by this great man! A true national hero, a savior!

The throng waved the flags, their handkerchiefs, their hats or their bare arms. With tears streaming down their faces, they continued on, "Wan-sui! Long life!"

The presidential couple was hard put to leave the balcony, called back repeatedly by the waves of cheers from people below. A grander welcome, one given with such heart, was never given in Taiwan's history.

Youde, pushed by the surging crowd, was now to the right, now to the front of his original spot. Suddenly, he heard somebody calling, "Youde!" and looked up in a tree nearby. Wu Che-fu, Cheng Wen-bang, and their classmate Yeh were smiling at Youde from their perch. When Youde clawed his way and got closer to the tree, Che-fu pointed to the tip of the tree branch, where Youde found Yu-kun precariously hanging to the end of the branch and was single-mindedly shouting "Long live President Chiang!" in an already hoarse voice. Yu-kun's face was drenched with sweat and tears. Yu-kun's hoarse voice of that day rang in Youde's ears as if it were yesterday. Counting the years, Youde realized that eight years had passed since that day of passionate frenzy.

Returning to reality, Youde lay down.

He listened indifferently to the receding band and the shouting of "Long live President Chiang!"

38

On the Night Train to Taipei

The day finally arrived for Youde to be sent to Taipei for arraignment. On October 14, after lights out and having just fallen asleep, he was roused by the guard ordering, "Tsai Youde, get up and be ready. You are going up for arraignment."

He got up right away and used the toilet. There was nothing to get ready for but to gather a few toiletries in a cloth scarf and tie it into a bundle. The time was twenty past ten.

At the desk, the guard handed back his money and his belt. Wasting no time, Youde put on his belt. He never appreciated the belt so much as he was again free to use both hands when standing. He found he could barely keep his pants on even when he tightened his belt to the last hole.

Two men in street clothes came in, one tall and stout with the obvious bearing of a judo expert, the other fair-skinned and short, wearing a plaid suit. The latter, so un-policemanlike, could easily be taken for a businessman if he were to go around without a pistol.

The stout one took out a pair of handcuffs, clicked one cuff over Youde's right wrist and slipped the other over his own left hand.

"Let's go," the stout policeman said. Youde hurriedly picked up his bundle with his left hand and took his steps, partly pulled by the handcuff. The policeman in the plaid suit stopped talking to the guard and scurried along. Youde saw the paled faces of Fu-lin and Sung-po peering out between the iron bars. As he stepped out the iron gate he heard somebody say "Good bye" in a timid voice.

Walking down the long corridor, the infirmary came to view. "Chuang is most likely still here," Youde observed. After a 90-degree turn, they came to the tall iron gate out of which the three silently passed. They climbed up the stairs and entered the front lobby. A jeep was waiting on the rain-slicked street.

"Beep, beep." The driver was impatient. He started the engine right away. The jeep with the three of them on board rolled toward the train station.

The outside world that greeted Youde after the long separation seemed sadly forlorn. Perhaps due to the late hour, only a few pedestrians were seen here and there. The rain-slicked street reflecting the neon signs aroused homesickness.

It took about ten minutes to get to the station. There were quite a bit of comings and goings and some people were talking loudly. It was a different world, after all, where people were free to carry on with their lives. The three entered the waiting room and waited for the train's arrival.

The businessman-like policeman sat down next to Youde and introduced himself.

"My name is also Tsai. He, over there, is Officer Chen. Chen is our judo coach. We are both 'sweet potatoes.'" The last sentence meant to put Youde at ease.

The two women sitting across first looked at Youde's face suspiciously, then discovering the handcuffs hurriedly moved to other seats. "Never before in my life was I ever feared like this!" Rather than feeling bad about it, Youde felt like breaking out laughing.

They passed through the ticket turnstile and waited for the train on the platform. Finally the night express to Taipei arrived at midnight, about twenty minutes late. They boarded the boxcar at the middle of the train and sat down in the first box seats next to the door. Youde had the window seat; Officer Chen sat next to Youde, while Officer Tsai sat across from them. Tsai, quite talkative, conversed easily with everybody, yet he studiously avoided talking to Youde. The two policemen took out cigarettes and started to smoke. Youde was offered a cigarette, but he refused because he had resolved not to touch cigarettes until he was again a free man. The train was scheduled to arrive at Taipei at five o'clock the next morning.

The tactful officer Tsai, of the plaid suit, put a handkerchief over the handcuffs to avoid attracting attention. Youde closed his eyes and listened to their conversation.

Even though they also worked at the Garrison Command Headquarters, these two were police officers and not secret police. As such, they sometimes helped in escorting political prisoners like Youde but never got involved in arrests or interrogations. Rather, their conversation centered on burglars and murderers.

In time, Li Ah-fu's story came up.

Officer Tsai said, "To tell you the truth, I fingered Li Ah-fu right after Ah-pin's death. So I suggested to the captain to arrest him. Do you remember?"

Tsai was referring to the captain who was in charge of the criminal section and not Captain T'ao, who handled the special cases.

"What did the captain do?" Officer Chen asked.

"Captain took a look at Ah-fu and right off he disregarded it. Captain said Ah-fu was just too boyish to be a killer. Besides, the guy never took a day off from work."

"Ha ha ha. While his gambling friends fled in fright."

"That's right. Those fools. If we were after gamblers we could have nabbed them in action anytime."

"I guess Yen-lo, the keeper of the Gate to Hell, was meant to add another name to his roster."

"Ha ha ha. Even though I couldn't care less if more guys like Big Head died, if the Captain had listened to me and arrested Ah-fu, Big Head would have been spared."

"He wouldn't have thanked you for being spared, anyway."

"But I kept my eyes on Ah-fu. Even without the second killing, I think I would have arrested him eventually."

"Too bad you missed the reward."

"Ha ha. What a story, though, don't you think? This Ah-fu, a born killer, isn't he? Even after killing Ah-pin, he was totally fearless toward us, so calm like he knows nothing about it."

"You don't deserve rewards! He fooled you all from the captain down!"

"Hey, don't forget that I was the only exception."

"Is that so?"

"Ironically, the prime suspect for Ah-pin's killing was actually the Big Head Chin-sheng. Ha ha."

"So instead of rewards, you ought to be fined. Ha ha."

When they became aware that Youde had awakened and was listening, the two men forced a smile. Youde again closed his eyes and pretended to sleep.

"Those guys would have arrested Ah-fu." Officer Tsai was not able to let go of the subject.

"Of course, they would have," Officer Chen answered and gave a huge yawn.

"Those guys" referred to the secret police, of course. It was reputed that within the Garrison Command Headquarters, there was friction between the regular police and the secret police. The latter, armed with the Sedition Law, could arrest with little regard for responsibility, while the former were not so free.

But there seemed to be a discrepancy between the Ah-fu that Youde knew and the Ah-fu described by Officer Tsai. Youde's Ah-fu was good, cautious and even somewhat timid, yet Officer Tsai's Ah-fu was bold, cold and insensitive. Which one was the real Ah-fu?

No matter, Ah-fu was absolutely not a "born killer," Youde believed. Ah-fu had said to Youde, "I am glad to have run into you, sir." It was a heart-felt utterance. It's possible he meant, "If I had met you earlier, I could have been better off." Indeed, if Ah-fu had the advantage of the counsel of a proper teacher-like person, he would have avoided becoming a killer. Youde was certain of that.

Youde opened his eyes. He asked Officer Tsai, "About Li Ah-fu, what kind of sentencing would he get?"

"He was charged yesterday. Of course, the prosecutor asked for death penalty."

"Isn't he still a minor?"

"No. Just turned twenty."

The train entered the tunnel, creating loud echoes. Soot poured in from some unclosed windows. Everybody hurried to cover their noses.

Youde suddenly noticed his own reflection in the window.

"Ah!" he cried out, shaken.

It's odd. Isn't it the face of Huang Sheng-san, the main character in *The Sunrise*, which Youde had once played? Isn't it the haggard and worn face of the man who was at the end of his rope because of joblessness and poverty who finally committed suicide? The made-up face from the past stage, stared with startled eyes at Youde, the actor who once played him, as if asking, "What happened?"

39

New Cellmates

The train arrived at Taipei at seven o'clock, two hours later than scheduled. A jeep took Youde to the Taipei Police Battalion of the Security Defense Headquarters. It was past nine when Youde was put into the prison cell after the usual admitting procedures.

The building was doughnut-shaped, like two opened fans put together, and was evenly divided into sixteen cells, each about twice the size of Chiayi's facility. When Youde entered Cell 12, he was greeted by ten existing inmates, who interrupted their conversations to look at the newcomer. Youde knew from the reflections in the train window that he possessed the looks of a veteran prison inmate. Following the unspoken rule of the prison, as the newcomer, he took the spot closest to the toilet and set down his bundle.

Self introductions followed.

"I am Tsai Youde from Putzu. How do you do?"

From the back of the cell came, "What's the charge?"

"Political crimes."

"Just as I thought."

A man who was sitting against the wall stood up. Since he occupied the spot furthest from the entrance, he must have been the first one there, the so-called dragon-head.

The dragon-head of Cell 12 came over to Youde and spoke in Mandarin Chinese, "I am a political prisoner too. I've been here for three months. My name is Peng." Peng extended his right hand for a handshake, a friendly gesture. It was apparent that he was a mainlander, a *waishengjen*. Many mainlanders had been arrested for political crimes, perhaps even more than the Taiwanese, percentage wise.

When Taiwan was first restored to Chinese rule, only Kuomintang members were allowed to come to Taiwan from the mainland. Eventually, many Communists disguising themselves as KMT entered Taiwan and positioned themselves in schools and various government organizations. They began collecting intelligence and started recruiting for the Party, Taiwanese and mainlanders alike.

On the other hand, driven to despair by the KMT government, the Taiwanese had seen new hope in the Communist regime. Wasn't the Communist's people's government our real motherland? So the motherland was not so ugly after all. In time, young people romanticized and sang praises of the Communist motherland. And in extension they considered heroes the mainlanders who risked their lives to come to Taiwan to do political work.

But the fate of a Communist cadre was a sad one. Eight, nine out of ten were captured by the secret police, who were fellow mainlanders. Only a lucky few were able to escape the dragnet and go back to the mainland. Awaiting those captured, without exception, was the overly harsh death penalty. With no families or friends to retrieve their corpses, they were usually buried in mass graves. How many were there? Nobody will ever know. Peng was to be one of them soon.

Peng kindly introduced the fellow cellmates one by one. There were two other mainlanders: Hsiao, who spoke in a heavy Cantonese accent, was charged with assault. Chen was a deserter and spoke good Taiwanese, as he was a native of Fukien Province. Tu, with an impressive build, was from Penghu and was in for smuggling. Three were in for drug-related charges and another three for burglary. Including Youde there were eleven in all. The eldest in age was Chin, a fifty-ish man on drug charges whom Peng had introduced as "ojisan" (*uncle* in Japanese). Chin was said to doze all day long, waxy-eyed, paying no attention to others. All in all, these were people Youde was not likely to meet on the outside.

"Except you and me, the rest of them are 'sundry criminals,'" Peng added after the introductions.

"Sundry criminals" was a somewhat contemptuous term to describe all but the ones on sedition charges. But Youde found them to be likable individuals. With the exception of ojisan, all took interest in the newcomer and asked all

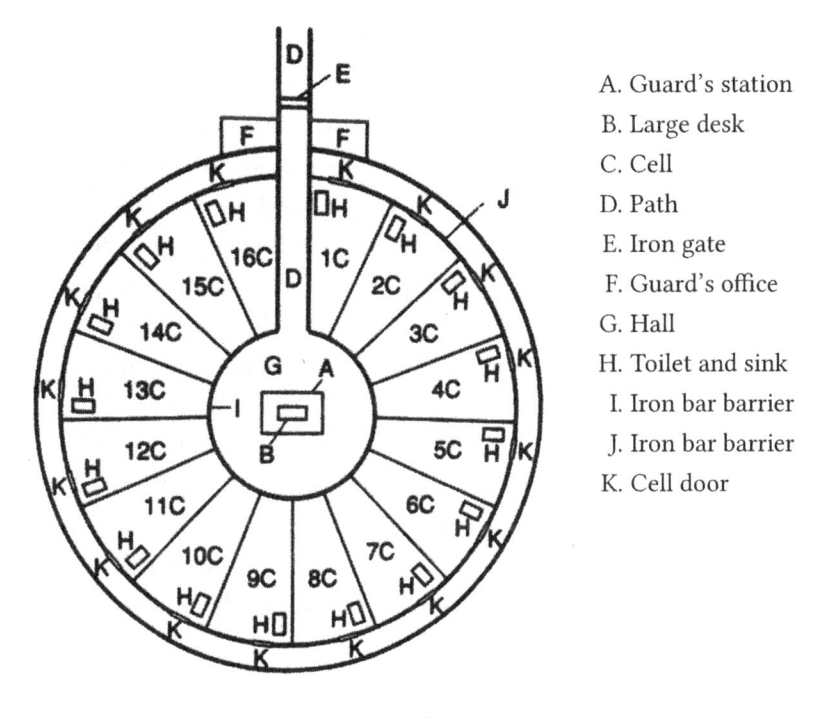

A. Guard's station
B. Large desk
C. Cell
D. Path
E. Iron gate
F. Guard's office
G. Hall
H. Toilet and sink
I. Iron bar barrier
J. Iron bar barrier
K. Cell door

Diagram of Taipei Police Detention Center

kinds of questions. Some brought up the names of Putzu townsfolk whom they knew, although Youde regrettably did not recognize any of them.

The prison was rather clamorous as there were nearly two hundred inmates living day and night in the sixteen cells, with some talking loudly to people in other cells. The place was boisterous like a market place; not a whiff of terror in the air. Perhaps, to somebody like Peng, who faced impending death, the noisiness was rather a salvation.

"Time to eat," announced a loud voice. Now the prison got even noisier. Everybody stood up and went to the far corner of the cell to pick out their crudely made enamel bowl and chopsticks from a large aluminum basin.

The guard opened the outside gate and the aids distributed two large wooden tubs to each cell. One tub contained rice, the other sloppy vegetable stew. Youde had heard the expression "prison's stinky rice." Indeed, the rice smelled mildewed. The vegetable stew was totally tasteless save for the smell that seeped from the wooden tub, not something palatable. Youde took one mouthful and quit. The food at Chiayi's facility was sumptuous compared to this!

Peng, who was eating standing up, said, "Nobody could eat this stuff at first."

Youde was hesitating about whether to try the second mouthful when somebody patted his shoulder from behind. The burglary suspect Yen was standing there holding a paper bag from which he proceeded to pick up something with his chopsticks and place in Youde's bowl. It was *bafu*, seasoned dried pork! Youde took a second look. *Bafu* was Youde's favorite food. He couldn't thank Yen enough for being able to eat such food, at such a place, at a time like this. Yen put some *bafu* in Peng's bowl also, then returned to his own seat. Youde realized that this place allowed care packages from home.

Thanks to the *bafu*, Youde was able to finish the mildew-smelling rice. Looking around, he found Peng getting his second bowl of rice, and even more amazingly, the runaway soldier from Fukien was on his third bowl of rice and vegetable stew with obvious enjoyment. These people have adapted to the environment and are stalwartly facing their lives head on. Youde felt acutely his own weakness; he was ashamed of already anticipating care packages from home.

40

Dragon-Head Peng

That night Peng told Youde his story. Peng was from a wealthy family of Shanghai. After the war he entered a university but, stirred by the unsettling political situation, he set his studies aside and instead participated day and night in anti-government demonstrations and eventually joined the Communist Party.

This was a road many a self-regarded intelligentsia, namely the college students, had traveled. They sang the praises of the Marxists and regarded them as progressives. These students were undeniably patriots imbued with a sense of justice, especially compared to the clique of high-ranking KMT government officials who busied themselves with accumulating personal fortunes. That mainland China turned red in such a short time was precisely because of believers like them.

Later, Peng came to Taiwan with a new mission and entered an intelligence organization, thus becoming something like a double agent. But soon, unable to endure the burden, he went to work for a newspaper. About a year after that he became aware that he was exposed and went into hiding. And three months later he was captured near the Kaohsiung train station when he had exhausted his money and had resorted to sleeping in a freight train box car.

Peng had two other comrades. Together they collected intelligence on Taiwan and sent it to the mainland authorities. One of them escaped successfully by boat from Kaohsiung, the other was still a fugitive. The reason Peng had been kept here for three months was to await the capture of the second cohort, so they could be charged together.

Three months with the "sundry criminals" made him the longest inhabitant of the entire prison, a dragon-head among all dragon-heads. But as long as he was in this prison, he did not have to worry about being called up for execution. Maybe that's why Peng did not seem to mind much about being here. Yet his fugitive comrade could not last too much longer outside. He would be recognized as a mainlander wherever he went and there was also a limit to his funds. It was only a matter of time before he was captured.

The burglary suspect Yen came over to Peng and Youde and offered them a banana. Yen always shared his food. He had the largest stock of food because his wife and his concubine outdid each other in sending care packages. Peng broke the banana in two halves and gave one to Youde. Youde took small bites of the banana. How delicious! He bowed to Yen repeatedly. In here, the professional burglar Yen was addressed as "Mr. Yen" and treated with much appreciation and respect. No wonder. Respect was indeed due to the provider of all-important nutrition.

Youde also summarized his case to Peng, who thereupon rendered his judgment.

"It won't amount to anything. You will get three years of re-education, the lightest they have. I sure am envious of you. But you are very lucky. Most people got trapped by the leading questioning, or succumbed to physical torture, and then pressed their thumbprints unwillingly. You did well to persevere on the assertion that you did not read *Mao Wenchi*."

Peng was impressed. He was once an insider and had a good understanding of these matters.

"But the book in fact did not exist."

"No matter how much you deny it, it's still the words of a suspect with nobody else to corroborate. They had the testament from Yu-kun, which was important to them."

"His testament could be just baloney, just trumped up."

"That's just it. Hundreds even thousands had died because of trumped-up testaments. Moreover, it is a common tactic to use baseless testaments to avenge political enemies. Chinese politics is far more complex than you Taiwanese think."

Peng gave examples of cases where high-ranking officials in the current government rose to their positions by dirty power tactics that caused the downfall of political enemies and sometimes even family and friends. Perhaps, in time, the Taiwanese would understand these kinds of political tactics, Youde surmised.

The drug addicts started to moan, Ojisan most loudly. With their faces down on the wooden floor, their bodies writhed, cursed and pounded the floors helplessly. Others, not knowing how to help, watched in silence even though the noise seriously interfered with their sleep. Even the guard could only check on them occasionally in silence.

Youde soon got used to the moaning and drifted into sleep, ending a long day.

41

The Sundry Criminals

WHEN Youde woke up early the next morning, the smuggler Tu from Penghu came to Youde's side right away and whispered, "Don't trust Dragon-head Peng. You must not forget that he is a pig."

"Pig" was already widely used as a substitute word for mainlander. Tu said that he was thoroughly distrustful of pigs because they had done him in repeatedly.

"First of all, look at him, no one can be so calm facing death."

"……"

"What he said to you last night was all made up. He was just trying to gain sympathy so he can share the food from the care packages."

"Isn't that a bit —"

"I think his real crime is bribe taking, a thing all pigs do given the opportunity."

Tu changed the topic when Peng walked by.

Tu himself was the captain of a five-man motorboat and was caught smuggling cigarettes. He had reconciled himself to a three-year sentence. He said that he had taken full responsibility so the other four shipmates were allowed to go home. Darkly suntanned, he was quite handsome and a straight talker. But his animosity toward the mainlanders was absolute. He not only called them pigs but disliked them so intensely that he seemed irritated by any Taiwanese who conversed with a pig.

"Don't tell much to the pig. You will regret it," Tu warned.

Several days later, the three drug addicts were sent away for arraignment, like all sundry criminals, to the prosecutor's office of the local justice department. With the moaning gone, everybody seemed to relax some.

Captain Tu reported to Youde, "According to Yen, Ojisan was a city councilman during the Japanese era." Then he added, "He was the Councilman Matsuoka, quite a snappy young politician."

Now reduced to a mere shabby old man, not a shred of dignity nor image remained of the old days. If he were to loiter in a subway passage, he would have been taken for a beggar. The pitiful ending of a drug addict. Since Ojisan moaned all the time, Youde had no chance to speak with him. Regardless, after the three left, Youde was able to move his place that much more to the back and quite a bit away from the toilet.

Hsiao, the Cantonese man, and Chen, the deserter, did their t'ai-chi boxing daily. Occasionally Yen and the other two burglar suspects joined in. The other two burglar suspects were like Yen's subordinates and did as Yen told them to.

Peng habitually sat in a Zen posture with his eyes closed occupying the innermost corner of the cell. As Tu had observed, Peng appeared calm to Youde. But might this be his way to pray to the gods? Or maybe he was practicing the art of dying.

"I sympathize with Dragon-head Peng," Youde declared to Tu. Youde and Tu spent lots of time sitting on the floor side by side against the wall, their legs stretched out in front of them — the most common posture for inmates — and talked.

One day Tu whispered to Youde, "Hsiao is really a murderer. He tried to kill his wife and her lover but failed, so was charged with assault, thanks to the police chief who was from his hometown."

According to Tu, Hsiao was a retired military man. He and a friend opened an eatery specializing in breakfast foods — fried dough, hot flat bread, and soymilk. Then, when he saved up fifty thousand yuan, he bought himself a wife who was a poor farmer's daughter from the country and twenty years younger than him. His wife helped in the store, where eventually she met a young mainlander who frequented the place, and the two started an affair. Hsiao found out the place of their illicit rendezvous and one day, after being fortified with some wine, assaulted the lovers' nest. He slashed the lover boy in the face and chest and inflicted wounds on his wife's hand.

It was quite common that some mainlanders purchased wives with money; and knifing incidences by jealous husbands were also common occurrences, as the young wives inevitably acquired lovers.

Hsiao suddenly stopped his t'ai-chi exercises and moved toward where Tu and Youde were. "No doubt Hsiao knew we were talking about him," Youde thought, because he couldn't help glancing at Hsiao several times during the conversation. Somewhat flustered, Youde quickly sat up. But Hsiao did not seem to be angry.

"I worked my butt off for three years to save the money; but her family wanted more, so I had to borrow from a friend to buy that woman. It cost fifty thousand, you know. If I added up all the other expenses, it came to about sixty thousand yuan." Youde relaxed. Hsiao interrupted his t'ai-chi just to add supplemental explanation.

"Did you mean to kill them both?" Youde asked.

"No. I might have killed the lover boy, but I didn't mean to kill my wife."

"I guess you loved her."

"Sure. I bought her because I loved her. Besides, what fool would throw away something that cost fifty thousand yuan?"

"But the lover boy did not die, right?"

"My hand went wild because I had a few drinks that night. But the bastard's fair face was messed up forever. The sight of him now would send shivers up women's spines. Boy, what a good feeling."

"So, what are you going to do with your wife?"

"I don't know. She's still my wife on the books. I will decide when I get out."

The deserter Chen who had continued on with the t'ai-chi by himself now cut in, "Hey, brother! If I get out first, can you lend her to me? Or maybe you can let me have her for ten thousand."

"You bastard! You don't have that kind of money." Hsiao went over to Chen and jokingly slapped his head.

"Since you had considerable use of her, what's wrong with sharing her with me a little? Call it a roommate's favor."

"Pigs!" Captain Tu sent Youde a side glance and muttered.

42

Long-Denied Enjoyment

"Tsai Youde." The guard called out the name and opened the cell gate, then he saw Youde's puzzled look and added impatiently, "haircut."

Youde Stepped into his shoes and followed the guard out to the hallway. He found that almost all the shoes lined up outside the cells had crushed heels and were turned into slippers. In the hallway that led to the prison gate, a barber was waiting beside a bamboo stool. The so-called barber was also an inmate who was on work release, surely a much-trusted inmate to be working with a razor.

Youde sat down on the bamboo stool. A slightly soiled white cloth was draped around him.

"Do you want to shave your head or do you want to keep the same hairstyle?" the barber asked.

"Keep it the same," Youde answered.

"All convicted felons have to have their heads shaved," the barber said as he started the clipper.

Two or three minutes for a haircut and a shave. In spite of the crudeness of the haircut, Youde felt lighter above his shoulders and felt very good. The guard took him back to his cell.

"Whew! Handsome!" he was teased by his cellmates.

"Look like somebody else entirely," Tu said.

"It took ten years off you," Yen also commented.

Thus, after a long wait, Youde was finally rid of the appearance of a prisoner. It was like taking off the makeup after playing Huang Sheng-san in *The Sunrise*.

Yen started to distribute crackers. "Tomorrow is Thursday. Let's finish all the food we have."

Thursday was the day for care packages. Yen shared the crackers all around, with Taiwanese and mainlanders alike. "Unless one has experienced poverty, he would never understand the grateful feeling one single cracker could bring," Youde thought to himself.

Yen had one extra cracker left. He brought it over to Youde and said, "To thank you for last night."

The night before, by happenstance, Youde started to relate the plot of the movie *Casablanca*, much to everybody's listening pleasure. The cracker was the gift offering for that.

"Please do it again tonight," Yen asked.

That night, Youde told them *For Whom the Bell Tolls*. Youde's movie-telling threatened to become a nightly routine.

Suddenly Youde's thoughts turned to tomorrow. "Will I get a care package? Does my wife know that I am here? Should she bother to come to Taipei all the way from Putzu just to send in a care package? She has her hands full just taking care of Ah-jing and my elderly mother, really. I would hate to cause her to overtax herself. Yet...."

Youde's heart was conflicted.

43

A Feast

THE next day, the care-package day, the prison was unaccountably restless from the morning on.

Care packages had to be taken to the Combined Service Center in the police station because the families usually did not know in which of the several detention facilities their loved ones were imprisoned.

At least three organizations vied with each other in arresting people. The Security Defense Command, which consisted of police and special agents in local residence, handled crimes of all kinds and hence had the greatest number of people in their custody. Past bodies such as the Railroad Police and the Salt Bureau Police were subsumed under this organization. The organization that specialized in the so-called thought crimes, or the political crimes, as well as the important national and international cases, was the Investigation Bureau, an equivalent of the FBI. But the most serious political crimes came under the domain of the Secret Protection Bureau. The organization was said to have its roots in Shanghai's CC clique or the Blueshirts. This last organization could arrest anybody it deemed suspicious, be the suspect a national assemblyman, a government minister, or a general in the military. In some cases it could "disappear" the people they arrested.

The three organizations operated independently of each other, but all reported directly to the president. Ordinarily they may appear to be competing for merit, yet they also kept a sharp eye on each other. The arrangement enabled any of them to directly inform the president if high officials or important figures in the rival organizations showed signs of disloyalty, and to arrest the suspects rapidly.

In other words, the president controlled the leashes of three vicious dogs, while allowing them to hold back each other lest any of them become too powerful. In this way the dictatorship was secured.

The Combined Service received and kept the care packages brought to it by prisoners' families. Once a week, on Thursdays, it dispatched the packages to various detention facilities.

It was not until about four in the afternoon that the odd-job man brought the packages in and put them on the desk that was in the center of the doughnut-shaped prison, in plain sight of all cells.

The prison stirred. No wonder, the food relief had arrived. The guard read the name on each package and called out the name together with the cell number. As the inmate answered, the guard then placed the package right outside the cell gate. One by one, the packages that had piled high atop of the desk and spilled over to the side had disappeared.

Youde tensed up every time "Cell 12" was called.

Yen was called five times. The fifth time, people uttered words of amazement. Captain Tu received one package too. Dragon-head Peng and deserter Chen nonchalantly observed from the sidelines, knowing well that they were not involved in this. Hsiao, however, was fidgety and restless. In his heart, he was secretly expecting a package from his wife after all.

Chen the deserter mimicked the guard, "Cell 12. Hsiao."

To Hsiao, the care package meant more than just that, it would signify that their relationship had gone back to before the incident, the reconciliation that he still wished for. Unfortunately, purchased wives usually would take advantage of opportunities like this to rid themselves of their aging husbands ... and end up in brothels eventually.

"Cell 12. Tsai Youde," the guard called suddenly.

"Good," Youde thought. At the same time, he felt painfully compassionate toward his wife. "Might she have traveled the long way to Taipei just to pass on the care package? In that case, she and little Ah-jing would have to stay at my brother's place and will be returning to Putzu without a chance to see me. How sad they must feel during their train ride home. Or maybe she contacted my brother and had him send the package. Really, that's the way I would have preferred."

At last, after disposing the mountains of packages, the guard came around and opened the cells one by one and had the odd-job man carry in the packages.

A FEAST

Yen gave something to the odd-job man. But Hsiao, who did not receive any, appeared disappointed.

Youde received one package wrapped in brown paper. The haphazard packaging showed the hands of rewrapping after inspection, a fact also testified by the inspection rubber stamp. Only one look and Youde knew that his wife had prepared the package in person, because he was familiar with the brown wrapping paper that she had reused, something he had brought back from America. Inside the package, he found a pair of sweatpants he had purchased in America and were yet unused. What appropriate apparel for prison life I bought! Youde chuckled inside. There were two winter undershirts in the package also.

Youde wondered if she expected his imprisonment to last awhile. In the food department, Youde found *bafu*, peanuts, and crackers.

Soon it was dinnertime. They placed the foods from home in the center and sat around in a circle. Taiwanese and mainlanders alike, together they talked, laughed, and ate. It was almost like a picnic.

To Youde it was the first feast in a long time.

The entire prison was more boisterous than usual.

44

Re-interrogation

ONE morning about ten days later Youde was summoned for interrogation. When he entered the interrogation room he found two special agents waiting for him by the desk, smoking cigarettes.

As usual one did the questioning and the other took notes. Youde was seated across from them. The notetaker took off Youde's handcuffs. Perhaps owing to prior experience, Youde did not feel as tense as he had been in Chiayi. Besides, there was no torture apparatus in sight.

The questioner spoke fluent Taiwanese though with an Amoy accent. The notetaker was plainly a "sweet potato."

The interrogation covered the same ground as that of the Chiayi branch office: about Li Shui-ching, Chang Yu-kun, Cheng Wen-bang, Chou Shen-yuan, Wu Che-fu, Tu Ping-lang, Yeh Chin-kuei ... more than twenty in all. Plowing through what looked like Chiayi's investigation report plus some other document, they asked questions methodically and took down answers. The interrogation progressed smoothly as there was almost no discrepancy between Youde's answers and what was in the report.

But trouble arose with *Mao Wenchi*.

"I don't buy that Chou Shen-yuan left the book *Mao Wenchi* in your place without telling you and again retrieved it without saying a word." The questioner persisted over and over, "You are covering up for somebody."

Youde decided to take the opportunity to clarify the matter. "The truth is nobody brought the book to me."

"......"

"Chang Yu-kun made it up to finger me for a Communist," Youde declared flatly with visible confidence.

The two special agents looked at each other, looking quite surprised. They must have examined the investigation report and considered many possibilities, including the possibility that Yu-kun had concocted the accusation, something any able agent would have entertained. "Could it be that they looked surprised not because I had said something unexpected, but rather precisely because I had said what they themselves had suspected?"

But the two did not seem to possess enough fortitude to overturn Chiayi's report to create favorable conditions for Youde. After all, they would gain nothing from it. On the contrary, if anything happened later, they would be saddled with the responsibility. Given the order they received — "Do not let one escape even if one hundred are killed mistakenly" — their behavior was to be expected.

The questioner stiffened his expression somewhat and said, "Are you trying to overturn the Chiayi confession?"

"No, it's just that I was so exhausted from repeated interrogation that I concurred that possibly it had happened that way. But when I thought it through later, I couldn't remember a book like that...."

"Does that mean you lied at the time?"

"I absolutely had no intention of lying."

"Then are you intending to lie to us here?"

"……"

"Besides, what you said about Yu-kun concocting the story is totally mistaken. That's not what happened."

The special agent who had been taking notes now interjected, "You don't gain anything by overturning your confession. It will only complicate what's simple."

"Then why are we going through with this re-interrogation anyway?" Youde restrained himself from shooting back lest they would turn red in anger. Instead, Youde said, "Since I came to Taipei, I've been pinning my hopes on the re-interrogation. Please do what you can for me."

"Can't do what's impossible," the "sweet potato" notetaker replied.

"You are being presumptuous," the questioning agent raised his voice slightly. "We trusted you and had made our report according to what you said, all favorable to you. But are you still dissatisfied?"

"……"

"If you insist on overturning your confession, we will have no choice but to send you to the *other* organization, even though that would make us look bad."

It did not sound like an empty threat. The "other" organization would have to be either the Investigation Bureau or the Secret Protection Bureau. Youde had never heard of anybody going free from either place. "Just what I need to aggravate the matter." A saying came to Youde's mind: "When bitten by a dog or a secret agent, better swallow the hurt and let the matter drop."

The notetaking "sweet potato" said, "You did not read the book anyway. It doesn't matter, does it? Why don't you just let it go?"

Consequently, this report said the same thing as Chiayi's.

As Youde glanced at the report and was putting his thumbprint on the document, the special agent who had been paging through some material, said in a sarcastic tone, "You are not much trusted by your colleagues."

Youde was stung by the words. After graduating from the Normal University, he had returned to his hometown to teach in the small-time middle school, spurning Taipei's famous schools, with only one thought in mind: to serve his hometown. At a time when certified teachers were in short supply, it could be said that his colleagues had fully trusted and even relied on him. He got along well with them and did nothing to betray their trust. When Youde's scholarship to America was announced, all his colleagues, Taiwanese and mainlanders alike, had been happy for him as if they themselves were the recipients of the good fortune. To be told now that his colleagues lacked confidence in him was rather unexpected.

But the school principal had changed during Youde's stay in America. The new principal had brought with him about ten new people, from the dean down to clerks, with whom Youde had worked for only about a month. Still, there couldn't be anything to cause them not to trust him.

The special agent must have detected Youde's disagreeing look because he slammed shut the file and briskly walked out of the room.

As he put the handcuffs back on Youde, the sweet potato agent said, "You shouldn't look so sullen. To end your interrogation with such a conclusion as yours, you should be grateful."

"……"

"You know, we did make quite an effort on your behalf."

How much of this is true and how much false? The special agents are the untrustworthy ones!

Youde was returned to his cell. It was after lunch. People were napping and the place was quiet.

45

Statue of Liberty

But Dragon-head Peng was up. He stood up and took out the lunch he had saved for Youde. Atop of the rice were vegetables and three chips of coveted, precious pork croutons (what's left of pork fat tissues after rendering). But Youde had no appetite so he put the food back. At that point, the presumably sleeping Chen the deserter sprang up from his pallet, excused himself to Youde, and started to eat the food.

Youde described the interrogation to Peng.

When Youde was finished, Peng said, "That's good. I was worried that you were going to be submitted to another fatigue-interrogation.... Anyway, that's good. I don't think you'll be sent to another investigative body from here. If anything, it would be the Military Court for prosecution. Of course, it is possible that the Military Court may in turn send you somewhere else, then the matter can get a bit sticky. But there isn't much evidence against you here; I don't think that will happen."

Peng, being a former intelligence man, was knowledgeable. He said decidedly, "Within a week, you will be sent to the prosecutor of the Military Justice Department, then in a month or two be given the sentence of 're-education without crime' and sent to the re-education center. Then, if nothing else happens, you will go home from there three years later. That's the outline."

"So it will be three years later?"

"At the Military Court Prison, anybody would jump with joy with a three-year sentence. At least you will not be exposed to fearing death on daily basis."

Silence prevailed for a while. The nap time was over and the prison started to stir. The only thing left for the inmates to do was to wait for supper.

Youde remembered the special agent's parting remark.

"When I was pressing my thumbprint after the interrogation, the special agent said that I lacked trust among my colleagues."

"Hmm."

"I wonder if they went to the school. My affair at school was already thoroughly investigated by the Chiayi branch."

"Not exactly. On each case, two agents were responsible for questioning; but the investigative team usually consists of seven or eight people. Maybe they didn't think Chiayi's job was thorough enough, so they sent some people down to Putzu."

"Hard to believe. If anything, the Chiayi interrogation was too thorough. You see, they did not arrest me right after my return from America in order to watch my behavior and observe my relationship with my colleagues. They knew every detail of my conduct at school."

"Is that so! It's fortunate that you didn't give them any handle during the month. Otherwise they would have plunged into that during the interrogation. But about your conduct at school, they probably looked at everything since you took the job and not just after your return."

The February 28 Incident and the April 6 student incident were like immunization shots to Youde: He had been extremely cautious in his speech and conduct. It had been a rather painful predicament for Youde, but it paid off.

Youde thought to himself, "But the more thorough the investigation, the less likely they could conclude that I am not trusted by my colleagues, because that is just exactly the opposite to the truth."

Suddenly, Peng slapped his thigh.

"I see. I know."

"What is that?"

"They had tried to release you."

"Oh?"

What a surprise! Even though release is the proper thing.

Peng said, "There is something called a 'workplace guarantee.' If the man in charge at the workplace was willing to put the seal on the 'mutual guarantee agreement,' people like you against whom they had insufficient evidence, were sometimes released. Of course, you were under surveillance. There was one recent case like that."

" ......"

"That's the reason the special agent went to your school — to secure the guarantee agreement."

Of course, that made sense. The sweet-potato agent had said, "We had made quite an effort on your behalf." Maybe it wasn't necessarily a lie.

"I guess the principal and the department head both refused to put the seal to the agreement. That is what they were referring to when they said that you were not much trusted by your colleagues."

"I see."

All public servants were assigned to groups of three to five people and were required to sign the "mutual guarantee agreement." If any among the group were to commit the crime of sedition, and the group members did not report it beforehand, the signatories of the agreement would be charged with the same crime — a law reminiscent of the mutual responsibility law (*lien-tso-fa*) of sixteenth-century China.

Youde thought it was reasonable that the new principal and the new department chairman refused to guarantee a person they knew for only a brief time. Besides, they considered Youde to be the big man in the previous principal's camp and could have wished that Youde did not return.

"Why did they consider releasing me?"

"Well...," Peng thought for a while, "I think it is because you are a returnee from America. The other case that I mentioned also involved a returnee."

To send someone who had just returned from learning the democratic process in America to a brainwashing program would require some explaining to the Americans, especially when the cause was only a thin pamphlet of uncertain existence. Americans would have a hard time understanding that.

"You are extremely lucky," Peng said, "If Yu-kun had been captured before your departure, the matter could have been entirely different. First of all, you couldn't have escaped physical torture. You came back just when they relaxed the torture policy."

"Why do you think they relaxed the torture policy?"

"I am not sure, but many people think it's due to Chiang Ching-kuo. Compared to his old man, Chiang Ching-kuo is quite a bit more enlightened. Besides, he is the only one who can change Chiang Kai-shek's rules. In any case, you are lucky."

"But the change of school principal during my absence was not so lucky."

They laughed together.

Unknown to Youde, the Statue of Liberty had come near and then, again without Youde's knowing, had abruptly departed.

46

The Doctor Who Was Not Immunized

During the following week, all of the cellmates except for Dragon-head Peng, Captain Tu, and Youde were sent to prosecution, and seven new "sundry criminals" took their places. By seniority, Captain Tu was number two and by rule should sleep next to Peng, which he was unwilling to do, so he changed places with Youde.

One afternoon another political prisoner arrived. From his clothing and mannerisms, it was apparent that he was a Taiwanese returnee from Japan.

"I am Kuo Wen-hsiung from Ts'aotun. How do you do? I don't think I did anything wrong, but the police brought me here."

"What's your profession?" Peng asked.

"I am a doctor. I just returned from Japan last month."

"Ooh!" words of lament came from the sundry criminals.

In Taiwan, the word "doctor" was synonymous with "elite." Most doctors were financially well off, well trusted, and well known in their localities. Also there had been many doctors who died working for political causes under colonial rule.

Peng first introduced the "sundry criminals" then at last brought Dr. Kuo and Youde together, who held each others' hands and talked like old friends.

Kuo was two years older than Youde and had graduated from Jikei Medical School of Tokyo, with surgery his specialty. He had come back to Taiwan swelled with hope and dedication. And upon his arrival, his high school classmates welcomed him with a party; but right there the problem occurred. It was not yet ten days after his return.

It happened that among Kuo's classmates was a man called Li, a grade school teacher who had secretly joined the Communist Party. What with frequent newspaper reports of arrests and executions of Communists, Li was driven to the verge of a nervous breakdown.

So when the Self-Renewal Policy was announced, he turned himself in, at around the same time as Chen Ming-chih. Implicated by Li's confession, two cell members of his who were also schoolteachers were arrested. One was sentenced to life; and Liao, the cell leader, was put to death. Liao and Dr. Kuo were bosom buddies in their high school days.

Dr. Kuo, ignorant of Taiwan's situation, had castigated Li at the welcoming party, partly aided by the wine he drank that night.

"It's the same as if you yourself had killed Liao." Kuo reproached Li, who did not respond except to put his head down on the table and sob. A few days later, Li took rat poison and killed himself, without leaving a suicide note. People thought Li might have committed suicide anyway, even without Kuo's reproach, suffering as he was from extreme nervous exhaustion.

Dr. Kuo was taken in by the police. There were many witnesses when Kuo reproached Li, hence he was detained. What could his crime be? It couldn't be anything other than "suicide assist," a common case that would be turned over to the local court and the offender released. But the problem cropped up in Kuo's answers during the police investigation. The naive Dr. Kuo had criticized the Self-Renewal Policy and, for good measure, threw in a few cases of official misconduct that he had observed since his return. Consequently, the case turned into a "political thought" case, too complicated or serious for the local police, so they sent him here.

"But can something like that constitute sedition?"

Peng replied, "It is likely that you will be charged with Article 7 of the Sedition Law."

"What is Article 7?" Dr. Kuo asked.

"Those who committed actions favorable to the enemy or of use to the Communists, should be sentenced to no less than seven years of confinement," Youde elaborated.

"Goodness, I thought I would get something like three months, even if I am convicted." Dr. Kuo's face visibly paled.

Feeling sorry for him, Youde said, "It's not like it's been decided. Maybe you will be turned over to re-education; then we could become classmates."

"How cruel, our government," Dr. Kuo muttered.

Dr. Kuo made the same mistake that Youde and his friends did before the Restoration. He had mistaken the foreign regime that landed on Taiwan's shore as the government of his country.

Dr. Kuo was not in Taiwan during the February 28 Incident nor during the April 6 student incident. Obviously he did not get the immunization shots against the reign of the White Terror.

47

Regrets

Naturally, Youde and Dr. Kuo got along famously. They never seemed to run out of things to talk about. They talked about the war, during which they both experienced a life of poverty — past sufferings now only fond memories. Kuo talked about postwar Japan, while Youde talked about Taiwan after the Restoration. In contrast to Youde, who was well informed about postwar Japan, Kuo, though a Taiwanese, did not at all comprehend Taiwan's situation after the Restoration.

Kuo said, "The newspaper from Taiwan never mentioned anything like that."

The newspapers were all owned by the KMT government and naturally only printed news favorable to the government. As for the editorials, they were truly a laughingstock. If one judged Taiwan by what was in the newspaper, he could run into real trouble.

"Letters from my family also never touched upon the so-called White Terror either."

If one wrote something like that and the letter happened to be inspected by the censor, he could be in big trouble. Nobody took pointless risks like that.

Kuo had married a Japanese nurse and had a child with her. He did not discuss Taiwanese politics with his wife either.

Occasionally, he and fellow Taiwanese in Japan had talked about Taiwan. But his acquaintances were also just as uninformed, so the talk was always limited to the fond memories of their homeland.

"It's understandable how Kuo came to be totally ignorant of the present Taiwan," Youde reflected.

Captain Tu, in language sprinkled here and there with "bastards," also related to Kuo the true stories of violence committed by the Kuomintang army that landed on Penghu, and the corruption of the government officials.

Peng nodded to Captain Tu's words. These days, Tu had dared to criticize the government in front of Peng. Perhaps he had second thoughts about Peng as days went by.

Dr. Kuo had an additional worry that Youde did not have. That was what to do with his wife. How was she going to live in a land of strange language and customs without a husband? Fortunately for her, Kuo's parents were still living and rather well off, so she would not end up on the streets. Nevertheless, to wait patiently for at least three years, or by chance ten years, couldn't be easy.

Kuo found the most reasonable answer, "Maybe I should let her go back to Japan. She is able to support herself as a nurse."

Peng immediately said, "That's no longer possible. The moment you were taken in, no family member of yours will be allowed to leave the country."

Kuo was speechless.

Tragedy begets tragedy, it was once said. From Li's Self-Renewal confession, unexpected tragedy had befallen the peaceful Kuo family.

"I wish I had never come back to Taiwan," the silent eyes of Dr. Kuo clearly indicated.

48

To the Military Court

One afternoon it came time for Dragon-head Peng to be sent to the prosecution. Youde untied his bundle and asked Peng to please pick out something from it. Peng took one of the two tubes of toothpaste and said, "All right. Thanks. I'll have this. It should be enough."

He meant by "enough" that the toothpaste should last till his execution.

To Youde's surprise, Captain Tu also insistently pressed a bag of crackers into Peng's bag. Mainlander or not, Peng was a fellow unfortunate soul with whom he had slept and eaten for the past twenty days. Naturally, Tu had feelings for him. Because Peng was a serious criminal, he went out not only with handcuffs but also with leg-irons.

As if to chase after Peng, several days later on November 18, Youde was sent to the Military Court, leaving the rueful Captain Tu and Dr. Kuo behind. The Military Court was located in the center of Taipei, on Chingtao East Road, in a compound refurbished from the former Japanese Army supply depot. The compound was as large as a middle school campus and consisted of business offices, military courts, and the prison barracks.

Youde was turned over to the receiving office. First he was fingerprinted, then photographed with a name plate around his neck — thus officially recorded as a suspect for sedition. The name plate had 107085 next to the name. Youde wondered if the number was going to take the place of his name from now on.

After the admission procedures, two soldiers took Youde out of the office from a side door. Just outside the office, a one-story portico building was visible to the right.

To the left, a high wall continued. A small, grassy courtyard lay between the wall and the building.

The building on the right had four rooms. At first glance, they could be taken for kindergarten classrooms. In front of each room a wooden plaque hung on the pillar under the portico: "No. X Courtroom."

"So this is the notorious Devil's Palace of Chingtao East Road," Youde muttered under his breath. Suspects were sentenced here, and those given death sentences were transported from here to the execution yard, while those sentenced to confinement were transferred from here to the military prisons. For such a terror-arousing Devil's Palace, the building was shabby indeed. "I guess it well serves its purpose," Youde thought.

In the middle of the high wall, there was a gate of iron bars from which a paved path directly led to the courtrooms. Prisoners were led into the courtrooms by this path.

Another paved path connected the offices to the gate. Youde, taken by the two soldiers, now passed through the iron gate and stepped into a guards' station. The other end of the guards' station was another wide entrance gated by a door made of thick planks. Through the gaps between the planks, one could peek at the inside of the yard. This wooden door separated the prison yard and the guards' station; guards were stationed on either side of it.

The other side of the wooden gate looked to be the prison yard. It was covered from corner to corner with sunshine. Youde couldn't wait to get there and soak up the sunshine.

The guard took off Youde's handcuffs and took him through the door. He was at last standing under the glare of the afternoon sun.

In front of him was a large open space, half of it occupied by three worn, concrete tennis courts in a row. On the other side of the tennis courts was a small pool-like structure. Originally this was probably an athletic field, too spacious for a garden, Youde surmised. To the right edge of the open space there was an asphalt path, and alongside of it stood two huge warehouses, towering over their surroundings. Youde had heard that the old warehouse buildings were used for prison housing and that in these buildings some one thousand people, each harboring his own tragedy, jostled each other like chickens in a chicken coop. But the thick walls prevented the voices inside from escaping.

TO THE MILITARY COURT 165

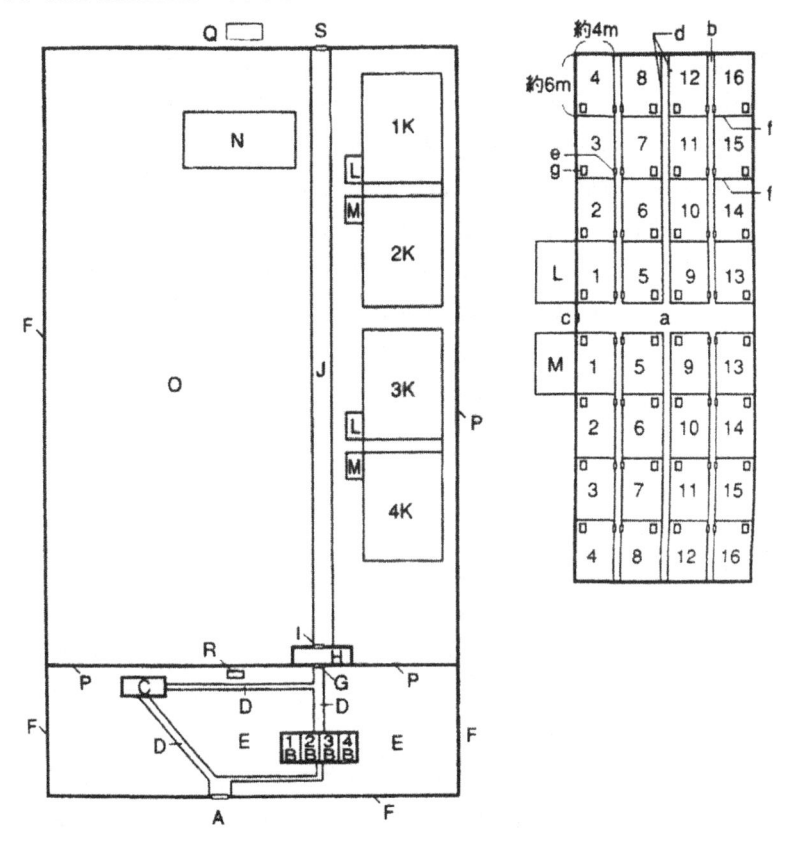

A. Front gate
B. Courtrooms
C. Office
D. Paved path
E. Lawn
F. Extra high wall
G. Gate to prison
H. Guard's station
I. Heavy wooden gate
J. Wide asphalth path
K. Prison barracks
   (formerly warehouses)
L. Guard's office
M. Guard's sleeping quarters
N. Cement water tank (bathing area)
O. Exercise grounds

P. High wall
Q. Machine gun platform
R. Watchtower
S. Gate to women's prison

(Detail of K)

a. Central hallway (2.5 m wide)
b. Corridor (1 m wide)
c. Entrance gate
d. Floor to ceiling cage divider made of lumber columns
e. Cage door
f. Wall
g. Matung (wooden tub for human waste)

Diagram of Taipei Military Court Prison

Youde walked on the asphalt path toward the warehouse, sandwiched by two soldiers. He walked as slowly as he could, swaying his body front, back, left, and right. While his body happily soaked up the sunlight, Youde felt an injection of new energy into his body, just like a battery being recharged. He was not aware that his body had craved the sunlight so.

He was taken past the first warehouse and headed toward the entrance of the one farther down. Step by step he approached yet another unknown world.

49

Unexpected Welcome

At about one hundred meters from the guards' station, they reached the entrance of the second warehouse building.

In front of it, several guards in shirtsleeves were sitting on low-swung bamboo chairs, puffing cigarettes. There were a few add-on structures on either side of the entrance. The structure to the left was the office. It contained four desks; and its walls were decked with handcuffs, keys, and flashlights. The room to the right looked to be the night guards' sleeping quarters. In it, several men could be seen spread out on the floor and snoring. Wooden plaques, marking "Area 1" and "Area 2," were on the sides of the entrance.

The pool-like structure that Youde saw earlier turned out to be a large cement water tank, situated straight across from the entrance on the other side of the asphalt path. A naked man was by the side of the water tank, scooping out the water from the tank and washing himself.

"*Panchang* Teng, I brought you a newcomer," the guard shouted.

From inside the warehouse-turned-prison barrack appeared a red-faced man of stout build who approached with jangling keys. The *panchang* (squad leader) took charge of Youde and ordered his man to get a new set of keys. While they were waiting, a different guard went through Youde's bundle again. The entrance to the prison barrack had a gate that was made of square lumber, but it was left open. One could hear the voices coming from inside.

"Come. Area 1, Cell 7."

Following the panchang, Youde entered the building. Two guards accompanied them from behind.

The entry area was bright but the interior was dark. Even in broad daylight, with the aid of several naked light bulbs switched on here and there, the inside was still rather dim. A putrid stuffiness overwhelmed, almost preventing one from breathing, as if entering a cellar. This ex-warehouse had been divided into numerous cages with rough, irregularly shaped lumber. The number 107085 probably signified the eighty-fifth inmate to enter Area 1 — Cell 7.

"Mr. Tsai Youde," somebody called from one of the cells when Youde passed by. Youde turned around to look, but the face was already obscured by the partitioning lumber and couldn't be seen.

They soon arrived at Cell 7, which was not far from the entrance. The cage door to the cell was not quite four feet high and was made of thick boards. Panchang Teng picked out the key to Cell 7 and unlocked the door.

The floor was maybe about two feet off the ground, under which the familiar shoes-turned-slippers were lined up in a row.

As Youde lowered his head and entered the door, he was pulled up by several helping hands and climbed onto the floor with ease.

"Mr. Tsai, how are you?"

It was evident that their smiles showed heartfelt welcome. Despite the November weather, these people wore almost nothing. To Youde's surprise, even without the customary self-introduction, they already knew his name, that he was from Putzu, about his study in America, and even that he was implicated by Chang Yu-kun. It was obvious that some kind of intelligence network was at work here. But Youde did not know any of them.

A dragon-head-like person introduced himself. "I am Liu Ming-hsiung. I am really glad that you came to this cell. We knew that you would be sent here sooner or later, but we did not know which cell you would be assigned to. We are very lucky to get you."

Although somewhat bewildered by the unexpected welcome, Youde was grateful for the goodwill.

"Well, let me make introductions."

Before Liu could finish the sentence, somebody had already taken Youde's hand.

"I am Lu Min-jen. Call me Little Lu."

Youde was taken aback when he saw the friendly, smiling face.

Why, isn't it identical to Ah-fu's? The shape of the face, the expressions and the open friendliness were much the same, the only difference between the two was that Little Lu was a bit shorter and that his eyes shined with intellect that had not been present in Ah-fu's.

"I see. How do you do." Youde returned a firm squeeze.

"Little Lu, at seventeen, is the youngest among us; yet he has been here the longest." Liu's words were startling. "It's been more than four years since he lost his freedom. Like me, he was transferred here four years ago."

That would put Little Lu at the age of twelve or thirteen when he was arrested. A mere child. But Youde did not have time to inquire, as Liu continued with the introductions.

"Here is ex-police officer Wu Wen-chin, charged with Article 4. He's been here nearly two years. Here is Chou Shui from the village of Luku, charged with Article 2.1. This is Mori, real name Lin Sun-shan. He was a bank clerk and is charged with Article 4. He has been here for two years. This here is Shen Shih-kai, a public scribe. He is the oldest among us, so we call him Ojisan. He is charged with Article 7. He will soon be here a year. This here is Chen Shih, also from Luku. He is charged with Article 2.1 in the same case as Chou Shui. He is a grown man with the mind of a ten-year-old. He has been here nearly two years. Here is Huang Chin-huo, an errand boy for a printshop. He is charged with Article 4 and has been here almost a year and a half. This is Kao Ching-chi, my colleague at a primary school in Feng-yuan. He is charged with Article 2.1 He has been here over four years."

After the straightforward introductions, Liu added, "These are all nice people with whom you can talk openly. You see, this place is probably freer than the outside in some respects since we can say whatever we want...."

"About the only place we can sing Communist songs aloud," the ex-policeman Wu chimed in and gave a throaty laugh.

Unlike previous places, this prison housed no "sundry criminals;" and since it was not an investigative organization, planted informants were not likely to be present either. A sentiment of brotherhood permeated the room.

While one could not see the inside of the adjacent cells on the same row, because they were separated by thick, solid planks, one could see clearly the cells across the hallway through the gaps between square lumber columns that were set about ten centimeters apart to form a wall.

"Tsai Youde, how are you?" Somebody stuck his hand through a gap and was waving it up and down.

The gap between columns barely accommodated a person's wrist, so unless two people faced the gap frontally, one side could not meet the other side's eyes. So, Youde walked around the cell and returned the greetings from his fellow "friends in misfortune" in the neighboring cells.

At one spot, the inmate from the opposite side said, "Cheng Chi-hsiang sends his regards."

"Oh? Cheng Chi-hsiang?" Youde repeated the name to himself but it did not click.

"He said he saw you earlier when you walked by."

"So that's the person who called my name. The message must have been relayed from cell to cell," Youde realized.

The fellow on the opposite side added, "He said that he helped when you performed *The Sunrise* in Chiayi."

That did it. That Cheng Chi-hsiang, Youde remembered. Cheng was a Christian like Wu Che-fu and Chen Ming-chih and was a promoter for the outreach program of the Chiayi Presbyterian Church. At the time, he was a student at National Taiwan University and helped Youde with various chores during the Chiayi production. Youde had learned that Cheng was arrested at about the same time as Wu Che-fu and they both were convicted and serving their sentences.

"But isn't Cheng Chi-hsiang already tried and sentenced?"

Liu took over and replied, "When he was serving his sentence on the 'island,' something else turned up that got him to be brought back on a separate charge. The investigation of that is completed, so he is here to await the second trial. He is in an extremely dangerous situation."

The "island" referred to Green Island, situated off the southeast coast of Taiwan. The Japanese named it "Burning Island," made infamous as the devil's island for serious criminals. Youde had heard that the facility had been expanded ten-fold in order to accommodate the continuous flow of political prisoners.

The fellow across the hall continued, "More. Wu Che-fu was also brought back from the island in the same case as Cheng Chi-hsiang. He lives in Area 4, so he doesn't know about your arrival yet. Do you want to send him a message?"

Liu again explained, "This building on the east end has Areas 1 and 2; the building to the west has Areas 3 and 4. As a rule, the authorities disperse people involved in the same case to different areas. Because Chang Yu-kun is in Area 3, you came to Area 1, you see."

"But would my message really reach Wu Che-fu in Area 4?" In any case, Youde couldn't think of anything at a moment's notice. Instead he asked, "Is Che-fu going to be all right?"

"I don't know about that. Since he is involved in the same case as Cheng Chi-hsiang, maybe fifty-fifty."

Of course, "fifty-fifty" meant that there was fifty percent chance Che-fu would be sentenced to death.

Youde's heart, just buoyed by unexpected welcome, was again heavy.

50

New Brothers

Youde put down his bundle and surveyed the room. The raised platform floor was made of a wooden plank, the size of two rows of five tatami mats laid side by side, upon which inmates were to sleep in pairs, touching head to head or toe to toe. On each of the side walls hung a foot-wide shelf at a height barely clearing a man's head. On the shelves sat inmates' belongings and each person's enamel mug. Under each shelf, a laundry line spanned the length of the shelf, on which hung undershirts and towels. At one corner of the room sat a large wooden tub — called the *matung* — to be used as a toilet. The *matung* was covered but still emitted foul smells. The room had no ventilation.

It looked to Youde that the warehouse was probably converted by some lumber-loving designer who used some eighteenth-century prisons for a blueprint. It was atrocious even for a temporary prison.

Nevertheless, the platform was spotless and shined to a sheen, perhaps owing to too much idle time on the inmates' part.

According to the unwritten rule, the newcomer must take the place next to the *matung*. But Little Lu had already switched Youde's bundle with his own pillow.

The oldest veteran Little Lu said with a smile, "I am too accustomed to sleeping at this spot to do otherwise."

There is a big difference between sleeping right next to the *matung* and to sleep a person away from it, because the person in between serves as a levee and greatly lessens the unpleasantness. Not to mention the occasional splattering caused by somebody urinating in the middle of the night. Youde was moved by the Little Lu, who had willingly slept for four years next to the *matung*. How would his parents feel if they knew that their son has been sleeping in the worst possible spot in the worst possible prison conditions?

"Are your parents in good health?" Youde asked.

"Oh yes. They are very well. But I heard that they think of us every day...."

"Us?"

"My older brother is in Area 3. He is doomed because he killed a KMT secret agent."

Youde couldn't imagine the tear-filled days of Little Lu's parents. There were so much more Youde would like to know, but it was dinnertime.

Four servants carried in two huge wooden tubs and placed them in the hallway. One tub contained rice, the other contained other foods. The tubs stayed in the hallway, while the inmates stuck out their enamel bowls through the gaps between square lumber columns and the servants by turn filled the bowls with rice and other accompanying foods — another eighteenth-century practice. Youde also stuck out his bowl that he received from Liu. He felt like a beggar.

Having skipped lunch, Youde was hungry. Today's accompanying dish was fried fish.

All sat down in a circle. Liu and Kao put two bowls in the middle, one contained peanuts and the other pickles. Youde hurriedly took out the small amount of food that remained of his last care package and placed them in the center.

"The food here is not too bad. We get the same food allowance as the soldiers," the ex-teacher Kao Ching-yuan said.

"No way. It can't be the same as the soldiers' because somebody is bound to take a cut somewhere. Take this fish. It is deep fried because it is not really fresh," the ex-policeman Wu Wen-chin rebuked.

No matter. The fried ocean eel suited Youde's palate just fine. He did not need the additional food from the care package. In this cell, all food from home was kept by the dragon-heads, Liu and Kao, and were shared by all. Youde's food too was put away by the two men.

The servants entered again with steaming wooden tubs, this time, to provide boiled water. All rose to fetch their enamel mugs from the shelves. Again, they stuck the mugs out from spaces between columns then retrieved the mugs carefully, taking care not to bump into the beams and spill the hot liquid on their hands.

The enamel mugs were large and even came with lids. There were a few mugs remaining on the shelves. Liu took one off the shelf and handed it to Youde.

"You may use this one. It was left by someone who was called out to execution from this room."

Putting his lips to the mug, Youde felt the last owner's pain and despair.

Sipping his hot water, Liu said, "When we first arrived here, the place was jam packed, about twenty people to one room."

Ex-policeman Wu, who was fanning his bare torso with a homemade fan said, "Even when I got here, the space per person for lying down was only this wide," and showed the width of the fan which looked tiny against the stout Wu.

How did they sleep in that space?

Liu explained to the perplexed Youde, "At night we took turns to either sit or lay down. Then our rank gradually dwindled, as one by one they were called out."

Ex-policeman Wu again interjected, "They went home. Home. The one in the other world."

"Sadly, though, the room became more spacious. You arrived at the emptiest time. Just ten to the room. It hasn't happened too many times."

After drinking hot water, cleaning started. Everybody took a rag and wiped the columns and the wooden platform with great care. The air was already extremely polluted with nitrogen; when dust was added to it, it would become intolerable. That was why they all had to work together to rid the place of dust. Indeed, cooperation was the only means for survival in this tragic condition.

Mori, the bank employee, stretched his arms through the gaps between the columns to wring the rags in a bucket of water that sat outside the cell, and handed them to his cellmates. For this task, even the long-armed Mori had to sprawl on the floor. They cleaned twice a day, once in the morning and once at night. After cleaning, it was time to walk. They formed an oval and sang as they walked. The Chinese Communists had numerous morale-raising songs that had circulated so widely on college campuses before the April 6 crackdown that Youde also knew them well. "This is probably the only place in Taiwan where songs like these can be sung aloud," Youde thought. Singing voices from other cells wafted through the air. Sometimes people from different cells joined in a chorus.

On Mori's suggestion, they decided to cut short the walking to twenty minutes and use the time to listen to Youde's story. Ordinarily they would have walked for one hour then read or written letters until lights-out at nine. This prison allowed simple correspondence, albeit under strict censorship, but prohibited newspapers and radios. Thus, in effect the inmates were isolated from the outside world.

Youde's arrival afforded a certain degree of contact with the outside. Youde understood the meaning of the outsized welcome.

What concerned his cellmates most were the developments of the international situation.

How much had the Communists' military been strengthened? When would the Chinese Communists move on Taiwan militarily? Would the United States and Taiwan sign a mutual defense treaty? Also, would the United States recognize the Communist regime? Was there room for compromise between the KMT and the Communists? And so forth. To the political prisoners, these were all pressing questions that could affect their life and death.

Suppose the Communists attacked, it was possible that all inmates would be lined up and executed. On the other hand, it was also possible that they could be rescued by the Communist army; a road for life could thus open up. If talks between the KMT and the Communists went well, they could be released. Then again, if the opposite happened, they would be the first to be offered up as sacrifices.

Youde, not being a political analyst, was not able to answer the questions to his new friends' satisfaction. He offered the latest — although already one month old — observations, in an objective manner, to their eager ears. Liu and Kao took notes and passed them on to neighboring cells.

The questions continued in whispers even after the lights were out and they lay down in pairs with their heads touching.

Before settling down to sleep, Youde got up, removed the lid of the *matung* and urinated. It took longer to perform this bodily function in front of others.

As he lay down again, the no-longer-used mugs on the shelves came in sight. Lined up neatly in a row and reflecting faintly the lights of the darkened room, the mugs resembled the ancestral alter plaques, unknowingly filling the room with sorrow.

51

Open-air Bath

Learning that he was allowed a postcard once a week, Youde wrote a letter right away to his wife the next morning. Youde did not have a postcard, but his cellmates offered theirs. This was the first letter since he lost his freedom; Youde's heart galloped. His cellmates informed him that prison conditions were not to be mentioned because the postcard could be confiscated and thrown into a wastepaper basket. Therefore, only mundane things could be written, such as, "I am fine, don't worry." Nevertheless, it was not hard to imagine that these pedestrian words in his own handwriting would, more than anything else, bring his family peace of mind. "Most likely, I will repeat the same words every week," Youde resigned himself. The next thing to put down would be to ask for necessities. But because this prison allowed inmates to withdraw their money that the office kept for them in order to purchase daily needs from the employee-benefit shop, there was not a thing Youde needed to ask from home. Books on religions and languages were allowed, so Youde asked for a dictionary. At the end, he added that he was concerned about his family and eagerly awaited her reply.

Breakfast was at six, followed by cleaning. After that, they waited for the biggest event of the day: to be let out in the yard. Forty to fifty inmates were let out at one time for about twenty minutes, during which the inmates bathed in the open, washed their clothes, or just walked.

Their turn arrived at nine. In their underwear, carrying washbasins, towels, and soap, they waited by the barred door. As soon as the panchang unlocked the door, they jumped out at once and rushed outside.

Fresh air, warm sun, and cold water were the most precious elements in human existence — a well-known fact that Youde had pretty much failed to appreciate in his past life. "I deserve to be punished for that," he thought.

Once outside, his lungs automatically rose and fell, full with fresh air.

"It's delicious!" Youde let out.

Then there was water. The water tank was already surrounded by naked prison friends.

"Come here," said ex-policeman Wu, who moved over some to make room for Youde.

"You are the newcomer, Mr. Tsai, right?" the man next to him greeted Youde right away.

The guards were stationed close by, so any inquisitive talks were out. Outside the wall, on a raised platform, machine guns could be seen pointing inward.

Youde scooped up the water and poured it over himself. Even in a southern country like Taiwan, the open-air bath under a November sky was a bit chilly. But this was hardly a time for nitpicking. This was the first bath since his arrest. He soaped himself and let the water wash away the grime. He felt literally lighter, several layers of grime gone.

Whenever Youde's eyes met those of other inmates, all replied with smiles and nods. These were true friends. Some had started to wash their clothes. Youde joined the threesome who were circling the yard. Little Lu joined Youde and followed him from behind. They walked rapidly, swinging their arms as high as they could. When he first arrived at this compound, Youde did not notice the hut-like watchtower sitting atop the wall, which was equipped with searchlights and machine guns. Now he could see the helmeted soldiers in the tower. But the fellow prison brothers walked intently, completely ignoring the tower. As the guards were stationed every ten meters or so, they were not able to converse as they walked abreast. But it was possible to mutter a word or two when passing the person in front.

"Mr. Tsai, keep well," two or three people had greeted Youde as they passed by. Youde thought of Cheng Chi-hsiang and looked around but was not able to locate him.

Twenty minutes soon passed. Panchang Teng blew the whistle and the inmates swarmed to the entrance like a flock of ushered ducks.

On his return trip, Youde paid special attention as he passed Area 2, Cell 5. As he expected, Cheng Chi-hsiang was waiting. Perhaps Cheng also waited on Youde's trip out to the yard, except Youde was so eager to get out that he failed to notice Cheng.

"Have you gotten used to it yet?" Cheng asked.

"Ya, thanks," Youde nodded.

From the fleeting glance of Cheng's face, Youde observed that Cheng hadn't changed at all from his student days despite years of suffering.

52

Lovable Little Lu

After being locked back in the cell, they answered the roll call. The period following was slated for free activities. Youde was impressed how they all started to study, except for Chou Shui, the woodcutter from Luku, who leaned against a pillar, seemingly deep in thought — or perhaps he was just sitting blankly. The group took out their books and proceeded to read.

The ex-bank employee Mori said to Little Lu, "Well, from today on, Mr. Tsai is your teacher, a bona fide English teacher at that. You must study hard."

Little Lu smiled widely and shyly took out his book and notebook. The book was a textbook for third-year middle school students. He said that he had been taking English lessons from Mori and Japanese lessons from Shen, the public scribe.

Mori said, "It's rather the case that I've been studying English together with Little Lu, not teaching him. Please let me be a student also." He bowed his head and took out an English textbook and a book on English grammar in Chinese.

"For me, the English grammar in Japanese would be easier to understand. But Japanese books are not allowed here."

Except for the four youngsters — namely Little Lu, the mentally retarded Chen Shih of Luku, the woodcutter Chou Shui, also from Luku, and the printshop errand boy Huang Chin-huo — all spoke Japanese with varying competence. For Taiwanese over the age of twenty, Japanese was still a more familiar language than Mandarin Chinese, which they studied only after the Restoration — a logical consequence from receiving their formal education in Japanese and through no fault of the "sweet potatoes." Yet the government was particularly hostile toward the Japanese language. Speaking Japanese in public places was prohibited; and sometimes the government even labeled Japanese speakers as "products of enslaved education" or "persons possessing a slave mentality" and treated them with hostility. The Taiwanese people were thus forced to speak only Chinese, faltering and stumbling, in public. Youde wondered if it was another kind of abuse of human rights.

Little Lu's notebook was crammed with English vocabulary, a considerable amount of it. Youde picked out a few words and gave Little Lu an impromptu test. Little Lu's spelling was very good, but his pronunciations were strange. Asked to construct a sentence or two with the words, he did not do well either. Yet he comprehended well and was able to quickly grasp the sentence patterns and apply them. At this rate, Little Lu could become an honors student. Youde praised him. At that, Little Lu gave out a "Wow!" and did a backflip from his sitting position, his special stunt when he was happy, according to Mori. Mori again said happily, "From now on, I can study live English."

After studying for a while, the talk turned to Little Lu's case.

"Why did your older brother kill a KMT secret agent?"

Mori answered for Little Lu, "His brother's name is Lu Kuo-jen. He was still a student in the First Taichung Middle School when he and five or six other students were recruited by a mainlander teacher into the Communist Party. About half a year later, the Communist teacher ordered his recruits to murder a teacher by the name of Sun who had been a KMT secret agent. Using the pistol and the three bullets given to him, Lu Kuo-jen ambushed the secret agent Sun in a Taichung park and shot him to death. It was written all over the papers at the time."

It happened in May 1948.

"Lu Kuo-jen accomplished his mission successfully," Mori said.

"That's right," Little Lu continued. "My brother got to the designated location, where he was supposed to report to the person who had ordered the murder and flee with him to the mainland."

"But," Mori resumed, "the person did not show up. He had already gone back to the mainland alone. So Lu kuo-jen and several of his comrades fled into the mountains and led subsistence lives as fugitives."

"But how did Little Lu get involved in this?"

"Little Lu was used as a messenger. The fugitives needed money, even in the mountains. After six months they were flat broke, the family sent money and medicine. Little Lu took on the role of the carrier. He was only a fifth grader at the time."

"I was young, but I was also alert and precocious."

"Did you know the way to their hiding place?" Youde asked.

"Not too well, but I did remember going there with my brother once."

It was Mori's turn to ask, "I heard that you dressed like a peasant boy and walked all day. It must have been dusk when you got to the location. Weren't you afraid at all?"

"No, not at all. It was for my brother and his friends."

Mori turned to Youde and said, "Little Lu stayed there that night and was supposed to return to Taichung the next morning. But he was persuaded to stay an extra night to rest up."

"I, too, was so happy to see my brother that I ended up staying the extra night."

"That's what's bad. Because of the additional night's stay, you ran into the policemen."

"Yes. When I emerged from the mountain path onto a road wide enough for automobiles, I saw five or six policemen checking the passersby. So I turned right around, before the policemen could detect me, and returned to my brother's hiding place."

After that, Little Lu shared his brother's fugitive life.

"What was the most difficult thing during hiding?" Youde asked.

"I missed my mother, so I cried a lot."

"And you haven't seen your mother since?"

"No. I haven't seen her since that fateful day when I left home."

Youde imagined: She must have felt the pain every time she recalled with regret to have sent such a young boy on a mission like that! On the other hand, if Little Lu had safely returned home that day but was later detained by the secret police and subjected to torture, the mother's suffering would have been even more unbearable. Pity the "sweet potatoes;" but the mothers of "sweet potatoes" were even more worthy of sympathy.

Youde remembered Liu's words at their introduction and asked, "Even so, that is not enough to be charged with Article 2.1."

Mori answered, "When Little Lu was living at the hiding place, brother Lu Kuo-jen's comrades jokingly said to Little Lu, "You are now the captain of the Youth Brigade." Little Lu was so pleased with the title that he wrote it down on a piece of paper: Captain of the Youth Brigade — Lu Min-jen. When the special agents ambushed the hiding place while the fugitives slept, the piece of paper was confiscated along with other evidence."

"Were you ambushed while you slept?"

Little Lu answered, scratching his head.

"That's just it. The special agents learned from somewhere of our whereabouts and in the middle of the night quietly surrounded our hiding place with the help from many policemen. We were fast asleep, owing to our own carelessness. We were still in bed when they broke down the door, pistols in hands. Then, under the flashlights, we were pinned to the bed and tied with ropes. When we were taken out of the house, I found the yard swarming with noisy policemen, leaving almost no room for another person to stand. Somebody probably informed on us. To this day I don't know who."

"I see. You must have been mighty surprised. But," Youde still couldn't quite comprehend, "you mean the piece of paper caused you to be charged with Article 2.1?"

"That's right. Just because of that slip of paper. I sure wrote down some weird thing, didn't I?" Little Lu scratched his head again.

Mori comforted Little Lu, "But no matter what, I don't think they can convict you on the basis of a slip of paper. Not like it was an official commission from Mao Tse-tung! Besides, you didn't even have a single underling, so you can't be a captain! I think they most likely will convict you on Article 4 — giving aid to bandits. You were just a child then. You will be given the lightest sentence of ten years. You will see."

Liu came over to use the *matung*. He said, "Hey, Little Lu, you should study hard for ten years and get yourself a Ph.D. from the Security Defense University."

The military prison was nicknamed "Security Defense University."

Using the *matung* after Liu, Little Lu recited, "Lu Min-jen, Doctor of Philosophy, Security Defense University. Ha ha ha."

Little Lu's fetching laughter was utterly innocent.

It seemed maybe Little Lu was no longer satisfied with the title of captain of the Youth Brigade.

53

Five-Star Flag on the Window

THE public scribe, Shen Shih-kai, who slept next to Youde, told his own story to Youde. Shen was a native of Hsinying and was called Ojisan (uncle) by his cellmates. But he was really in his early forties. His balding hairline made him appear older than his age.

Shen entered school at an older age. He graduated from a preparatory school in Tokyo and at age thirty entered Chien-kuo University in Manchuria, a university established by the Japanese in order to develop Manchuria and maybe even China. Hence, the university was viewed by the KMT government with hostility — a place to develop human resources for the invasion of China. Some even called it a spy university. The true nature of the institution can only await future historical research. Meanwhile, the several hundred Taiwanese students who attended the university became victims.

After the war, Manchuria was the first area taken over by the Communists. The students that remained there, as a matter of course, worked under Communists; and many of them probably joined the Party. But the ones who chose to return to Taiwan did so because they loved Taiwan. Or it could even be argued that they did so because they were against the Communists. Yet the KMT government, lacking self-confidence, suspected them to be advance teams for the Communists.

Shen learned Chinese in Manchuria; that enabled him to take up being a public scribe as his profession. Public scribes in Taiwan are highly regarded. They sometimes take on lawyer-like functions.

One day, Shen was summoned by the Investigative Bureau. This was not an official summons; rather, he was asked to show up at a certain place and time for an "appointment," an innocent enough event from which not many people returned home. Just like Dr. Kuo, most Manchurian returnees were ignorant of the practices of the White Terror and walked into the traps set by the special agents' interrogations. They either refuted or gave answers critical of the government. Without comprehending what had happened, they were sent to the re-education centers to be brainwashed. Shen was one of them.

Then, one day at the re-education center, a pane of glass on a window cracked. Glass panels were precious. Shen cut out five paper stars and mended the glass by pasting the paper stars along the cracked arc. And this act invited the unthinkable calamity.

Somebody said, "It looks like the five-star flag of the Chinese Communists."

The director of the center came to the room. He took a photograph of the window and turned Shen in on the charge of Article 7: committing actions beneficial to the enemy. That's how Shen came to Cell 7 and became everybody's *ojisan*. That was almost a year ago. Only once was he called to appear in court; then nothing.

Nobody knew if Shen would be set free or sentenced to a heavy penalty. His fate depended entirely on how the young, uniformed military judge would interpret his action.

After the story, Shen said, "I try not to think about it."

Shen took out a book on Zen, put on his spectacles, and started to read.

54

The Village of Luku

YOUDE was concerned about Chou Shui, the woodcutter from Luku who sat at all hours against a pillar with his eyes closed. A man not yet twenty, he did not join the group's post-walk conversations. He sometimes seemed to be listening to the others talk; yet he also seemed to let it all pass by. And from time to time he sighed silently.

Youde asked Mori, "What's the matter with Chou Shui? Is he always like this?"

"No. He was quite lively up till a while back. He and Little Lu were always fooling around. He was an especially strong arm-wrestler, beating even policeman Wu."

It figured. Chou's well-proportioned body looked fast and agile. But right now he looked more like a sick leopard.

Mori dropped his voice and explained.

"The date of his sentencing is approaching. There is no hope for him. Several weeks ago he shaved his head and since then has had few words."

A death-penalty-convict was immediately executed after the sentencing. He first received the death sentence in the courtroom on the other side of the high wall; then, with his hands tied to his back and his body coiled in ropes, would be turned over to the white-helmeted military police. The MPs would receive a *chan-pan* from the uniformed military court judge. A chan-pan is a thin, narrow paddle about 2.5 feet long, with one end wider than the other, on which, or sometimes pasted on a piece of paper on top, the name of the convict and his crime was written in red and black ink. The MPs would then insert the chan-pan under the rope in the convict's back, thus completing the executionee's attire according to Chinese custom. Next, the MPs would take the doomed man from the courtroom, put him on the waiting truck, and lower the truck's canvas flap. The truck then would start toward the execution yard.

Before execution, the convict would be given a "death banquet." In ancient times, proffering good food to a doomed man for the last time was an expression of sympathy as the guilty faced death, a virtuous custom born out of human considerateness.

But some time ago this turned into a superstition. It was believed that a hungry dead person would turn into a foraging ghost. Consequently, the executioners had to make sure the doomed men had plenty to eat, lest they turn into avenging ghosts. Ordinarily, the banquet consisted of a bottle of kaoliang wine, hot braised pork liver, poached chicken, and either steamed buns or rice. Some men enjoyed the meal; but most soon-to-be-executed men were too nervous to have any appetite and would eat only a slice of meat or a mouthful of rice, if any. But if one refused to eat, two MPs would force open his mouth and pour the kaoliang into his throat, sometimes causing the man to choke and suffer. Virtue had been turned into yet another trampling of human rights.

After the death banquet, the convict would be taken to the execution yard, which was encircled by red bricks and suggested a children's sandbox. An MP would pull out the chan-pan and make the doomed man kneel in the sand. Then aiming for the heart from close range, the MP would pull the trigger. If one shot did not kill, then a second. If the second did not kill, the third.

Up until three years ago, executions took place under the levee at Machangting, by the bank of the Hsintien River. The bodies were left in the open for twenty-four hours as object lessons; and the chan-pans that were removed before execution were discarded in prominent places, where they could better be noticed — another eighteenth-century practice. But the frequent executions reaped the opposite effects. Nowadays the executions take place in the execution yard of the Ankang military prison in Hsintien.

At Machangting, the executions always took place at dawn. After the new execution yard was built, the time of executions was not limited to dawn anymore. The number of Taiwanese whose lives evaporated with the dews of the execution yard would compare favorably with any other police state in the world.

THE VILLAGE OF LUKU

Among the cases, that of Luku was particularly monstrous. Luku was an almost forgotten poor village of fewer than two hundred families. It was situated in a Taipei prefecture, whose inhabitants tilled the small plots of land between mountains for a living. Although they possessed little money, they led a peaceful, happy existence, a shade of the Peach Blossom Utopia of classical Chinese literature.

In this village, a group of young men fleeing from the secret agents appeared. The kind villagers hid them and fed them. Since only a lone road connected the village to the outside and visitors from other villages were rare and easily spotted, the fugitives were able to lead carefree lives. And their ranks increased rapidly. However, the fugitives were not idle. They worked the fields and integrated themselves into village life, especially contributing much to the village's intellectual life. The villagers liked them and were much moved by the young people's passion that sought valiantly for a "better country."

Among the fugitives, a few were activists. They lectured about Marxism in simple, easy-to-understand terms and started to recruit the villagers into the Communist Party. The rank of Party members increased geometrically; soon the entire village turned red. From the village head down to the school principal, to the teachers and farmers, to even the only policeman, all joined the Communist Party. Chen Shih, the man-child, also was persuaded and joined the Party.

The woodcutter Chou Shui also joined. A young man of vigor, Chou was a mainstay of the Youth Corps. He was also one of the vanguards of the Armed Defense Team.

In January 1953 the army surrounded the village and bagged about one hundred people in one swoop. Then, one by one, the ones who got away during the dragnet were captured.

Luku, after the arrests, was too sad to mention. Having lost so many hands at once, the fields sat fallow. The village, which was poor to start with, became poorer still. And the village women shed tears day and night over their husbands, fathers, and sons. On top of that, they had to put up with the hostility of the new conquerors.

On some days, the sad news of the execution of a husband, a father, or a son would reach the village. The wailing reverberated among the mountains, day and night. That was so sad that even the ghosts might have been reduced to tears, it was said.

The whole tragedy sprang from the villagers' kindness toward the fugitives from other villages. "Isn't God too unfair?" Youde reflected.

Suddenly, the sound of "Hee-it, hee-it" broke the silence. Chen Shih, the man-child, was having a seizure, perhaps a nightmare.

"Mommy, I am afraid." Finally, a cry came out of his mouth and it continued.

"Hey, wake up." Chou Shui, who was sleeping next to Chen, shook Chen's body.

"Brother, I am afraid." Chen Shih rose and put his arms around Chou Shui.

"It's all right. It's all right." Chou Shui rubbed Chen's back as he laid Chen down again. Chou Shui's hand, a woodcutter's muscular hand, stroked back and forth along Chen Shui's back. The hand of a caring mother, it appeared.

"Chou Shui lived with his mother alone since he was five," Mori said. "A very considerate son he is. His mother, too, almost every week, traveled the long distance from the mountains to bring him care packages, sometimes carrying just a bunch of bananas in her hands. She has never been allowed to see her son, you know. I guess she just wants to be near him."

With an embarrassed smile, Chou Shui turned his head to look at Youde and Mori, his eyes gleaming with tears.

55

Flimflam Loo

ONE morning while Youde was teaching English to Little Lu after their outing, running footsteps approached suddenly and somebody said, "Hi, Youde, how — do — I am Loo."

Youde quickly turned to look. He got only a glimpse of the smiling face of a smallish man who wore a headband around his forehead.

"Hey!" The panchang's angry voice followed.

"Oops, mistake, mistake," the man's voice replied.

Obviously, he was someone who knew Youde and was on his way back from a bath or something.

The ex-policeman Wu said, "That was Loo."

Youde thought the face was familiar but was not able to place him, maybe because of the headband.

Wu added, "He is also from Putzu."

"Oh?"

"Ha ha ha. He thinks that the whole town knows him. I am inclined to doubt it now that you did not recognize him."

Others in the room laughed too.

"He is here in relation to Yu-kun's case."

That made it even more confusing. An unusual name like Loo (deer) was not easily forgotten; but, wracking his brain, Youde still could not think of the person.

Youde's puzzled expression, growing even more puzzled by the minute, must have appeared comical to the others, because even the woodcutter Chou Shui finally laughed.

Wu dropped another hint.

"This is not the first time he's been jailed. He has a prior record."

Youde still couldn't recall.

"Was his incarceration related to the February 28 Incident?"

Youde's question was greeted with loud laughter.

"Ha ha ha. He is not that kind of fellow. He was arrested for perpetrating a sham in the marketplace."

Finally, it came to Youde.

"I got it." Youde broke into a wide smile. So it was Flimflam Loo! He was not a friend exactly, but Youde surely knew his face and his name.

Loo used to set up a simple folding table in the middle of the market, on which he lined up three identical tobacco boxes, one of them marked by a seal at the bottom. The game was for the customer to guess the marked box while Loo slowly switched the boxes around. It's an innocent game that looks easy but was hard to win. If the police showed up, Loo only had to fold up his table and quickly run away. The townsfolk had caught on to him, so were not taken in by him anymore; but eight or nine out of ten farmers from the countryside would be flimflammed into losing their money. For somebody who engaged in dishonest business, Loo was a jocular and comical fellow; and there was something about him that deflected hatred.

Still, how did he end up here, a place that takes no "sundry criminals"?

Wu said, "You know, he is the happiest person around. He has no wife, no children or parents — not a care in the world. The food is free. On top of that, he gets twenty-four hours of private lessons."

Mori cut in, "Even Loo transmits his special skills here. He is a professor of rare values in this Security Defense University of ours. They say that his cellmates will never have to worry about a livelihood when they return to the outside."

Everybody laughed.

Liu said, "Now he is able to read, write letters, even say a few English sentences nicely."

It clicked. Youde mused, so what I heard earlier, 'How — do' was really 'How do you do?' Loo had pretended to lose his way while in fact he came to see Youde, his fellow townsman. His room was in the back, so he had to take quite a detour to get to Youde's — not at all a likely mistake. Ordinarily, an act like that could cost an inmate a week's outing privileges, a penalty meted out by the panchang. But being commonly regarded as a clown worked to his advantage. Even so, he wouldn't be able to repeat the same "mistake" too many times. Youde regretted that he did not show any response earlier.

Liu told Youde about Loo's case.

Loo was a distant relative of Yu-kun on his mother's side. When Yu-kun escaped successfully for the second time and fled to the base camp in the mountains, he beseeched his family for money. Loo was asked to be the carrier. He took Yu-kun the money and returned home without incident, although he did not exactly reach the base camp like Little Lu. He just went to a designated location on the mountainside, some distance from Chiayi and handed the money to Yu-kun himself. Loo accomplished his mission splendidly and kept the secret well too, for the clownish person he was.

But soon after Yu-kun's capture, Loo was arrested, implicated by Yu-kun's confession. Loo admitted to the crime frankly and was charged with Article 4.1. He was awaiting sentencing.

Mori said, "But even Loo desires freedom. He appears so cheerful, but I wonder how he really feels inside. The outside world is better, definitely. For one, he can hold a woman. Loo never married but knew many women."

Liu agreed, "Of course, you are right. From time to time, Loo would think of it and start to curse Yu-kun."

Wu said, "There are many people here who curse Yu-kun. If Yu-kun was not seduced by the Self-Renewal Policy, many people here would have been spared." Then, pointing at Youde with his fan, he said, "You are one of them."

Liu said, "But Mr. Tsai is very cultivated. He hasn't said anything hateful, let alone cursing."

Self-consciously, Youde said, "It's not a question of cultivation. I curse people too sometimes. But I really can't hate Yu-kun even though it's a fact that he implicated many people after his arrest, myself included. In spite of that, his love for Taiwan, his love for his people, and his revulsion toward the corrupt government were pure and true. I know it the best. If his life can be saved, as a friend I shall endure this misfortune."

After a pause, Mori said, "Mr. Tsai, you are a nice person."

"He is," Little Lu also nodded.

"Ha ha. Too nice," Wu laughed sardonically.

Youde really wanted to add something but thought better of it for fear of sounding too sanctimonious: "Who I really curse and hate are the people in this dictatorship we once welcomed as blood brothers; who betrayed our expectations only to turn into violent, imperial rulers; who manufactured arbitrary, cruel laws for the purpose of killing off political dissidents. Yu-kun is but a sorry victim."

56

The Permanently Un-sentenced

WHEN Liu and Kao were together, Youde took the opportunity to ask, "How about your case? I understand that you are charged with Article 2.1."

Liu grinned sardonically and said, "I am almost too ashamed to talk about it. Hey, why don't you tell Mr. Tsai?" Liu urged Kao, who, a man of few words, scratched his head.

The talkative Mori interjected. "These two, they are fake Communists. Ha ha ha."

Youde laughed too. In this day and age, what fools would disguise themselves as Communists and get arrested?

"Because we are only fakes, we don't carry much weight around here," Kao made a rare joke.

"The whole thing started with a man called Lo Wen-hsueh."

Youde asked, "Lo Wen-hsueh? Was he once a student in the Chinese Literature Department at the Normal University?"

"Yes," Kao answered.

Youde remembered Lo Wen-hsueh. He was a beanpole of a guy and a conspicuous presence at the Normal University. Maybe he was devoted to books, but he always walked around with books under his arm. He didn't seem to take much interest in student activities. Instead, he stood on the side and eyed coldly the others who were active.

"Was he also a Communist?"

"No. Well...." Kao was hard pressed for an answer.

Liu explained, "You see, to this day nobody knows if he was a Communist. Before he entered the Normal University, he taught with us at a primary school in Fengyuan. So afterward he frequented our school, bringing us many books of all kinds. He would sort of show off the book titles on purpose, all but saying, 'I am reading such difficult stuff.'"

"Most of his books were banned books," Kao added.

"Maybe only the covers were from the banned books and nothing but ordinary books under the covers," Mori teased, laughing.

Liu continued, "Even so, he didn't discuss the books with us, let alone persuade us to join the Party. I think he just enjoyed being mysterious."

"What a strange fellow," Mori again laughed.

Lo Wen-hsueh was three years ahead of Youde at the Normal University. Come to think of it, Lo did look somewhat old-man-like for a college student, Youde mused. For sure, his nickname was "Opium Head." His unkempt beard, his philosopher's pretension, and the way he sometimes stretched his torso and cackled fit the label "mysterious fellow" to a tee. To take a kinder view, he could be the ivory tower researcher type who considered activities like demonstrations rather childish.

Liu said, "There was an informer at our school who reported Lo Wen-hsueh to the authorities right before the April 6 crackdown. Maybe Lo knew about it, or maybe he didn't. In any case, Lo disappeared after the April 6 incident."

Many university students disappeared after that incident — not a particularly rare occurrence. As a matter of fact, from the incident's aftermath, Youde's class lost half of its members.

Liu and Kao took turns continuing the story.

"To tell you the truth, we were actually relieved when Lo disappeared. We didn't want him to flaunt the banned books in our face; but it would be painful to watch him being arrested too."

"But before we had time to relax, unthinkable tragedy fell on us."

"The secret police took it out on us because Lo escaped."

"All Lo's so-called friends were arrested."

"We were so simple-minded that we admitted to having seen the books. You know, it's true what they say that one becomes a fool after being a teacher for too long. Those who denied having seen the books to the end were let go. What was left were we ten, foolishly honest teachers."

"After that, things got worse."

"The investigators insisted that Lo had not only showed us the books but also persuaded us to join the Communist Party."

Having gone through the same thing, Youde understood perfectly.

"No matter how we denied it, it was no use. We ended up being tortured. I am ashamed to admit it, but we were weak in the face of torture."

"They laid us out on a long bench and tied right here solidly to it," Liu grabbed his thigh.

"And, between here and the chair," this time, pointing to his heels, "they hammered in two-inch thick wooden planks, one after another, all the time, berating 'How about it? Ready to confess yet?' The pain was something else, to have your knees bent backward."

Human legs from the knee down are made to bend to the back. The torture forced them to go the other way. Youde could imagine how excruciating it must have been.

"If one plank did not induce confession, the second plank was hammered in. Most people lose consciousness after three planks."

"Sorry to say, I surrendered after the first plank."

"Kao is not alone. We all admitted that we joined the Communist Party."

"Just like Mori said, we all became fake Communists."

"But that's not the end of it. Now they wanted to know the names of people we had recruited, and the activities we had engaged in. How could we oblige? So the second round of torture started."

"After that, everything was a mess."

"We fell into a self-abandoning funk — let whatever would happen, happen — and acknowledged everything the interrogator wanted us to."

"Consequently, ten more fake Communists were manufactured. The ones who were let go after the first investigation were brought back."

Mori interjected, laughing, "Ha ha ha. This is no joke. They will be treated even more harshly the second time around. Ha ha ha."

"To sum it up: one person was to have written Communist propaganda, another created the galley, yet another made copies using the school's copy machine, and, finally, one pasted the flyers on the utility poles. We made them all up."

"We followed the plot the secret police wanted."

"When we found out later that we were charged with Article 2.1, we were stunned and devastated. We ended up being accused of joining the Communist Party and participating in political activities."

The ex-policeman Wu said loudly, "Ha ha ha. It's truly the comical story of the century, worthy of being passed on to the later generations."

But this was not a matter that could be laughed off. No fewer than twenty men had already been imprisoned since May 1948, a duration of six and a half years, their futures still hanging in the air.

"For the first six months, days were filled with fear," Liu said.

"We were put in the same cell as death-sentenced convicts, and every day someone was called out for execution. We imagined constantly that we would be the next."

At this, Liu abruptly closed his mouth. He had noticed Chou Shui, the woodcutter of Luku. Liu changed the topic.

"By any chance, do you know a Putzu native called Cheng Wen-bang?"

"Sure. I more than know him."

"I met him at the theater in Hsintien."

"Oh? At a theater?"

"Ha ha ha. We weren't there to see a play. You see, at the time all the available jails were filled to the limits, so they remodeled the theater to take in more prisoners."

"Which part of the theater?"

"There is the stage, right? The stage was about one and a half meters off the ground. We were packed like sardines under the stage."

"How inhumane...."

"We were treated like animals, nothing like it is here. We could have been smothered by each other's body heat. Because we couldn't stand up straight, we had to walk around bent over. And the smell of urine and feces stunk to high heaven."

"And you met Wen-bang there?"

"Yes. He was among the ones who went to the execution yard from that place. But he carried himself splendidly. He gave away his personal belongings before he went. He was calm and majestic, befitting a patriot going to battle for justice."

"I see."

Wen-bang of yesterday came to Youde's mind. He who wheeled around the town on its only child-size bicycle. He who could have lived a carefree life, wanting for nothing. Yet he suffered underneath the theater stage.

Liu and Kao continued.

"In the end, we survived despite living in fear. The goddess of good luck did not abandon us after all. We were transferred to the crypt of East Penyuan Temple. Then, again four years later, transferred here. Everyplace we've been was jam-packed.

"When we first arrived here this place was jam packed too. But it was a step up compared to the space under the stage."

"There are many contradictions in our case. For example, when they compared our investigation reports, they found the same person was said to be at two different places at the same time. Or the date February 29 showed up despite the fact that it was not a leap year. Or we were supposed to have pasted the flyers all over the place, yet no one ever saw them nor traces of them being removed either. Or where we supposedly had pasted the flyers, no utility pole stood."

"In the military court, we unanimously recanted the previous statements. All of us, in one voice, insisted vigorously that we were forced into confession by torture."

"We also showed them the scars from the torture."

"Still the judge would not believe us easily. Or maybe he did believe us in his heart, but he might not have had the power to release us. Finally, he just quit hearing our case."

"In the four years since we came here, we have been called to the court only twice."

Mori jumped in, "If they start to release people on the basis of torture-induced confession, this place will empty out in no time."

"One is not allowed to hire a defense lawyer in the military court. But if you read the sentencing document, you will find the name of the public defender. So we requested to meet with our defense lawyer. Many times we applied, to no avail."

"We are," Liu and Kao smiled mockingly, "the permanently unsentenced."

57

Letters

The long-awaited letter arrived from his wife, Panto. It was already opened and had an inspector's rubber stamp on it. As incoming letters were not limited to postcards, Youde's wife filled two pages of the stationery. One word about the case or about the political situation outside, and her letter would go straight into a wastepaper basket. A snapshot was enclosed, showing Panto, his daughter, and his mother under the pomelo tree, taken after Youde's arrest. His wife and mother looked thinner — no doubt a result of the anxiety of the past two months. Youde was moved by the sight of his daughter fearfully clinging to her mother.

She wrote that she was very happy to receive the letter from Youde, that everything was fine and everybody was healthy, and asked him not to worry about things at home. Then she reported some unexpected good news — she was pregnant, conceived right after his return from America. She said she was wishing for a boy this time. Youde took a second look at the snapshot. Indeed, her stomach appeared thickened somewhat.

She then wrote about life at home, about the daughter's activities — all the inconsequential details of life. Still, Youde read it over and over.

On this day, four prison friends — Little Lu, Chou Shui the woodcutter, man-child Chen Shih, and the printshop apprentice Chin-huo — did not receive a letter. Chou Shui and Little Lu, on the latter's urging, started to play chess while Chen Shih and Chin-huo watched, a rather heartening sight in a prison. Yet whenever there was a loud noise outside, Chou Shui jumped and his hand froze over the chessboard. No doubt Chou was distracted by worries that somebody had come to call him out for execution.

Mori, the bank employee, was reading the letter from his wife with a wide grin. He was jailed soon after his marriage and was therefore childless. His newlywed wife — even though it had been two years since his incarceration — must have written sweet talk.

Liu said, "Hey, let's have it," and stretched out his hand toward Mori.

Mori handed over the letter without embarrassment. The cellmates shared letters here, it seemed.

Liu read Mori's letter and passed it to Youde. The letter from Mori's wife was indeed filled with sweet talk. She wrote unabashedly of her longing for her husband. Youde passed it on to Shen, the public scribe. Youde also shared his wife's letter and the snapshot with everybody.

"She writes very well," they praised Youde's wife.

Little Lu lifted his hand from the chessboard to look at the snapshot.

"The little girl is cute," he praised Youde's daughter.

Amid happy goings-on, Youde noticed that the usually lively ex-policeman Wu, he of the "ha ha" laugh, was sitting by himself with a dark, threatening expression. Youde asked Mori about Wu's story.

Wu once worked in a police station where a policeman Liang, a native of Luku and a Communist, was among his colleagues. They were not particularly close. But maybe it was because Liang trusted Wu for also being a clean cop — a rare find among policemen — that one day Liang came to recruit Wu. Wu rejected Liang's overture on the spot but alas did not immediately report Liang to the authorities. While Wu was still brooding over if he should go to the authorities about Liang, Liang was arrested.

Interrogated under torture, Liang gave the names of his recruits. Wu was soon arrested and investigated on suspicion of Article 9 of the Statutes for the Denunciation and Punishment of Bandit Spies: Failure to Report. The Statutes for the Denunciation and Punishment of Bandit Spies were supplemental laws put into effect one year after the publication of Laws on Sedition, in June 1950, in order to thoroughly rout out Communist spies.

But to a rational mind, the article of "Failure to Report," a crime unknown in civilized countries, contained much irrationality. For example, everybody knew that Mao Tse-tung and Chou En-lai were Communists. But, abiding by the rule, all who failed to go to the police and report the fact were guilty.

Maybe it was all right not to report the well-known big fish, but then what were the criteria that distinguished the big fish from the small fries? What happened if the Communist suspect was arrested before one could report him, as in Wu's case? Were there standards on how soon one was supposed to report the spy? Suppose one wrongly reported a person, was one liable for slander? If not, then one was free to report those he hated. On the other hand, if one was liable for slander, one would need to make sure of the facts before going to the police. What if the spy was arrested while one was looking into it further?

Wu, it may be said, was a victim of an irrational law.

But the matter did not end there. During his interrogation, Wu, with his usual openness, admitted having given objects to Liang. That led to an additional charge of Article 4: Giving Aid to the Enemy. This kind of escalation of charges was a common development. On top of that, because Wu was a police officer, the seriousness of his crime was doubled. In short, Wu drew the worst possible lot.

Wu finished reading his letter and handed it over to Liu. The letter was fairly short. Liu read it and gave it back to Wu without passing it around to others.

"Some letter!" Wu retrieved the letter and stood up.

Aware that everybody was looking at him, he said, "She said that she is having a hard time and that I should do something about it. What can I do? Doesn't she know that I am in jail?"

Wu started to pace the room.

The once friendly and happy air turned precarious.

"She is not an understanding woman," Shen the public scribe whispered to Youde. "She always writes something that upsets him."

Suddenly, the angry shouts of Wu broke through the air, "Damn! Go be a whore!"

58

Reward for a Favor

Mori's case was simple. To make it short, he lent money to a friend from the past for old time's sake who turned out to be a Communist. But the act altered the course of Mori's smooth-sailing life. His was a destiny changed by coincidence on top of coincidence.

One day, on a whim, his newlywed wife said she wanted to visit her family. So they decided to go to the train station in Taichung to catch a train. On the way, they stopped by the market to buy some fruit to take along as presents and missed the train. As they were waiting for the next train at the station's waiting room, Mori went to the men's room. While there, Mori noticed a drifter-like man. The man approached Mori and called him in Japanese "Mori kun," the way his schoolmates from grade school did. A surprised Mori quickly shook hands with the man, whom he recalled to be quite retiring even in the old days. The man said that he would like to go to Taipei to look for a job but was short of money. A newlywed, on-top-of-the-world Mori felt for the man and generously handed him one hundred yuan. Mori was a big-hearted man to start with. Besides, he had just deposited his wife's dowry in the bank, and one hundred yuan was just peanuts compared to the expected bank interest. The man thanked Mori and said he would definitely pay back the money. And they parted.

Three months had passed. One night, the man came to Mori's house with Mori's calling card in hand. Mori thought maybe the man had come to pay back the one hundred yuan; yet something told Mori otherwise. In fact, judging from the scarf-tied bundle he was carrying, the man could very well be on the lam. Mori did not let the man in the house. Instead he stood at the door to talk to the man. The man gave an incoherent explanation as to why he was not able to repay his debt.

Mori said to him clearly, "I gave you the hundred yuan. Don't worry about it." But the man would not leave. Finally, Mori gave the man another fifty yuan. The man entered it in his shabby memo book:

Date xxx   100 yuan   From Lin Sun-shan
Date xxx   50 yuan   From Lin Sun-shan

What an unnecessary thing he did!

A month later the man was arrested and the memo book that he carried wherever he went got Mori in trouble.

Mori was called in for investigation and then transferred here, having been charged with Article 4 of the Laws on Sedition. Those who supplied money to rebels could be sentenced to death, life, or prison terms of no less than ten years.

Mori tried denying knowing the man, but the memo book had Mori's name in black and white. Also, Mori did not escape torture. After torture, Mori did what the secret agents wanted.

The fact that Mori's story could happen to anybody with a compassionate nature made it all the more terrifying. Since Mori gave money to the man twice, he was considered a repeat offender — liable to be sentenced to death.

Meanwhile, Mori's newlywed wife, probably still in the dark about the seriousness of the matter, filled her letter with sweet nothings. She wrote, "I want to gaze at the moon with you on the first full moon."

So be it. But if she hadn't capriciously decided to visit her family that day, or if they hadn't stopped by the market to pick up some fruit, or if Mori hadn't gone to the men's room, or if the man hadn't been at the men's room, or if Mori hadn't given the man money, or if the man hadn't entered the gift unnecessarily in his memo book, Mori and his wife could be gazing at the moon right now and not to have to wait until the first full moon next year.

But Mori was a born optimist, not one to brood. "To receive agreeably what is thrust against you" being his stated philosophy of life, Mori lived his every day to the fullest with a happy heart.

Mori said, "The man was a Communist! Can you believe that? Totally unexpected. But I don't think he joined the Party for idealistic convictions.

Neither can I believe that he harbored any idea of sacrificing himself for the sake of Taiwan. He was a loser. That's the most fitting description of him!"

How did the man end up a Communist then? Mori diagnosed: "Precisely because he is a loser, lacking in self-confidence, he joined the Communist Party. I think he was trying to get in with what he thought would be a new regime, so as to secure himself a position for the future."

It was a sad truth, but some Taiwanese were just such opportunists, Youde knew.

59

A Mistake of One Character

The printshop apprentice Huang Chin-huo was a quiet and inconspicuous fellow, often neglected by others. He was over twenty, but owing to his small stature everybody called him "boy." Chen Shih the man-child and he made a good pair, often off to a corner whispering and snickering by themselves. Chin-huo was also teaching Chen Shih new Chinese characters and some new songs. Having worked in typesetting, Chin-huo did seem to know a lot of Chinese characters.

Youde asked Chin-huo how he ended up here.

Chin-huo shyly answered in an almost inaudible voice, "A mistake I made in typesetting came out as 'Oppose Communism, Surrender to Russia.'"

Liu explained to a puzzled Youde, "See, in typesetting the phrase 'Oppose Communism, Resist Russia,' Chin-huo transplanted the character for *surrender*, 投, for the character for *resist*, 抗, and ended up distributing flyers that said 'Oppose Communism, Surrender to Russia.'"

"Is that all?" Youde was dumbfounded. A mistake of one character in typesetting and he was turned over to the military court.

Chin-huo nodded.

Wu said to a still perplexed Youde, "Ha ha ha. Mr. Tsai, do you understand now what is meant by arbitrary?"

Indeed, until learning about various cases in this prison, Youde, a person living in Taiwan, did not know the extent of the arbitrariness of the arrests.

"Then you must be charged with Article 7: Making Propaganda Beneficial to the Enemy."

Chin-huo shook his head.

"Article 4."

Article 4 was "Giving Aid to the Enemy." Youde thought that was possible too, since it all depended on how the judge interpreted the circumstances.

"Either way, it doesn't sound very serious. You should just study hard and not worry about it," Liu comforted Chin-huo.

Mori said, "We are here because we did bad things in our previous lives. Isn't that so, Ojisan?" Mori solicited agreement from Shen the public scribe, who was immersed in Zen books.

"Therefore, even if one did nothing bad in this life, or should I say, even if one did something good, one still gets put in here to suffer. It's all karma. Take Chin-huo, why did he mistype the all-important character? He wouldn't do it on purpose, right?"

Chin-huo quickly shook his head.

Wu defended Chin-huo, "So he distributed the flyers with the mistake. So what? Are people going to surrender to the Soviet Union after reading them, like there's magic in typesetting?"

"On the other hand," Mori put his hand on Youde's back and said, "Mr. Tsai's karma is just the opposite. He must have done good deeds in his previous life; that's why he will get only three years of re-education."

Youde had already told everybody about his case. Indeed, compared to these prison friends, Youde's various activities were numerous, yet it was the others who would receive much heavier sentences. Youde remembered Peng's words with renewed appreciation — "In the Military Court Detention, people would jump up and down with joy if they heard a sentence of three years."

Little Lu pulled on Youde's hand.

"It's about time, don't you think, Mr. Tsai?"

"For what? For studying?"

"No. For telling us movie stories."

Since some time ago, Youde's movie telling had become a routine here also. By now, not only was he scraping the bottom of the barrel to come up with a movie, but since all the movies were from so long ago, Youde had to improvise and invent the plots as he went along. This day he picked *High Noon*.

Little Lu always smiled and nodded through any story Youde told. And when a story came to an exciting part, he would do his special stunt of back-flipping from the sitting position with a "Wow!" He was a perfect audience.

As that night's story progressed, Chin-huo left Chen Shih and moved from the corner to Little Lu's side and listened.

60

A Puzzling Message

One day after supper, a voice came from the cell to the right, "Mr. Tsai Youde." The usual message transmitter, Sung, was waving at Youde.

"Yes, what is it?"

"Well, Wu Che-fu said something about you."

"I guess he learned that I am here."

"Yes. He said the following: 'Tsai Youde is an anti-Communist. He used to always engage in heated argument with Cheng Wen-bang.'"

"What?"

Youde doubted his ears. For these were unexpected words. Youde was not a Communist nor was he an anti-Communist. If anything, he was sympathetic to the Communists because of his disgust with the government in power. In this, he was in the same boat as the great majority of university students. Moreover, he absolutely was not one of those favor-courting, anti-Communist ideologues who attributed all evils to the Communists and advocated their total annihilation. On the contrary, he had always totally despised the secret agents and professional students who committed atrocious acts all in the name of anti-Communism. And he also had nothing but contempt for those who had risen to ever higher and better positions by flaunting their anti-Communist stands. Indeed, to be taken as one of them was more than Youde could bear. How he had shed sorrowful tears, time and again, when friends were executed or sentenced to long prison terms, snared by the Law of Sedition!

At a minimum, Che-fu must know this about me. Why is he saying such a thing now?

Youde sat down weakly and leaned his head against a pillar just like Chou Shui. Youde sank into his own thoughts.

Is Che-fu jealous of my light sentencing as he himself faces death? It was true that while Che-fu was suffering in prison, I was enjoying a leisurely life in America, paid for by public funds. Therefore, it was perhaps reasonable that he eyed me with suspicion and envy, and maybe his envy turned into jealousy and those were the words of the moment. Then again, it was also conceivable that Che-fu was changed by the long suffering.

He said that I argued heatedly with Wen-bang, certainly possible during our fairly lengthy association. But discussions yes, heated arguments not likely. Because I had always listened quietly when Wen-bang expounded on his beliefs, and on occasions when I spoke Wen-bang had always respected my opinions. As a matter of fact, we never exchanged a harsh word. First of all, I was not in the same league to carry a heated argument with a well-versed Marxist like Wen-bang, who impressed even the secret police with his zealotry. Maybe on literature, but on political ideologies, I was always just listening. Did Che-fu confused me with somebody else, putting out such incomprehensible words?

In any case, Che-fu sure said something troublesome. Wen-bang is an acknowledged patriot in this prison. I could be taken as a traitor who had argued against the beloved patriot! Besides, anti-Communists are clearly disliked by the inmates here. Who can blame them, since these people are accomplices of the inmates' persecutors? Just as I settled into a life of easy familiarity with everybody, this thing could cause a crack in our relationships!

Little Lu's sad face peered into Youde's.

"Mr. Tsai, were you really an anti-Communist?" A glint of hostility shot through his teary eyes.

Silently, Youde shook his head sideways.

Liu came over and said, "There's a communication network between the east area and the west area. I don't know for sure, but some said that it's done through echoes from the beams, while others said that it's done with Morse code. Sometimes the communication was carried out by trustworthy prison guards. No matter what, only brief messages were possible. Incomplete information had caused misunderstandings in the past."

That night, Little Lu did not beseech Youde for a movie story.

61

A Spy-Judge

After several uncomfortable days, the life in the cell returned to its old, easy ways. Mori pointed to the prison cell at the right and said, "Do you see the man with the eyeglasses?"

Youde looked through the gap in the wall toward where Mori pointed and saw a balding, bespectacled man sitting there writing.

"The man's name is Tang. He was a judge right here in this military court."

"Is that so? Surely he was not a Communist, was he?"

"It turned out he was a card-carrying Communist."

"……"

"He infiltrated the Military Justice Department by faking it as a KMT while in reality he was dispatched straight from the Central Committee of the Chinese Communist Party."

Since only KMT members were allowed entry to Taiwan, Communists came under double identities.

"So he was a spy then."

"Yes, the most incomparable, world-class, cruelest kind he was."

Youde peered at Tang anew and found him still writing intently and unaware of the attention paid him from this side.

"I wonder what kind of mission made him infiltrate the Military Justice Department?"

"To disturb domestic politics."

"Was it to let the important Communists escape in case they were exposed?"

"Ya. I heard something like that did take place. Let's ask Liu."

Liu answered, "There was a case like that quite a while back. The judge who let the big fish escape was executed for it though. But it is not possible to do something like that anymore."

Then Liu caught on to the subject of the conversation and added, "That one over there is a vicious one. He is not a human being."

Wu chimed in, "Ha ha. Only a Chinese could do things like that."

"What vicious things did he do?"

Mori replied, "He sentenced his own comrades to death, one after another, including the ones who could have gotten away with less. That's what. He did it to fan the people's hatred toward the government. That's what they meant by 'disturbing domestic politics.'"

"That's outrageous, even as the so-called bitter-flesh tactic: to inflict harm to oneself in order to win sympathy."

"And Tang was not alone. There is a large group of these spy-judges. In this prison alone, there are more than I can count on my five fingers. And there must be many other Communist moles in other intelligence organizations. Should you be so unlucky as to run into one, a death sentence is a certainty regardless of your crime. Worthless are the lives of Taiwanese who were sacrificed for the sake of political struggles, I should say."

"That's why I say, Youde, that you must have done lots of good deeds in your previous life. Suppose you had been arrested together with Yu-kun and Wen-bang. And let's say you ran into one of these spy-judges. I can tell you that you wouldn't be here today. Especially because you had studied in America."

Again Youde looked at Tang, who had taken off his glasses and was wiping them. Upon closer examination, Youde saw his buck teeth and thought the man looked like a beastly ghost. Perhaps becoming aware of the scrutiny from across the corridor, Tang also raised his head and looked straight into Youde's eyes.

"You beast!" Youde blurted.

Tang lowered his eyes, swiftly stood up and left his place.

"Why don't his cellmates beat him up?"

Youde, who had never thrown a punch in his life, was at this moment driven by the impulse to do violence. An avid reader of spy novels, he never read about a spy who intentionally killed as many comrades as he could.

"At first, he was beat up quite often, but it has since calmed down. You see, even a guy like that is still a man awaiting execution."

"I really don't want to say this here, but," Shen the public scribe prefaced his remark, "really, the bad guys are the folks at headquarters who sent him. The Chinese, be they Communists or KMT, don't consider Taiwanese their fellow countrymen. Isn't that something? Living as they do in a less civilized society, they still consider the Taiwanese lesser people who are outside the benevolent reign of the great Chinese civilization. I know it well, you see, because I was in China."

Bad-mouthing Communists made Little Lu uneasy.

"Is the Communist Party also bad?"

Mori answered, "There are good guys and bad guys in any party."

Youde also wanted to make Little Lu feel at ease again, so he said, "Except for fellows like Tang, folks here are all good people."

Little Lu broke into a smile.

All of a sudden, Wu's manly laughter rang out.

"Ha ha ha. Mr. Shen is probably sore at his business being taken away. You see, for whatever reason, maybe to assuage his conscience, Tang writes appeals for the fellow inmates here. He is the public scribe with the most business. So, Youde, instead of being angry at him, why don't you ask him to write you an appeal?"

Wu's jokes were sometimes grist for bitter smiles.

62

Talk of Divorce

The third letter from Youde's wife Panto arrived. The content was much the same, but knowing everybody was fine at home gave Youde peace of mind.

This day Wu the ex-policeman again received a letter. Everybody stared at Wu when he continued to read the letter with a menacing expression. Was he going to break out in his patented "ha ha" laugh, or was he going to start cursing; Youde could not read his face. But it turned out to be neither.

Wu stood up without a word, handed the letter to Liu and started to pace the room, which appeared to be a habit of his when agitated. Liu read the letter then returned it directly to Wu.

"She did it to me," Wu muttered, not aiming his remark at Liu in particular.

Whatever it was, surely it was not good news.

Liu began to pace too. Everybody now stared at the two men. There was no protecting privacy here.

Liu said quietly, "His wife asked for a divorce."

The air turned turgid.

Wu forced a smile and said despairingly, "She said that she has no means of support and wanted a divorce to marry somebody else."

Liu corrected Wu, "She didn't say anything about marrying somebody else."

"Same thing."

Wu handed the letter to Youde. Mori and Shen came over and the three read the letter together.

"During the past two years, I have borrowed money from relatives of all kinds and friends of all descriptions, and haven't been able to pay back a penny. Nowadays, learning about my visit, people either pretend they are not home or close the door right in my face. It's hard to take. Even if I had wanted to work, no decent place would touch me when they find out that my husband is imprisoned for sedition. I even tried peddling homemade stuffed rice balls, but it caused me back pain and I ended up incurring medical bills.

"I don't want to engage in degrading work. After giving it considerable thought, I decided that I would like a divorce and try to support myself. I think jobs would come easier after divorce.

"This is better for the children too. I will be able to feed them good-tasting food again. I've cried untold tears before coming to this conclusion." She laid out her main points thus in an awkward hand.

The unreasonable woman in Shen's words was no more; rather, a weak and helpless female came to Youde's mind.

Liu said, "This kind of thing happens a lot. So far three or four people have signed the divorce papers."

But Shen the public scribe said, "However, the others all came after sentencing, after the husbands been sentenced to life, no less. Their divorces are understandable since there's no chance to be together again. Asking for divorce when he is still awaiting trial, it's.... I think she should wait a little longer. Hey, Wu, tell her to wait till after sentencing."

Mori said, "But some people just can't wait when they don't even know how many more years till sentencing. Don't you say 'case by case' in English for something like this, Mr. Tsai?"

Suddenly, Wu burst out laughing.

"Ha ha. Some women can't wait because of livelihood, then there are others who can't because of sex." Then, after a brief pause, Wu added an even more stinging remark, "Mori, for the time being, your wealthy wife is still writing you sweet stuff. But someday she might ask for a divorce too. Ha ha."

His laughter was as loud as ever, but it had a ring of self mockery.

Mori didn't seem to take offence.

"Ya, I guess you are right. Since we don't have children, it may be even easier to bring up the subject of divorce."

Liu asked seriously, "What will you do if it happens?"

"It depends on the sentence I get. I'll sign the divorce papers without a word if I get ten years or more. It's unreasonable to ask this wife of mine to be celibate for more than ten years."

There was laughter, but not from Wu.

Special amnesty does not apply to people imprisoned for sedition. If one got to go home straight after serving a sentence, that was cause for celebration because many had three years of re-education tagged on after their actual sentences. They said that whether or not one would be slapped with additional re-education was not written on the verdict, although the decision was made at the time of sentencing.

"Ha ha," Wu belatedly laughed.

"Mori, you don't have to worry about your wife being lonely. The special agent will take care of that. Ha ha. My wife has already been done in by the special agent. A husband's sixth sense told me so."

Wu turned toward Youde and went on, "When I was first interrogated, there was this special agent, a mainlander also named Wu, who showed special kindness toward me. He said it was because we shared the same last name. The fellow went to my house to let my family know about my whereabouts."

"A fellow playing the same role as Ho in Chiayi," Youde thought.

"The fellow visited my family many times since. He must have gotten close to my wife by telling her that he was working for my release. Well, my wife has nothing else but her pussy to offer! As the days went by, the two of them became intimate. He is probably sleeping with her at this very moment."

Liu opened his mouth, "Hey, hey, you imagine too much."

"No, that's not so. She wants a divorce in order to marry the guy. It may even be the case that her stomach is swollen with child and can't wait any longer. Ha ha. Just you wait. Her next letter will include the divorce papers."

"You imagine too much. Your wife is not a bad woman like that." Liu and Kao took turns to comfort Wu. But Shen concurred with Wu.

Youde held on to the letter, not knowing what to say, as he never intruded in others' private matters.

Shen said to Youde in a whisper, "It's not rare that special agents visit the homes of the prisoners. Some go to check out the women folk; some do so for money. They would cheat the family out of a few thousand yuan by wantonly promising to work for the release of the loved ones. The families, who are usually grasping at straws, would hand over the money they don't have. Especially easy prey are the families of the would-be-death-sentenced. They often go to all lengths to get the money to satisfy the arbitrary demands and hand it to them, bowing their heads over and over. But these agents, they don't ever feel the sting of their own conscience as they take advantage of another's misfortune and extort money or steal women from their victims. I guess the relentless competition for survival on the Chinese mainland formed this kind of character in them. What beasts!"

Shen, who had started out whispering, was now speaking in an uncharacteristically loud, irate voice.

63

A Momentary Reunion

ONE sunny day after lunch, a guard came to Cell 7 and called Youde's name in a brusque manner.

"Tsai Youde, you are to appear in court."

Youde hurriedly stood up. First, he put on the pants of the leisure suit that he brought back from America, then he searched his bundle and took out the carefully prepared photograph and put it in his breast pocket.

The guard thought Youde was taking too long. "Hurry up," he said.

Youde put on the top of his leisure suit, but alas there was no time to button it up. Youde had heard that most people appeared in court in their pajamas. How unreasonable! After making the prisoners wait for months, even years, they themselves were not willing to wait for an extra minute? Youde started to put on his socks.

"You don't need to do that. Just hurry up and get out of there."

Finally, in his bare feet, Youde stepped out of the cell, slipped on his shoes with crushed heels and started out for the court.

At the office by the prison entrance, the panchang checked Youde against a photograph.

"Nice clothes," the panchang remarked. The smart leisurewear was still rare in Taiwan.

"Where did you get it?" A pointless question.

"In America."

"Oh. You are a returned student from America." The panchang took another look at Youde.

A guard led Youde out of the East Area office. In the compound, forty some inmates were out taking their baths or walking. All unfamiliar faces. Youde realized that it was time for the West Area inmates' outing.

Sandwiched between two guards, Youde walked along the hundred-meter path, the same path that he traversed about a month ago coming in. Now he walked in the opposite direction toward the courtroom. Groups of inmates who had already bathed walked pass Youde as they circled the compound. Naked from the waist up they were enjoying the sunlight. Youde was preoccupied with rehearsing his answers for the courtroom. When the time comes, one tenses up nonetheless, he thought.

Youde passed the mid-point of the path and was moving toward the gate. Suddenly, from behind, "Tsai Youde," a rapid, crisp voice came.

A familiar voice! Youde reflexively halted and turned his head. At that moment, the owner of the voice abruptly turned his head away. Their eyes did not meet; nor did Youde catch the other's face. But the back of the slowly retreating figure was unmistakably that of Yu-kun himself.

At the moment Yu-kun turned his head away, Youde had shouted at Yu-kun's back, "I do not hate you." Those were words from his heart.

But the guard had stopped him, so Youde was not able to enunciate the words clearly; and there was no reaction from Yu-kun either. With his arms held tightly by the now-angry guards, Youde had to resume his steps forward. Behind him, a whistle sounded.

He'd had only a brief glance, but the image of the back of Yu-kun, whom Youde hadn't seen in five years, was burned firmly into Youde's brain as if on film. Yu-kun was bare from the waist up, wearing only white, short pants and carrying in one hand the undershirt that he had shed. The naked back was still of the dark shade, well proportioned, and retained its leopard-like alertness; yet Yu-kun's arms hung helplessly from his shoulders.

Because Yu-kun averted his face as Youde turned around to look, Youde did not catch Yu-kun's face. But Yu-kun surely had seen Youde's face. Why did Yu-kun turn away? The answer was obvious. He must have been ashamed to face Youde. Youde had understood and instantaneously shouted, "I don't hate you." If Yu-kun had not turned away, Youde might have said something different entirely.

Yu-kun must have noticed Youde the moment he stepped out the gate of the East Area. People naturally turned their attention to the person being led by the guards. Besides, the bright, colorful leisure suit should have caught their eyes in this dull, drab landscape. But Yu-kun did not call Youde's name at the earliest opportunity. He must have hesitated.

And when Youde passed him by, just before he was about to lose his last chance, Yu-kun called Youde's name — a cry that he could no longer suppress. Then he turned his face away. The once fearless Yu-kun, bravery personified, was afraid of me, Youde realized. Youde's breast was tight with emotion.

They arrived at the gate of the high wall. As he stepped inside, Youde was immediately handcuffed. Youde quickly turned his head to peek at the compound through the gaps between the pillars of timber. But Yu-kun and the bathers had, like a mirage, disappeared altogether. Only the brilliant sun of high noon filled the compound.

64

Questioning in Court

Youde was led through the gate to the other side of the high wall. Then they followed the narrow, paved path and entered one of the four courtrooms that sat in a row. The courtroom was smaller than a regular classroom.

On the platform, three tall built-in desks sat side by side. On the front wall hung a portrait of Sun Yat-sen and above, a blue-sky/white-sun national flag and a KMT flag were pasted on the wall. Chiang Kai-shek's portrait hung on the back wall, across from Sun Yat-sen's. Was this done intentionally to intimidate the judge, who would face Chiang's portrait when sitting down? Youde chuckled to himself. Chiang smiled benevolently in his portrait, like a kind father. Yet several thousand people had stood at this very spot and received death sentences before being taken to the execution yard.

Three rows of benches occupied either side of the central aisle, making the room look cramped. The trials were not open to outside audiences anyway, so why the need for the benches? Youde was seated in the front row, between the two guards.

Youde had rehearsed several times the possible questions and his replies, so there was no reason to be uptight. Yet, as he sat there, he felt mounting tension. Time seemed to drag ever slower. At last, three men in olive green uniforms carrying white-covered folders swaggered into the room and took their seats. The man in the middle wore a colonel's insignia and looked to be the judge. On his right sat another colonel; and to his left sat a young man wearing the insignia of a lieutenant colonel. The other colonel looked to be the public defendant; the lieutenant colonel was probably a scribe. The guards took off Youde's handcuffs and ordered him to stand in front of the judge. Two guards stood behind Youde.

The judge opened the file, cleared his throat and asked in a deliberate, businesslike manner.

"What is your name?"

"Tsai Youde."

"Where were you born?"

"I was born in Putzu, Chiayi Prefecture."

"Your birthdate?"

"December 6, 1925."

The judge then asked about Youde's schooling and work history, ascertained that Youde studied in America, then started on the main topic.

One by one, and thoroughly, the judge went over Youde's friends and associates mentioned in the investigation report. Youde replied that none of them had tried to persuade him to join the Communist Party and that he was not aware that any of them was a Party member. The judge did not interrupt Youde's replies, merely carried on patiently and matter-of-factly, inquiring about one person after another. The judge's manner was unexpectedly gentlemanlike, quite a departure from the sharp inquisitions and distrustful bearings that Youde had experienced in other intelligence organizations. Thanks to that, the tense feeling in Youde ebbed considerably.

Next, the judge asked about Youde's activities during his student days. On his part, Youde looked for a chance to put forth his refutation as he answered the judge's questions.

"Your Drama Society and the Student Friendship Association both had many Communist Party members. Yet you claim neither was a Communist front organization. Maybe they were used as front organizations, were they?"

Youde replied, "In those days, many government and private organizations alike were infiltrated by many Communists. So it was unavoidable that the Drama Society and the Student Friendship Association too had Communist members among their ranks. For the same reason that the Railroad Bureau, the Telegraph Bureau, and schools, which had all been infiltrated, were not front organizations, my Drama Society and the Student Friendship Association were not either.

"On the contrary, despite having so many of them in my organization, I, the president, was not controlled by them. Doesn't that prove that their effort was thwarted because I was too staunch an anti-Communist? I think I should be lauded for that, so it is entirely unexpected that I am charged with a crime."

The judge grinned a mysterious grin.

"You read *A Reader in Materialist Dialectics*, did you not?"

"Yes, I read it. But the book did not appeal to me. As you know, many turned against materialism after reading the book, and I am one of them. Besides, books of that nature constitute but a speck of what I read. You can see from the list of books in my file that my interests lie elsewhere."

The judge's sharp questioning was again reserved for *Mao Wenchi*.

"You stated that you did not read the plain-covered *Mao Wenchi*. But if you did not open the book, how did you know it was *Mao Wenchi*?"

The question was to be expected. Since the whole story about *Mao Wenchi* was a result of compromise with truth, the argument did not hold water.

Youde recounted to the judge the course of the investigation at Chiayi and denied the existence of the book on his bookshelf. The judge was not pleased and obviously unbelieving. Youde knew that it was extremely difficult to overturn one's confession. Besides, the judge's mindset took confessions for evidence — not something easily changed. In Youde's case, the contention was only about the existence of a book; but in other cases, such as those of teachers Liu and Kao, who had confessed under torture to serious crimes, the concocted confession could cost them their lives. Youde could not begin to imagine the unimaginable bitterness of those who had cried and pleaded their innocence as they were dragged to the execution yard.

At one point, the judge showed signs of wrapping up the questioning. Wasting no time, Youde straightened his posture and raised his hand.

"Your honor, I have something to say."

"……"

"I am suspected of being a Communist, but up to now only matters unfavorable to me have been taken up by the investigation. While plenty of evidence exists to support my anti-Communist stance, none was taken into consideration. I think this is rather unfair," Youde rapidly stated his case in one breath.

But the judge would not have anything to do with that. He slammed the file shut with a loud thump.

Youde took out the photograph from his pocket, the one his wife had sent under his instructions.

For just such an occasion as this day's, Youde had asked a friend to snap this picture after learning of Yu-kun's capture. Such preparedness may seem laughable today, but for people under the reign of the White Terror, it was the wisdom of self-preservation acquired through personal experience — not really uncommon at all.

The snapshot showed Youde making a speech on top of a lectern in the China booth at a college international fair, his back against a blue-sky/white-sun national flag.

"Here I have a photograph taken when I made a speech to urge support for the Republic of China at an occasion where many pro-Communist students and the red five-star flags were present, something I couldn't have done if my thoughts were left-leaning."

To be truthful, it wasn't really a speech, but rather a talk to explain the cultural items on display.

Youde put on the best performance of his life.

Then the public defender, who had been silent all along, took interest in the picture and stretched his hand out toward Youde. The guard took the picture from Youde and handed it over.

"I have," Youde continued his acting, "always been anti-Communist. That is why none of my associates revealed his Communist identity to me, nor did anybody try to recruit me."

Suddenly a light went on in Youde's head.

"Cheng Wen-bang and Chou Shen-yuan, people you asked about earlier — I had many heated arguments with them."

The judge again grinned. Maybe he thought Youde childish, or, maybe he thought it comical to drag dead men out to prove a point.

The public defender put the photograph down and opened his mouth for the first time.

"A dead man has no mouth. Do you have a witness?"

"Yes, I do."

"Who?"

"Wu Che-fu. Wu was always by Cheng Wen-bang's side, so he knows well that I had always argued vociferously with Wen-bang."

The judge rose deliberately to his feet and announced the conclusion of the questioning.

The public defender returned the photograph to Youde. Then the three left the courtroom. Escorted by the guards, Youde again headed for the prison.

A new group of inmates were bathing and walking in the compound. Youde searched intently for Che-fu but did not find him.

Youde's heart felt lighter, like after shedding a heavy burden. He was especially glad that he had figured out Che-fu's intent. Turning his body toward the West Area where Che-fu was housed, Youde raised both his arm high in the air and laughed a hearty laugh, the first happy laugh since he was imprisoned.

A week later, a message came from the West Area.

"Today Wu Che-fu was called as witness with regard to your case."

Youde found out much later that, coincidentally, Youde's judge and public defender switched their roles and were Che-fu's public defender and judge, respectively.

65

Petacos (White Helmets) Are Here

One dark, cloudy morning, even though the time was past eight, the guards had not yet opened the door to let out the first group of inmates, who, towels and dirty laundry in hand waited by the door. Usually, the door opened at seven on the dot. Anxiety turned into terror.

A prison servant told the inmates in Cell 1, "Petacos are here."

The word *petaco*, literally "white head" in Taiwanese, was also the name of a small bird with a white patch on its head. The petaco is the most common bird in Taiwan next to the sparrow. Because the MPs wore white helmets, petaco became their nickname. Petacos came here for one special mission only: to take custody of the inmates sentenced to death and escort them to the execution yard.

In other words, they were messengers from hell.

"Petacos are here," the message was relayed from cell to cell through the entire prison.

According to fellow inmates, MPs were supposed to wait in the courtroom; but maybe to supplement the shortage of guards, or to avoid any unexpected resistance, they had been coming inside the high wall.

Immediately, the question turned to "how many of them?" For every two petacos, one inmate would be sent to execution. Therefore, by the number of petacos one could get an idea of whose case was involved.

The inmates of each cell set aside their towels and laundry. And they waited for the next piece of news, holding their breath. The atmosphere in the room turned turgid all of a sudden, filled with sorrowful anguish.

Chou Shui the woodcutter, awaiting a death sentence, sat leaning against the wall. He closed his eyes and dropped his head as if he were praying. Chen Shih the man-child moved close to Chou, fearful of losing him.

"Brother Chou!" Chen called Chou timidly.

Chou Shui did not move a muscle. In Chen Shih's mind, Chou was the most dependable protector next to his mother. Youde was afraid that when the time came for Chou to go Chen might hold on to Chou and not let go.

The prison friends in Cell 7 threw glances at Chou Shui from time to time. As much as they tried not to, they couldn't help themselves because everybody knew that his sentencing was near.

Silence dominated. When Youde looked around, he found the teachers Liu and Kao were visibly paler than usual. There was a probability that they could be called today, Youde realized. After all, their case was still open and they were charged with Article 2.1, for which the death sentence was the only possible outcome.

Youde noticed that even the ordinarily jocular Mori begin to pace up and down. Come to think of it, a repeat offender of "Aid to Bandits" could draw a death sentence. Youde joined Mori, who said to Youde in a whisper, "It must be nice not to have to worry." Somehow Youde felt embarrassed for his good fortune and apologetic toward the others.

Little Lu was nervous — standing then sitting. His eyes were already welling up. He was thinking about his brother.

Wu sat on his pillow, facing the corridor. Chin-huo, kneeling by Wu's side, also peered in the same direction. As one's vision was severely limited by the bulky columns from any angle, the most one could see was a portion of the cell straight across the corridor and the immediate area of the corridor. Finally the guards could be heard approaching, jangling handcuffs and leg-irons.

Shen sat upright and started to read in his Zen book. He looked different. In a worst-case scenario, even Shen could be the intended victim today, Youde thought.

That left Youde and Chin-huo, who had no fear of being called.

Were this the United States or any democratic country, none of them would be guilty of the charges. What a sad destiny for the Taiwanese people, Youde contemplated.

Perhaps rattled by the ever-silent Chou Shui, Chen Shih shook Chou's knees and insistently called "Brother Chou" ever more frequently. Still, there was no response from Chou. At last, Chen began to cry aloud.

"Don't cry, Chen Shih!" Uncharacteristically, Liu raised his voice and glared at Chen.

As if to escape the unbearable silence, a chorus rose from one cell. Then, answering the chorus, singing voices rang out from two or three other cells. The song was a rousing Communist tune. Yet for some reason the voices sounded hollow. They did nothing to uplift morale. Instead, it added an air of desolation.

In this anxiety and terror, the second piece of information came through.

"There are eight petacos."

That meant four people from the same case would be called for execution this morning.

Nobody in Cell 7 fit the bill, as four was too many for Mori's case, or for Wu's or Shen's, while it was too low for Liu and Kao's case because at least twenty petacos would be needed to handle the case of these beloved teachers who were fated to live or die together.

Four was also too small a number for Chou Shui's case, the case of the Luku villagers. Even though more than thirty people had already been put to death in two rounds, a third round involving at least ten more was expected.

The chorus had subsided. The prison was dead still.

"Here they come," somebody in Cell 3 shouted. But there were no guards' footsteps. Had there been a mistake? Or did they hear phantom footsteps due to extreme tension?

A metallic clinking sound broke the prison's stillness.

"Cell 5." The message spread by relay. Cell 5 was the cell close to the entrance.

"Chung Chi-hsiang." Youde heard Panchang Teng's Hunan-accented voice — a colder voice than he had ever heard in his life. In the next instant, Youde realized the squad leader meant his friend Cheng Chi-hsiang and shuddered.

"It's patriot Tei Keisho." Cheng's name in Japanese came over by relay. Suddenly and spontaneously, the singing of "The Horse-Drawn Wagon" (Horo-basha) in Japanese surged and enveloped the entire prison.

To the distant sunset, the leaves scatter.
Along the tree-lined road, swaying to and fro,
You in a horse-drawn wagon, I see you off.
Parting of yesteryear, became forever.

The supposedly sorrowful song was sung matter-of-factly and in full throttle as if it were a military march. Everybody including Chou Shui, Shen the public scribe, and Chen Shih stood up and marched in a circle as they sang.

It had become a custom for the prison friends to sing the doomed man's favorite song as a send-off. It was a sad fact that because Taiwanese historically had been prohibited from using their own language, there were few well-known popular songs in Taiwanese. Consequently, most of their favorite songs were Japanese; for some reason, "The Horse-Drawn Wagon" was the most popular.

Perhaps the song's words "Parting of yesteryear, became forever" matched their feelings all too well. Whose parting did they lament so, these passionate, virginal young men of this tropical country, who were fated to scatter before knowing any woman? Was it parting from their parents or sisters? Or was it the young girls who were their secret first loves?

As the singing continued, bits of intelligence continued to flow.

"He has been handcuffed."

"They put leg-irons on him."

The singing grew ever louder.

"He is raising his voice to say goodbye."

But Cheng's voice was lost amid the singing and did not reach Cell 7.

"He was taken outside."

The singing, now soaked with tears, grew even louder, crashing and shaking the prison walls like an angry ocean wave. They wanted so much to present their unfortunate friend the gift of his favorite song as he walked, handcuffed and shackled, the hundred meters to the courtroom, despite the thick walls of prison.

Youde's heartstring was taut with emotion, for he had crossed paths with Cheng, remembering vividly that Cheng was the first person to greet him by calling his name when he first came here. Drops of tears silently coursed down Youde's cheeks.

"Oh, my goodness. What happened to Wu Che-fu?"

Suddenly, Youde remembered Che-fu who was routed back here from the "island" on the same case as Cheng Chi-hsiang. Three people were taken out from the West Area today. Is Che-fu among them? Youde's heart pounded violently from the new worry.

Youde left the singing column and shouted at the messenger in the opposite cell, Cell 3.

"What happened to Wu Che-fu?"

But the messenger merely shook his head sideways, either because he couldn't hear the question above the singing or because he did not know the answer.

Eventually "The Horse-Drawn Wagon" turned into a Communist song.

It said:

Sleep peacefully, comrade of fatal disaster.

Many other songs followed, and the singing continued until the first group of inmates were belatedly let out to the compound.

Later, bathers returned and sent over the names of the four who were executed that day. Che-fu's was not one of them.

66

The True Meaning of *Zaijian* (Meet Again)

THE next day a circular about the four executed came around.

Cheng Chi-hsiang was a student of National Taiwan University. He was a Christian and had organized Chiayi's Taiwanese Christian Youth Corps, which consisted mostly of young students. The corps was formed around the same time as Youde's Putzu Student Friendship Association. This was before the April 6 student crackdown and also before the Law on Sedition went into effect, so associations could still be formed.

One day, Cheng's group invited a mainlander student to give a talk. The speaker criticized the government's corruption and received enthusiastic applause from the audience. After the April 6 incident, this very student was arrested for being a Communist; subsequently, Cheng Chi-hsiang and many of the Taiwanese Christian Youth Corps' young men and women were investigated and sentenced.

Cheng was sentenced to twelve years and sent to Green Island to serve his time.

Several years later, however, Cheng was brought back to the military court, this time, for conspiring in the prison uprising. The so-called separate case referred to this conspiracy.

According to the circular, the conspirators planned to first seize the guns from the guards, follow it with an attack on the armory, then distribute the firearms to the inmates, and, finally, occupy the entire island. The plan was exposed by an informer. Yesterday's execution put to death the four ringleaders.

An additional ten people or so, including Che-fu, were implicated in this "separate case." Being veterans of interrogation, they denied to the end any knowledge of the plan, while the four leaders took full responsibility and sacrificed their own lives. The fact that only four people were executed was the only consolation in this calamity. Che-fu received a judgment of not guilty.

By an odd coincidence several days after the execution, Youde saw the not-guilty defendants unexpectedly. As he dashed out to bathe on his outing rotation, Youde saw ten or so inmates, all clad in the grey prison uniform of the "island," standing in a corner of the compound. Even prison garb, when worn by a group of people, looked rather good. Several of them had white cloth bags swung over their backs. As they talked and laughed among themselves, they did not resemble prison inmates. If anything, they could have been taken for a group of students on a school trip.

Youde and his friends barely splashed themselves with water and hurried to approach the group.

Che-fu raised his hand and stepped out from the group.

"Hey, Youde!"

"Ya, Che-fu."

Their exchange was cut short by the guard. Youde got a warning and Che-fu was yanked back to the fold.

Other people, too, waved and greeted their acquaintances. On the one side were people who, though not guilty on the "separate case," still had to return to the hellish island, which kept only people sentenced to ten years or more, to serve out their long sentences. No doubt there were life termers among them. On the other side were people awaiting sentences of unknown severity. Some like Chou Shui faced certain death. Would there be another day for these friends to meet again?

Meeting in sorrowful circumstances was especially precious.

Che-fu broke into a wide grin and shouted from the crowd, "It's going to be OK."

Youde knew he meant "Your case will go well. I've testified for you. So don't worry." Youde shouted in return, "I am glad for you too."

Che-fu did not appear changed at all by years of hardship on the "island," still looking like the fair-faced, handsome young man of his student days.

"Let's meet outside!" Youde yelled.

Che-fu's "Let's meet outside" echoed back.

The guards divided the group into two lines and ushered them toward the gate.

"Sayonara!"

"*Zaijian!*" Shouts of farewells in both Japanese and Chinese followed the group. The group waved and shouted *zaijian* in return.

Would there really be days to meet again? Youde wondered.

Youde was in the habit of using *zaijian* — meet again, the term for farewell in Chinese — interchangeably with sayonara, or goodbye in Japanese, without giving it much thought. Never before, did he wish more for the true meaning of the words as he did now.

67

Sending Chin-huo Off

THE year 1954 was drawing to a close, and everybody figured that Chou Shui the woodcutter would be able to reach age twenty after all.

The first group of bathers came back hastily and passed the words "We saw four petacos."

As if to confirm their words, the second group's outing was suspended. Four petacos were seen, but more could have followed.

Chou Shui was carrying a towel and his laundry in his hand. The blood drained from his face.

"This must be it," everybody thought, staring at Chou Shui with frozen faces. Chou Shui quietly put down the towel and laundry, reached up to the shelf, and took down his bundle.

As Chou Shui took a deep breath, his face regained some color. He said clearly, "It seems that our parting has finally come," and took out a set of freshly laundered clothes from the bundle.

"Brother Chou! Brother Chou! Ah …ah…," Chen Shih the man-child clung to Chou.

"You must not cry. It looks bad," Chou Shui scolded Chen in an unexpectedly calm voice.

Unable to bear watching Chou Shui any longer, Mori also started to sob loudly. Meanwhile, Chou began to change his clothes.

The sight of Chou Shui dressing for his crude, impending death was unbearably sad. Chou's shaved head intensified the sorrow even more. All watched him through their tears.

Liu tried to comfort him, "There were only four petacos."

"No," Chou said, "It has to be this time. I have long ago resigned myself not to see twenty."

Once a person is resigned to the prospect of death, he seems to gain strength. Chou Shui's face had a determined look, not at all like when he slumped against the column.

Chou Shui said gently to the still crying Chen Shih, "Now, how about you stop your crying and see your Brother Chou off with a smile, huh?"

Chen Shih instantly stopped his crying and lifted his face toward Chou, whose smile and dry eyes seemed to set Chen at ease.

Using this interlude, Little Lu and Chin-huo pulled Chen away from Chou.

Now, Chou Shui sat on the floor and started to put on his socks with some difficulty. Maybe the white socks he'd been pulling on were too small for him, or maybe the outwardly calm Chou was unsteady after all. He took another deep breath and started all over again.

"His feet have grown, because he was still a teenager when he entered here," The ex-policeman Wu said.

No wonder. This was probably the first time in many years that he had socks on since he was imprisoned. After putting on his socks, Chou Shui sprung up from the floor, brushing aside helping hands from Youde and Shen.

Chou Shui started to shake hands with his prison friends, one by one.

"Thanks for taking care of me," he said in a firm voice. Chou was the only one with dry eyes.

"Please take care of my parting note," he said to Liu to whom he had entrusted the note sometime ago.

Liu said, "You are wrong. It's not your turn. There are only four petacos."

"No," Chou Shui said, "I would rather they execute me early. I got that premonition today. No, actually, I had the feeling since last night because today is my birthday."

"Your birthday! Is that so!" Everybody sighed audibly.

The second piece of intelligence reached Cell 7 — the panchang finished his drink and had come out of his office.

Panchang Teng had at last stepped out of his office and was ready to open the barred gates of the cells.

Footsteps of two or three people echoed in the now-stilled prison. They were approaching Youde's Cell 7. Panchang Teng and two guards appeared in the corridor and stopped squarely in front of Cell 7. Chou Shui's premonition was accurate after all.

Panchang Teng inserted the key in the lock and with a loud clank opened the lock.

Chou Shui stood like a wax statue right in the center of the room.

"Brother!" Chen Shih the man-child wrestled away from Little Lu's hold and clung to Chou's legs.

Creak! The door opened halfway. Panchang Teng yelled in a loud voice, "Huang Chin-huo. Come out."

Totally unexpected words. All stood speechless and doubted their ears.

"Huang Chin-huo. Come out!" Panchang Teng yelled again.

Audible sighs echoed through the prison. What's going on? Is this a mistake? All looked toward Huang Chin-huo, the printshop apprentice.

"Huh?" Chin-huo uttered and remained glued to the spot, his face deadly pale.

"I ... I...." At long last, sounds came out of Chin-huo's throat.

The front of Chin-huo's khaki shorts changed color as wetness spread and eventually drops of water dripped to the floor.

Chou Shui came over to Chin-huo. At the same moment, Mori walked over to the shelf.

"You must get a hold of yourself, all right? Brother Lung is waiting for you out there, and I will follow you soon."

Mention of Brother Lung made Chin-huo shudder.

Mori took a bundle down from the shelf and took out a change of clothes.

In front of everybody's eyes, Chin-huo stripped from the waist down and started to get into the clean clothes. His penis had shrunk pitifully. His hands were unsteady. Chou Shui, Mori, and Little Lu helped him.

"Brother Lung is with you. Don't worry."

"Brother Lung," at long last, words came out of Chin-huo.

"Chin-huo, Chin-huo!" Chen Shih started to cry and reached to cling to Chin-huo, but was held back by Wu and Little Lu.

Liu stood next to Chin-huo and said, "Chin-huo, is there anything you want to say?"

Chin-huo's vacant eyes looked toward the front of the room. He shook his head slightly.

Shen also moved next to Chin-huo, took his hand and said, "Chant *namuamitofu*, OK? It's *namuamitofu*, don't forget."

"Hurry up," Panchang Teng pounded on the door and shouted.

The face of the squad leader was red like a red ghost. It was said that the panchang customarily downed a bottle of wine before carrying out his duty of taking the condemned prisoners.

Youde firmly squeezed Chin-huo's cold hands as the latter left the cell. He did not know what to say, this being his first experience seeing somebody off to execution. Chin-huo did not return Youde's handshake.

From the cell across the corridor, rose the song "Our Youth." Soon other people joined in the singing.

Chin-huo was handcuffed at the entrance to the cell block. Panchang Teng held back the guards from putting leg-irons on him, perhaps because he thought it an extra nuisance to shackle a person already having difficulty moving his feet.

Accompanied by the singing, his wrists held by the guards from each side, Chin-huo gradually disappeared from view.

Youde's eyes were flooded anew with tears of regret. "Why didn't I show more concern for Chin-huo, who was fated to live a short life of scant affection? I had plenty of opportunities to do so," he thought.

The song "Our Youth" continued:

Our youthful lives, bright yellow like fire
Burning in the fields of battle

Crashing through the pounding waves of the chorus, Chin-huo's give-it-all, top-of-the-lung cry reached Cell 7.

"Brother Lung!"

68

Brother Lung

Chin-huo's execution was a shocking event to some inmates because it meant that, depending on the judge, people charged with even not-so-serious crimes could still end up receiving a death sentence. In other words, people with not-so-serious charges couldn't relax anymore.

Youde, too, had to contemplate the worst prospect. "Do I really face no danger of losing my life? Suppose that young judge had reasoned, 'Tsai Youde did join the Communist Party. No evidence, but we got a witness. And so if this were a mistaken execution, wasn't he the person responsible for producing the leftist plays?' One's life is never absolutely safe as long as one is in this place."

The air in Cell 7, its ranks now reduced by one, was heavy as lead. Nobody touched lunch; dinner, too, was mostly left uneaten. Youde had not seen this happen before.

Liu and Kao were conferring with each other; but they appeared to be in a quandary. It turned out that they needed to write up a circular about Chin-huo's life but were having difficulty coming up with anything. Besides, Chin-huo did not leave a parting note. What an oversight it was. It was hard for them to believe that Chin-huo was sentenced to death for transposing the character "surrender" in place of the character "resist," rendering the phrase to read "Oppose Communism, Surrender to Russia." No, Brother Lung, who was executed the same day, held the key to the puzzle. Again, the available information about Brother Lung was sketchy; only that he was a fellow townsman of Chin-huo from Yuan-lin and that he had run a printshop.

Everybody turned to Chou Shui, for he seemed to possess privileged knowledge about Brother Lung. Still dressed in the attire he changed into for his own execution, Chou, who was not a good talker, spoke haltingly.

"Brother Lung was an extremely intelligent person. His full name was Huang Chi-lung. After finishing only grade school, he left home for Taipei and became a printshop apprentice. While there he read vociferously as he set type for a living. According to Chin-huo, Brother Lung was as well educated as any college man. Brother Lung must have been the most learned person Chin-huo had come in contact with. Chin-huo's parents died long ago, and his only older brother used to beat him up; so Brother Lung was like a surrogate parent to Chin-huo, although Brother Lung was barely ten years his elder."

Youde reasoned that Brother Lung was the person who had given Chin-huo the most love, thus naturally had become his idol; and Chin-huo, in turn, had listened to Lung on everything.

Chou continued, "Brother Lung eventually opened his own printshop, and Chin-huo followed him there. Then, beseeched by someone, they printed the anti-government flyers."

As conjectured, Chin-huo's case was more than the mistake of one character. That also explained why he was charged with Article 4: Aid to Bandits.

"Why didn't Chin-huo say anything about Lung to us?" Liu asked.

Chou Shui grinned as he said, "Brother Lung had once told Chin-huo not to tell anybody in the prison about the case, because there might be spies."

"So that was why," someone sighed.

Loyal Chin-huo had kept his promise to the end. Except he did tell his secret to Chou Shui. Yet, despite living in such intimacy twenty-four hours a day, nobody was aware that Chin-huo trusted Chou Shui the most, a person who faced the death sentence. When and where did Chin-huo tell his story to Chou Shui? A meaningless pursuit now. Simple-looking Chin-huo turned out to be quite thoughtful after all. He told Chou Shui, fully anticipating that Chou would tell the truth about him if he were to be executed first.

For his part, Chou Shui also kept Chin-huo's secret well. Suppose Chou Shui was the one to be executed first, would Chin-huo's secret have been lost? Not likely. If that had come to pass, Chin-huo probably would have confided in someone else, again unbeknown to others.

"He could have told me," Little Lu dropped a line, showing his displeasure.

Right away, Wu teased him, "You can't keep a secret. Chin-huo saw right through you."

Chou Shui said, "If I were to go ahead of him, Chin-huo was going to tell you, Little Lu."

Little Lu gave a small smile, perhaps drawing comfort for being the runner-up.

"Chin-huo said that he needed no parting note, since Brother Lung was the only person in the world to whom he would have left his note...." Chou Shui choked up.

Youde asked Liu, "How long was Chin-huo here?"

"A year and seven months."

"During that time, didn't he receive any word from Brother Lung? Chin-huo must have longed for words from him."

"There was nothing. That's why we didn't know anything about him," Liu replied.

Messenger Sung interjected from the next cell. He must have been eavesdropping on the conversation on this side of the wall. "It was impossible for him to do that had he even wanted to do so. When Huang Chi-lung was brought over to this prison, his mind was already gone from severe beatings. All day long, he did not say a word. It's doubtful that he even remembered Chin-huo."

Youde could imagine the extraordinarily severe torture that the interrogator employed as they relentlessly pursued the identity of the customer who had ordered the anti-government flyers. But Lung did not break. For if he had, the customer would also be among the executed today. Youde figured Brother Lung to be a man of noble ideals and not one to print flyers merely for money. He also was not a man to betray his comrades lightly.

Youde saw in his mind's eye the noble young Huang Chi-lung whom he had never met and would never meet. New tears flowed into his eyes. In any decent society, a young person of such high-mindedness would probably be in *Who's Who*. The fact that he cautioned Chin-huo not to tell showed his cautious side. How sad that another excellent "sweet potato" expired with the dew of the execution yard.

At last, Liu and Kao finished writing Chin-huo's life story and passed a copy of the hand-copied circular to each neighboring cell.

That night, when they lay down to sleep, they left Chin-huo's place open. Everybody had a hard time falling asleep as their thoughts lingered on Chin-huo.

"When Chin-huo was about to leave the prison today," Youde thought, "he had shouted with all his strength 'Brother Lung!' But he couldn't have seen Brother Lung in person, because Lung was then waiting either at the courtroom or at the entrance to the West Area, a distance away. Did the shackled and handcuffed Chin-huo shout because he couldn't contain himself, or did he imagine that he saw his idol? Did he even hear the singing of 'Our Youth,' since he was totally preoccupied by the thought of Brother Lung?

"Chin-huo worked and died for Brother Lung's sake. What was on the anti-government flyers was of no concern to him.

"But what did he feel when he saw Brother Lung without any memory?

"The Brother Lung of yesterday, once the pillar of his existence, was no more.

"Brother Lung probably did not say one word when he saw Chin-huo. Having lost his psychological support, did Chin-huo collapse in sobs?

"When the two of them were made to kneel side by side in the sands of the execution yard, what did he make of the expressionless profile of Brother Lung?

"Did he repeatedly cry, 'Brother Lung!' or did he plunge into despair and chant *namuamitofu, namuamitofu?*"

69

New Year's Day

Day after day, Chen Shih the man-child continued to weep, until it was time to greet the New Year. New Year's Day in prison was particularly lonely.

Early in the morning, some people started to sing the Japanese New Year's song:

To greet the beginning of the year,
Wishing for endless universe.
Stands of pines and bamboo at the entrance,
We celebrate a happy New Year's Day.

Many who knew the song — there were at least a few in each cell — joined in the singing. How surprising it was to hear people singing such songs in prison, the oldies that were no longer sung in Japan. Were they perhaps remembering their innocent childhood as they sang?

Why do Taiwanese remember with such fondness an era during which they were considered to be inferior, colonial subjects and educated as such? Is it because it was peaceful, despite Taiwan being Japan's colony? Or is it because the present reign of Chinese rule is far more miserable and terrifying? Or perhaps anyone under any circumstances remembers his youth with fond memories. No matter what the case, if the past colonial rulers were to witness the singing scene, they would no doubt be greatly perplexed.

Each fell into his own reveries as the singing continued.

The song stirred in Youde the memories of his first New Year's Day in Japan. At a young age, Youde had left Taiwan to live with his brother's family in Moji, Japan, where he entered the sixth grade co-ed class at Junjo Elementary School. He had chosen this course on his own, over his parents' objections, simply because he had single-mindedly adored Japan. In fact, there was not a single, special reason that he had to go to Japan. Still, like all Taiwanese children, Youde had harbored an inferiority complex for being a Taiwanese since he was a little child. By going to Japan, Youde, in his child's mind, was perhaps trying to escape to a place where he did not have to feel that way.

It turned out that the Japanese people in Japan, unlike the ones in Taiwan, did not have superior attitudes toward the Taiwanese at all. Youde's young friends, as well as their parents, treated Youde as their equal. If anything, they showed a special kindness to a new friend who came from afar and had yet to experience his first snow. As young as he was, Youde keenly felt the kindness and, as a result, his inferiority complex gradually disappeared. Then came the New Year.

Youde remembered being warmly welcomed into friends' homes, where he enjoyed traditional hot-pot and played the karuta poetry card game, the sugoroku monopoly game, and shuttlecock paddling with his friends, who had no idea that their kindness had healed Youde of his inferiority complex. He remembered how as a young boy, while still tearfully longing for his mother, he also shed tears of joy for the new world he had discovered. Thinking back now, he felt fortunate that he had lived part of his youth in a society in which different peoples were treated with equality.

The New Year's songs brought back deep emotions.

"Mr. Tsai, what are you thinking?" Little Lu asked with an innocent smile.

"I was thinking about a New Year's from my childhood."

Responding to Little Lu's request, Youde told about the New Year's celebration in Japan.

In Taiwan, people celebrate the Lunar New Year instead of the Western New Year. But somehow confusing the two, Little Lu said, "I also have happy memories of New Year's."

"That's nice. I am glad."

Little Lu told of happy New Year from his childhood, then added, "The New Year I had in the mountains was also great."

"Oh, you mean your last New Year on the outside," Mori joined in.

"Yes. That turned out to be my last New Year in the real world. We dressed up like peasants and walked the five kilometers of mountain path to the town. It was around five o'clock in the afternoon when we got there. The town was small, but it was all lit up with many lights. Boy, was I happy. You see, we didn't have electricity in our mountain hideout. I thought towns were really wonderful. Night market stands lined both sides of the only street, and there was a lot going on. I bought a pack of cigarettes; after safely stashing it away in my breast pocket, I drew one out and tried it. I figured I was already fourteen, after all. My brother did not object either. The cigarette tasted good — indescribable, but good. I puffed up my chest, touching my breast pocket from time to time, and walked the only street back and forth, back and forth, for at least a score of times. I felt great. There were traveling salesmen and gambling among the night market stands; but we just watched, because my brother cautioned us not to attract attention. Besides, games like the ring toss looked childish to me, a smoking man! Still, that was a great New Year's."

"That was nice," Youde and Mori said in one voice.

70

Sent to the Investigation Bureau

Prison life passes rapidly once one gets used to it. It was after the lunar New Year and during a cold front when the panchang came to Cell 7 and called Youde's name one morning.

"Tsai Youde, we are sending you for further investigation. Gather your things and come out."

Everybody was startled by the unexpected event.

"Mr. Tsai...," Little Lu choked as he spoke; the eyes that met Youde's were already flooded with tears.

Youde took the bundle off the shelf and started to pack his belongings. Mori got the mug off the shelf, emptied it, and handed it to Youde.

"I'll truly miss you," he said.

Chou Shui was the first to grasp Youde's hands and said "sayonara," deliberately and slowly in Japanese. Most likely he did not use the Chinese *zaijian* (meet again), for he knew that they were not likely to see each other ever again. "Sayonara," which means "well, if so...," seemed to be made for the occasion. In return, Youde squeezed Chou Shui's hands tightly.

Liu, Kao, the public scribe Shen, ex-policeman Wu, Mori, and then, shyly, Chen Shih took turns taking Youde's hands and bid him goodbye. On his way out, Youde took Little Lu into his arms and hugged him with all his strength. Wiping away his tears with his fist, Little Lu said, "Mr. Tsai, take care of yourself. And thank you. I'll never forget you as long as I live."

Youde couldn't contain his own tears.

Prompted by the guards, Youde stepped through the door, put on his shoes, and started toward the exit.

Shouts of "*zaijian*," "sayonara," and "take care" came from other prison cells. As he was not handcuffed, Youde was able to raise his hands to answer the farewells. He passed by Cheng Chi-hsiang's old cell; but Cheng, the first person to greet Youde upon his arrival, was no longer there.

"Where are they sending me for further investigation?" Since neither the panchang nor the guard seemed to know, it was a waste of time to ask. One thing was certain: the destination was not the re-education center, because one was sent there only after receiving the court decision. "Why am I being sent to another investigative organization? Is it going to be the Investigation Bureau of the Interior Ministry, or is it going to be the Secret Protection Bureau? Or has there been some new development?" Youde's mind was dogged by questions.

The guard took Youde across the prison compound; they passed through the gate of the tall wall and stepped out of the iron gate and into the office — a route in the exact reverse order from the time he came in.

Youde was handcuffed after the routine procedures and was taken out of the building and put on a jeep. Two plainclothes guards sat on each side of Youde. The jeep passed by the front of the Military Court Building and turned onto Chingtao East Road.

"Where are we going?" Youde ventured on a dare. No answer.

The outside world that Youde saw anew was a different world entirely. Bicycle riders and pedicabs with their fares passed them by seemingly so carefree. Youde also thought everybody dressed well.

The jeep moved slowly, turning left once then right, and came out on the crowded streets of Taipei, where the world looked even more different and remote. Happy faces of people in colorful attire was something Youde had not seen for a while. But, most of all, the sight of women attracted Youde's eyes. He realized that he had not seen a female face or a female figure for a long time and was grateful for a world where there were women.

The jeep stopped suddenly at a red light, throwing the passengers forward. Youde looked up. Right in front of him was a truck loaded with bronze statues. "Where did the truck come from? I must have been so taken by the female passersby that I did not notice it."

The truck was filled with full-length statues of Chiang Kai-shek, which were lassoed together by a heavy rope to prevent them from toppling. The statues, which had kindly smiles on their faces, had outstretched arms, as if they were about to embrace a schoolchild. Still, the sight of a dozen or more statues of identical pose bundled together made for a comical scene. Youde gathered that the truck must be delivering them from manufacturers to different schools.

In order to demonstrate their loyalty toward the president, school principals often outdid each other ordering Chiang's statues to stand in front of the school buildings.

Chiang's picture was already ubiquitous in schools. It was to be found in the assembly hall and meeting room, even the principal's office, the school's administrative office, and every classroom. Still, the principals planted the bronze statues lest they be suspected of disloyalty. And on the statues' platforms they had the carvers inscribe phrases such as "Savior of the People" or "The Number One Great Man in the World."

The light turned green. The truck started to move, and the jeep followed. As the statues swayed, the bald heads of the statues glistened in the sun. Youde chuckled at the thought that his prison friends called this savior of the people "Baldy."

All death sentences of political prisoners were required to be finalized by the president's signature. Youde figured that every day from 1949 to 1952, the namesake of this kindly smiling statue with outstretched arms, must have put his name on at least one, sometimes as many as ten, death sentence decisions. In this way, he sent the sweet youth of Taiwan, who had once welcomed him with open arms, to the execution yard.

The statues swayed back and forth in front of Youde. Are they on their way to save the people or are they on their way to solidify the dictatorship?

The jeep turned right and stopped in front of a temple with a green dome.

"It's the Investigation Bureau," the plainclothes guard finally answered Youde's earlier question.

71

Little Devils

Due to the shortage of jail facilities, the Investigation Bureau had taken over the East Penyuan Temple to use for both interrogation and detention.

The East Penyuan Temple, along with the West Penyuan Temple, was the largest Japanese temple in Taipei. Its main building was a modern, domed structure of poured concrete, while its basement housed a crypt in which the ash urns of the deceased, mostly Japanese, were stored. Not many urns belonged to Taiwanese, as cremation was not commonly accepted in Taiwan then.

The Investigation Bureau moved the ash urns left behind by the repatriated Japanese elsewhere and converted the crypt into many tiny prison cells — a place for the dead was thus turned into a place for the living. Interestingly enough, some claimed that more people than before avoided passing by the place now.

Youde was taken by the guard into the temple office, which was to the side of the main building. A wooden plaque on the door said "reception room." Inside, he saw a sofa set and a few long benches. One of the guards gestured to Youde and the other guard to sit on a bench, while he headed toward the main building.

On the sofa sat five students in their school uniforms and a man in a Sun Yat-sen suit, sharing friendly conversation. The high schoolers hardly stopped to pay attention to Youde, a handcuffed man who had just sat down in a prominent spot. Instead, they continued bantering with each other, portraying not a shred of fear despite being in the Investigation Bureau, a place that was said to still a crying child. These are not your ordinary high school students,

Youde realized. Rather, they must be the professional students who received monthly stipends to be secret agents' eyes and ears, and to snitch on any inappropriate speech or actions by classmates or teachers. And for their effort, they would receive rewards if the victims were convicted. Not only that, they would be placed in plum jobs after graduation — if working in a school, soon promoted to a principal. In other words, it was the shortest course to success, with pay, no less, albeit not one a young man of conscience could take. Youde remembered that there were many professional students on college campuses and it was due to their actions that many able and patriotic Taiwanese youths were plucked from schools and thrown into jail, some even losing their lives in the execution yard. Some malicious informers were known to send their love rivals to the execution yard by false accusations.

Soon the five students stood up, put on their caps, picked up their book bags, and saluted the Sun Yat-sen suit in a cheerful voice, "Thank you. *Zaijian*, see you later." Youde figured that they had already received their stipends. This was the first time Youde encountered professional students of high school age, barely old enough to be his students. He was saddened.

The students walked by Youde, jostling each other, without even a glance at Youde. At the door, they turned to wave again at the man in the Sun Yat-sen suit, then changed into small, quick steps. Youde was reminded of the frenzied dance of little devils after they had finished sucking blood.

72

People at the Crypt

At last, the plainclothes man came back with a uniformed guard, who carried a bunch of keys in his hand. Youde was turned over to the guard and taken to the office. After finishing the admission procedures, they headed toward the basement. The place was cool and bleak, befitting a crypt, and the cold front outside made the place feel extra chilling.

Youde was assigned to Cell 2, a short distance from the entrance. The elongated cell was wide enough to accommodate ten tatamis across, and its sidewalls were of plastered brick. The front of the cell was formed by a row of a dozen or so square timbers, all reaching from ground to ceiling. This place could use some ventilation, Youde thought.

The guard opened the cell door and Youde stepped into it in one big stride. The wooden floor, which rose two feet off the ground, defined the living space, leaving a narrow strip of concrete floor between the wall and the raised floor. Thank goodness, there is a separate space for the *matung*! Youde observed.

The inmates were most likely all Chinese, because the conversations were in Mandarin Chinese.

Somebody asked, "Where's your home?"

"Putzu."

At once, a loud voice came from the back of the room.

"Yo! You must be Tsai Youde."

A stocky man rose from the spot customarily occupied by the dragon-head and approached Youde.

"Hmm, you are exactly as I imagined." He slapped Youde's back familiarly and introduced himself.

"I am Lin Jin-so. You may not have heard of me, but I've heard a lot about you. You see, I lived in the cell next to Chang Yu-kun."

"In the West Area?"

"Yes. I also saw a lot of Che-fu during bathing times. I was transferred here only a week ago myself. Come over here. Am I glad to have somebody to talk to!"

Lin Jin-so picked up Youde's bundle and briskly led the way to the back of the room, next to dragon-head's seat. This was breaking the unspoken law of the prison, but nobody seemed to mind. Perhaps, having the *matung* on a separate floor space had something to do with it, or maybe because the room was quite spacious relative to the number of inmates, they were not stuck on seniority.

But how did Lin, who just arrived a week ago, come to occupy the dragon-head's seat? Youde's perplexed look prompted Lin to explain.

"You see, I was here for two years previously. Then I was in the Military Court Prison for more than a year before coming back a week ago. Old Wang, a servant here, remembered me and told everybody that I was the dragon-head among dragon-heads. That's because during my last stay I did not hesitate to rough up the selfish guys. Besides, I was known for enduring horrendous torture. Even the secret agents referred to me as 'the Bull.'"

"Ya, I have heard about 'the Bull' at the Military Court Prison. You are the guy who owns a six-star black belt in judo."

"No, no, no. Actually, I was only a three-star black belt, but I was still the highest ranked in central Taiwan at the time. My judo rank got escalated as the word spread, I guess. Ha ha ha. Well, the upshot is that they forced me to take this seat and they listened to me well too."

The servant Old Wang appeared in the hallway, dragging a tub that contained lunch. The inmates interrupted their conversations to eat. A mainlander inmate kindly handed Youde an aluminum bowl and a pair of chopsticks.

As they ate, dragon-head Lin, a.k.a "the Bull," introduced the rest of the cast.

"Mr. Lai is the only Taiwanese, other than me."

A thin, gangling, helpless-looking man bowed his head, his face twitched sporadically.

"He was a pharmacy apprentice at a doctor's clinic. When the doctor got arrested, Lai became so afraid that he went into hiding, not that there was much of a reason for it. For three years, he went from place to place, then was arrested six months ago."

No wonder he looked like a man exhausted of spirit and soul. Three years on the lam would do that to anyone.

Lai himself said, "It was probably a good thing that I got caught." It was a sour-grapes like lament, yet it did not sound entirely false.

Pointing to a group of four mainlanders who were eating together, Lin the Bull said, "Those over there were POWs from the Korean War. After the truce, they chose to come to Taiwan instead of returning to China."

They were the people the government had labeled as Anti-Communist Freedom Fighters because they had denounced the Communist regime and joined the side of freedom. A national holiday was specially proclaimed, called 1-2-3 Freedom Day, to commemorate the date of their arrival in Taiwan: January 23.

"How did they...?"

The person who had handed Youde the bowl and chopsticks answered, "Those guys lied to us. They told us that Taiwan was an Asian paradise. It turned out to be not so different from China — no personal freedoms to speak of, our salaries were meager, and nobody wanted to marry us. We were fed up and angry, so we demanded that our superiors fulfill their promises. That's all we did."

"For mouthing off," a different man added.

"Old (=Mr.) Shih, Old Chen, Old Chi, Old Li," Lin introduced the group one by one.

"And here is Mr. Ma. He is also from the mainland," Lin pointed to a man in a black sweater.

"Ma worked in the police bureau and rose to the rank of assistant bureau chief. But he took a knife to the bureau chief and ended up a political prisoner."

Ma greeted Youde, "My name is Ma. I am a native of Tientsin."

Youde sized him up. Ma looked honest. But how much should he be trusted? A rare policeman indeed, if he had actually faced his superior with a knife to protest the chief's misbehavior.

Or he may just have confronted the chief, a fellow mainlander, because he was short changed in splitting up the bribe and the chief got the upper hand by reporting him to the authorities for political crimes. Like everybody else, Youde's distrust of mainlander government officials had deepened with time. Still, Ma the prisoner was worthy of sympathy.

Cell 2 had eight members all together.

Youde started anew the group living that was forced upon him.

73

The Bull's Final Struggle

THAT night, Youde did as urged and slept next to Lin the Bull, replacing Lai the pharmacy apprentice. Now Lai had twice vacated the spot of dragon-head since he was the longest inhabitant of this cell. But Lai did not seem to mind, rather, he seemed to much prefer having Lin as the dragon-head. Lai was happy, though, about having Youde, whose presence increased the rank of Taiwanese inmates by one.

Lin said to Lai and Youde, "You both are pretty lucky. If you were here three years ago, you wouldn't be able to sprawl out like this. The central area of this prison is partitioned into many tiny cells, and they packed six people into each two-tatami space. That meant that if three were to lie down, there would be no place to stand for the other three. So, they had to sleep in three shifts — two lying, two sitting and two standing. And the ones standing had to move the hand-rigged fans to move the air, and one of the sitting men actually had to sit on the *matung* cover and he would stand up when somebody wanted to pee. What's worse is that because we had no timepiece, sometimes the shifts could not be alternated fairly and that, sadly, caused conflicts and fistfights among the supposed comrades. Compared to that, we are in heaven now. Back then, this cell on the end was called the big room and had thirty people — one tatami space per three people. Also, the wooden floor sat right on top of the concrete.

"In the summer, it was hellishly hot. Even in winter, I was always stripped down to my waist. Speaking of hell, the inmates then must have looked like ghosts. Look, do you see Old Chen's pants? They're an old, tan-colored military uniform with writing on it. The right leg says 'Oppose Communism' and the left leg says 'Resist Russia' in large characters. That particular pair was a leftover from the old days. It was given to Old Chen by the servant Old Wang. But in those days, our own clothes were taken away and we were forced to wear those pants with half-sleeve shirts in bright red. I was naked most of the time, so I did not wear the shirt much. But when we went out, I had to put on the prison garb."

"What's the reason for making people dress like that?" Youde asked.

"To prevent escape. They figured a person in a bright red shirt and funny-looking pants would stand out like a sore thumb, even if he made it out and snuck into a crowd. Besides, from lack of exposure to sunshine, the inmates usually had pale faces and arms. On top of that, they also had bushy beards and overgrown hair. What else could it be but a ghost from hell? Enough to scare a timid person away!"

Lai the pharmacy apprentice took a deep breath and said with a twitch, "So, it wasn't exactly a waste, being on the lam for three years."

"You are right, Lai. First of all, torture was a given back then. You would have folded."

"Ya, I wouldn't bear up well."

"I am not confident that I would either," Youde chimed in.

"But Youde, you did endure five days of continuous fatigue-interrogation. You did great." Lin knew a lot about Youde.

Lin talked about torture, about having water poured into his nostrils, about being whipped with a hose or beaten with a bat, about having fingernails pulled out, etc. Lin stood up and stretched out his two hands to show Youde the crushed nails on his index fingers. Then he lowered his pants to show a large, dark purplish scar stretching from his waist to his buttock. The part right above the split of his buttock cheeks looked most painful. Lin said it was caused by a beating with a bat. Why his tailbone didn't break was anybody's guess.

"I walk sort of funny. Have you noticed? No? It's because I was beaten around the waist."

Lai's face twitched again.

"But the irony is," Lin continued, "that I gave them everything about myself right off. The fact that I joined the Communist Party after the February 28 Incident, that I became a Marxist, and that I carried arms. I confessed everything because I thought what the hell, I am going to die anyway. Still, I did not escape torture. They wanted to know the whereabouts of my comrades who were still at large. They pushed a list of seven or eight names in front of me, but I had nothing to say because I really didn't know their whereabouts. Even if I did, I don't think I would have spilled the beans. I did not give them anything about people who had given me money or hidden me."

Lin rolled on his back, turned slightly toward Youde and said, "That's where I am different from Yu-kun."

That's exactly what popped into Youde's mind. Lin the Bull and Yu-kun had a lot in common. They were both judo experts, joined the Communist Party, and were open and generous in their personalities. But Lin did not implicate even one person. Youde looked at Lin's profile with renewed respect.

Staring at the ceiling, Lin said softly as if to himself, "But now I am making my final struggle here." The word "struggle" was used fondly by Communists.

What he meant by his final struggle, Youde did not understand. Yet Lin's expression as he said it was dead serious and commingled with pain.

Youde rolled over to his side and closed his eyes.

74

Picture

The next morning, immediately after the outdoor exercise period, a curious Youde asked Lin the Bull, "But how did you hide from the authorities for three years without help from anybody?"

Lin smiled and answered, "After graduating from Chiayi Agricultural School I went to work for the Agricultural Laboratory, so I was familiar with all manner of crops. When the time came to flee, I dressed like a peasant and ran into the mountains. Not much to it really. You can see that I am built like a peasant to start with. I soon got work helping the farmers extract oil from the Yu-mao grass. In fact, I was quite in demand. I used an alias and moved from place to place, and I never had a problem making a living. There was one troublesome thing that stumped me, though. Do you know what it was?"

"Well, was it the sexual urge? Did you get married while you were hiding in the mountains?"

"Ha ha. It's nothing romantic like that. The problem was with my weapon. I inherited a pistol from my partner who drowned in a storm. It came with about ten bullets. I had to carry the pistol all the time, for I couldn't very well throw it away. I thought about burying it, but I thought what a shame it would be when the time came and I couldn't use the few weapons we had. It was a constant headache for me to find a place to hide the pistol. I didn't want my fellow workers to see the pistol and turn suspicious."

"But were you a married man?" Youde tried again.

"Yes. I was married before I went into hiding. But barely six months after the wedding, I left without a word. It was horrible."

"So you left without a word."

"Ya, without even a parting word. I feel very sorry all the time about that. I guess a revolutionary should never marry, really."

"That day, as a typhoon had landed on the east coast, we were covering up the seedlings as a protective measure at the laboratory. Then at the end of the work day, as dusk set in, a comrade by the name of Shih came to me quietly and told me to get ready to flee. Thinking back, I realized that Shih was too panicky a fellow. He was the one from whom I got the pistol that I was telling you about. You see, because he talked as if the secret agents were to descend upon us any minute, I gathered together a raincoat — it was not raining yet — a flashlight and, wearing what I had on my back, jumped on my bicycle and sped toward the mountains. We had previously prepared to meet others at a safe house, so we abandoned the bicycles and headed into the mountain path. When we were halfway up the mountain, we ran into a downpour. Shih lost his footing and fell into the river and disappeared into the darkness. I decided then and there to pitch the identification papers that I no longer needed. So you see, as far as the authorities were concerned, Shih died of drowning and I had disappeared.

"That turned out to be a convenient situation for me. The secret agents did not pursue me tenaciously, thinking that I was drowned also; and my boss at the Agricultural Lab kindly acquired some sort of compensation for my wife.

"But when I arrived at the safe house, there was no one there and the food we had carefully stored had spoiled from mildew. That's why I had to change into peasant's clothes, put on a bamboo hat, and leave the safe house to make a living. I could go on and on about my story. It would fill a book."

"So, all the time, your wife did not know that you were alive."

"No, she did not. I had no way to contact her. I moved deeper and deeper into the mountains. There were no post offices where I was, not even a mail drop, let alone telephones. Of course, my house didn't have a telephone anyway. Also, I was afraid that the police would keep watch at my house, so I couldn't very well send a messenger either. But my wife told me later that she had always believed that I was alive."

"When did she learn the truth?"

"Quite a bit later, not until I got captured after three years on the lam. I first learned that she knew when I received her care package here. You know, I wept when I ate the cake she brought me. Call it a speechless love, but it made me feel warm all over. But we were not able to correspond until I was transferred to the Military Court Prison."

"Is that so!"

"In her first letter she told me that she was so happy about me being alive that she had gone to various temples to say thanks. She said she was never happier, but...." Lin paused.

"Even though we are both alive now, we will never see each other again. Eventually she will be notified of my death and asked to come to retrieve my body. Poor woman. It might have been better for her if I had died in the storm that night."

Youde had to move his eyes away from Lin's clouded face.

"I almost forgot, I have a picture to show you."

From his bundle turned pillow, Lin took out a snapshot. A cute little girl in a pageboy haircut wearing a dress was standing in front of a fence smiling, holding a jump rope in her hands.

Lin said thoughtfully, "This picture was enclosed with my wife's first letter. That was the first I learned that I have a six-year old daughter. You see, I didn't know about it, but I was already a dad, a useless daddy who hadn't been able to do anything for her from the day she was born."

Youde examined the picture once more. When he turned it over, he found a line of writing in a child's hand — "Dear Father: From Ah-bi, your daughter."

75

Anti-Communist Freedom Fighters

THE POWs, now the Anti-Communist Freedom Fighters, appeared to lead happy lives in prison.

These were the POWs that the United States Army turned over to Taiwan's KMT government after the truce was declared in the Korean war, because they, twelve thousand in all, had refused to return to China and had chosen to live in the free world. The film *Twelve Thousand Witnesses* was based on their story. The relocation was said to be motivated by humanitarian reasons, but political consideration must have also played a part. In any event, their lives took a drastically different turn by this action.

When they arrived in Taiwan, they were lauded as Anti-Communist Freedom Fighters and were incorporated into the regular army units. While they were able to resume their lives of military service, they soon found the reality to be far different from what they had dreamed of — a situation that left many of them disgruntled. Those who mouthed complaints or took actions against the system were charged with violation of military codes and sent to the Investigation Bureau or the Military Court prisons. But they came in such great numbers that even the government was having a difficult time dealing with them.

That's how a devoted Communist like Lin the Bull and these Anti-Communist Freedom Fighters came to share their lives in the same prison cell, each awaiting the court's decision. How ironic! Still, human beings develop affections and strive to get along with each other when they share the same misfortune. The Chinese word, *nanyou*, or, "friends in misfortune," is indeed a fitting one. Lin arm-wrestled, engaged in games of push-pull with them, or joked around with them.

Youde found that the Anti-Communist Freedom Fighters were simple folks. As such, they were much more lovable than the sly bureaucrats from the mainland. Besides taking great interest in Taiwan's old customs and its modern way of living, they wanted to know about Youde's family life at home. Youde, too, asked them about their hometowns and life under Communism. The conversation was interesting enough.

On the contrary, the assistant bureau chief Ma, their fellow mainlander, derided the Anti-Communist Freedom Fighters as a bunch of country bumpkins and showed nothing but contempt for them. It was not clear if Ma was trying to draw a line between himself and the ex-POWs.

Old Shih, a man from Manchuria, once said to Youde, "My village had electricity but no water lines. I never rode in an automobile or a train before I enlisted in the army. My special skill was to shoot from horseback."

All of the ex-POWs had tattoos on their wrists — either of the characters "Oppose Communism, Resist Russia" or "Eliminate and Destroy Chu and Mao." They said that they tattooed themselves while still in the Korean camp to show their anti-Communist resolve. But now, because of the tattoos, they will not be able to go home again.

"Do you dislike your country so much?" Youde asked.

"Sure. Because the Communists are totalitarian and cruel and they killed a lot of people. Of course, I didn't know that they arrested and killed so many people here too."

Old Chi, who was in for striking a superior, expressed his opinion.

"I don't understand the deep stuff. But, you see, I came only because they told us Taiwan was an Asian paradise. I thought I could find myself a wife, get some kind of job, and settle down to a stable living."

Alas, brides for them were not to be found so easily.

It's true that when they first arrived at Keelung's waterfront, a line of Taiwanese maidens welcomed them. The girls hung leis over their necks, smiled at them, and shook their hands. But the girls were there under official order to play their parts and were never seen again. In truth, no Taiwanese girls were foolhardy enough to be interested in marrying country bumpkins who came from an undeveloped part of the world and had no position, education, or money.

POWs, however, were less burdened than the Taiwanese inmates, as they had no worries about their families, and their lives were not in danger. They may have been dissatisfied in the service, but there were no stunted ambitions there. Besides, for them, serving prison terms was not much different from living in the army barracks. "No wonder they were able to live happily here," Youde thought.

Their one collective shortcoming, however, was that they talked loudly. So loudly that Youde had the urge to tell them to cut it out.

Meanwhile, Old Shih and Old Chi began to play Chinese chess. Old Chen and Old Lee again started to play husband and wife, rolling around on the floor entangled and fondling each others' sexual organs.

76

It's Wiser to Let the Matter Drop

Lin the Bull knew Youde's case well. He said, "When I heard about you from Yu-kun, I thought then that you would be sent to the Military Court sooner or later. However, I did not expect to see you here. I guess you and I are fated to meet."

"I didn't expect to be returned to another investigative organization either."

"I heard that you tried to overturn your confession in court."

"Overturn is too grandiose a word for what I did. I just told them the truth, that I never had *Mao Wenchi* in my house."

"Ha ha ha. That's what irked them. Don't you think even they knew that confessions were mostly nonsense? After all, many people carry around scars from tortures they received.

"You can't expect conscience nor reason from these guys. These judges are not human beings. They are but rubber stamps that affirm the conclusions reached by the investigative bodies."

"I can't bear to dance to the arbitrary tunes of the investigative bodies, to be convicted and sentenced without a reason that's understandable to myself. I can't help but feel that to do so is not being fair to myself."

"Ha ha. I can see that you studied abroad, because you think in foreign terms. You may not know it, but our country, though a democratic country in name, is in its core a country ruled by warlords, and for that matter, hasn't evolved much since the Three Kingdoms period in the second century. It's going to take total reconstruction to destroy the feudal system and in its place establish a truly democratic people's government. That was what we sought in the Chinese Communist Party."

He paused a bit then continued, "This government is corrupt to its core. The judges have all lost their consciences. No, rather I should say, only people without a conscience can become judges. They have not a speck of considerateness to help the innocent. On the contrary, they push anything sticky onto others for they are unwilling to take any responsibilities themselves."

"I guess that's why the accused are passed from one place to another and why it takes them several years to reach arbitrary and baseless decisions."

"That's right. Your case is a one-person case. That's why it proceeded rather speedily."

"……"

"Had you repeated obediently in court what was in the confession, you could have been sent to re-education shortly after the court appearance and be home in three years. Of course, who knows if this government will last another three years."

"I guess I said something unnecessary in court, didn't I?"

"Ya. As a result, you will be kept here for two, three, or even six months for re-investigation, then eventually you will be sent back to the Military Court. Since the sentencing is rendered only by the Military Court, there's no way they will send you to re-education directly from here."

"It looks like the time I will spend here is a total waste of time."

"I guess so."

Youde muttered the old saying with self-mockery, "It was wiser to let the matter drop after all."

77

Life-Extending Tactic

Youde and Lin the Bull became fast friends. They talked about everything. Youde asked Lin, "I've heard different numbers, but how many people did Yu-kun actually implicate?"

"As far as I know, it's fifteen or sixteen. He confessed all of his vertical connections."

"And he still was not able to save his life, with that kind of number?"

"No way. It doesn't make any difference how many people one implicates. Reduced sentences cannot be granted to political prisoners just because they told it all."

"How about the Self-Renewal policy?"

"Well, the policy is on the books, but it does not apply to confessing one's vertical connections. Yu-kun was taken in by the investigators."

"How about his confession about me?"

"Your relation with him is a lateral one; as such, the Self-Renewal policy should be applicable. But then, it's only helpful if you were a big fish that escaped the dragnet. Well, you turned out to be not much of a big shot. Ha ha ha."

"Ha ha. Well excuse me that I am not a big fish!"

"But Yu-kun did not tell about you to take advantage of the Self-Renewal policy."

"How's that?" This was a different take from what Youde thought.

"I think Yu-kun brought up my affairs because he was lured by the Self-Renewal policy. Suppose, as a result of his informing, I was exposed to be a Communist and was captured, he would be saved from death, wouldn't he?

You know, paying back one's crime with merit. Don't you think that's what he had expected?"

Lin said with confidence, "I rather think his was a tactic to extend his life."

"Life-extending tactic?"

"You see, the only way people like Yu-kun and me can be saved is the upheaval in the international situation. In essence, it depends on whether we can stay alive until something happens, be it a military confrontation or a political upheaval. I know it is maybe only one in ten thousand chances that it will happen, but we must wait patiently."

"Speaking of a change in the military situation, do you think there's a chance that Communist China will attack Taiwan?"

"That's what I wanted to ask you, since you are the most recent arrival."

"I think it will be very difficult for them to do anything at least in the next few years. Especially since the signing of the U.S.–Sino Mutual Defense Treaty, I should think the possibility of a Communist attack is almost non-existent."

As soon as he said it, Youde knew he had disappointed Lin and regretted it. What bungling! Youde continued, "But the situation changes constantly. Maybe no military invasion will occur, but political changes are still possible. The Korean War has ended; but the Cold War nevertheless seems to escalate. The United States may want to help solve the 'Taiwan Problem' as a way to embrace the Communist Chinese."

"In my view, the United States is a totally unreliable country. Didn't the U.S. hand Taiwan over to the Chiang Kai-shek regime? Yet it closed its eyes to the February 28 massacre and keeps mum about the current dictatorship. The U.S. would acquiesce to any inhumane behavior under the excuse of anti-Communism."

"That may be so, but the United States is the only country that will stand up for international justice."

However, Lin had hung his hopes on a military solution, instead of a political one. He said, "As we while away our idle days here, Communist China is strengthening its military power. I think China will begin its attack as soon as the U.S. forces withdraw from Taiwan. It's true that they lack battle ships of their own, but they can borrow from the Soviet Union. And as soon as the Communist Chinese land on Taiwan, the battle would be over in a matter of days."

That was but Lin's wishful observation. "Should Taiwan ever become a battlefield, it would truly be a disaster," Youde thought.

The conversation doubled back to Yu-Kun. It seemed rather pointless for two people who had no access to newspapers or a radio to contemplate the developments of international affairs.

78

A Helplessly Nice Guy

Youde asked Lin, "I wonder where Yu-kun told them about me. I've thought maybe he did it during the interrogation by the investigative organizations."

"No, he informed on you while he was in the Military Court Prison. I'm sure about that. He never mentioned you during interrogation."

"In that case, you were in the next cell when he was writing his secret report to inform against me."

"That's right. I saw for sure that he was writing a report. Though he did not tell me the content nor did he mention your name, my sixth sense told me that he was informing on somebody."

"Did you watch his actions in silence?"

"I sort of warned him that he would come to regret it if he wrote some funny report. He immediately tore up the paper. After that, several times, he would write then tear it up, then write again. I think he agonized over it a great deal. Then, sometime later, he intuited that his time was almost up. Finally, he handed the report to the panchang."

At that very moment, the course of Youde's life changed. "Several days after he handed over the report, he secretly told me your name. That's the first I heard of you. Yu-kun told me that he had a friend from the old days by the name of Youde who was studying in America. He also said that you might not return home. I thought then that you were the most suitable candidate to be used in his life-extending tactic. Granted it was a cowardly, dirty trick and sure to cause you trouble, but by reporting you he could at least extend his life until your return, And, if it happened that you did not come home, his execution could be repeatedly put off until the matter reached some kind of closure."

At the time, not a few Taiwanese, having gone through stringent screening to be allowed to go abroad and having breathed the air of freedom, refused to return home and lived abroad.

Lin continued, "Soon after informing on you, Yu-kun was called up by Chiayi's investigation organization, and while there, I think he was questioned for one whole week about you. He never told anybody how he answered the questions. But I can sort of guess, so when he returned to the Military Court Prison after a week I gave him a piece of my mind. I predicted that Youde would be handcuffed the moment he stepped off the plane at the Sungshan airport and taken to Security Headquarters. As it happened, I was off the mark. The authorities left you free to roam so as to trap more victims — a malicious ploy, indeed."

"......"

"I also said that Youde would be sent to the Military Court in a month or six weeks. This part I guessed right."

"Yes. My arrest was on October 2, and I was sent to the Military Court Prison on November 8."

"On the other hand, suppose you had implicated others and the interrogation of these people somehow took longer than usual. Who knows, maybe it can take upward of one year."

"......"

"In any case, Yu-kun's life-extending tactic worked to a certain extent. If he hadn't sacrificed you, he might have been executed before you returned to Taiwan. Of course, it would be much better for his purpose if you had not returned."

"But, Youde, don't you hate Yu-kun? You've got plenty of reasons to do so."

"No," Youde replied instantly. "If it will help save Yu-kun's life, this is not too much of an ordeal for me to endure."

Those were Youde's true feelings. He desperately did not want Yu-kun to die. Youde told Lin about the chance encounter, about how on the day of his court appearance, he turned his head in response to Yu-kun calling his name, and that he had then shouted after Yu-kun, "I do not hate you."

"I see. I haven't heard that one. Maybe your shouting voice did not reach his ears, or, maybe what you said touched him so deeply that he did not want to relate it to anybody. For all we know, he may have wept over what you said to him."

After a brief silence, Lin put his hand on Youde's knee and said, "You really are a helplessly nice person. Youde, I would also like to have a friend like you."

Inexplicably, Lin's eyes shined with tears as he said it.

79

Favorite Songs

Youde and Lin knew a lot of songs in common. Adding Lai to make a threesome, they often sang together.

Lin's favorite song was an Indonesian folk song, "Bengawan Solo." Youde knew its Japanese words :

Bengawan Solo runs without end,
Unable to hear the ancient past.

Lin sang it in Indonesian and taught it to other inmates:

Bengawan Solo, riwajatmu ini,
Sedari dulu djadi perhatian insani.

The POWs preferred the Indonesian verse better than the Japanese version.

Lin said, "This is the song I would like you to sing for me when I am taken out to be executed."

Youde asked him, "I am impressed that you can sing in the original verse. When and where did you learn it?"

"I learned it in Indonesia when I was in the Japanese Navy.

You see, during the war, I enlisted as a Navy volunteer."

The so-called Taiwanese volunteers were in reality halfway conscripted to join.

"I learned this song when I was stationed in Indonesia for a time. Wherever we went in the South Pacific, people were singing this song. As we watched the young men and women dancing to the music under the shades of coconut trees, we couldn't believe that we were in a war."

Speaking of the Navy, Youde inexplicably thought of Ho, perhaps because he also spoke of the South Pacific.

"When I was being interrogated in the Chiayi station, a man by the name of Ho, also an ex-Navy man, was among the special agents there."

Youde told Lin about his dealings with Ho.

"He must be Ho Chih-mo. I've no doubt about it," Lin said with cockiness. "I heard that he had become a special agent. As I recall, I met him once in the Navy Club in Singapore. The guy and I were in the same class, as we were both corporals then. Others called him 'Ho the Lecher,' because he took advantage of the fact that he knew the language in Singapore and often procured women for his superiors, taking kickbacks sometimes."

"At first I thought he was a kind and considerate man. I even thanked him."

"No way. No kind person ever becomes a special agent. A person possessing even a smidgen of kindness can't last in that job. I am glad that you were not taken in by him."

Lai, who ordinarily listened quietly interjected, "The guy is probably taking advantage of his position and fooling around with women as we speak."

Lin changed the subject and asked Youde, "Do you by any chance know what songs Yu-kun likes to sing?"

"Hmm. He favored military marches. He also sang the march in *Aida* and the 'Drinking Song'. Among popular songs, we used to sing 'Under an Apple Tree,' 'Red Roses,' 'Inn by the Lake,' sometimes under the pomelo tree in my backyard."

Never again will we ever share happy times like that, Youde realized, pained by the thought.

"I don't know the name of the song, but do you remember this one?"

Lin sang the first few stanzas of the song.

"Nice song. But this is the first time I've heard it. I've never heard Yu-kun sing it."

"Well, maybe it's a song he picked up after his flight into the mountains. Anyway, he sings this song every day. We will probably see him off with this song when he is called out for execution."

Youde took out a pencil and a piece of paper and wrote down the words to the song:

Runs, runs, to no end,
The river of my longing;
In the moonlight,
Longing for your image,
I walk and walk.

The last two verses touched Youde's heart. A lone Yu-kun had walked the moonlit mountain path, remembering the "you" in the song. Who might the person of his longing be? Youde knew she was Wen-bang's sister Su-yun, and the image of a smiling, elegant woman came to his mind.

Did she know about Yu-kun's unrequited love for her? Did he ever confess his love to her? Or was he captured before he had a chance to do so? When did they last see each other? Although somewhat embarrassed to be conjecturing about others' affairs, Youde continued to contemplate: Yu-kun was a fugitive for five years and it had been two more years since his capture. So, their last meeting, if it did take place at all, would be at least seven years ago. And during all this time, Yu-kun had held fast to her image, which no doubt added a splash of color to the grayish life of a fugitive. And the image of her no doubt sometimes smiled at him and quietly talked to him. And in those moments, Yu-kun was not alone.

Each harboring his own thoughts, the three "sweet potatoes" sang the songs over and over, "Bengawan Solo" and Yu-kun's favorite song.

80

A Forerunner of the Independence Movement

ONE morning the inmates of Cell 2 were let outside to exercise, which was not a regularly scheduled routine. Instead, here in the Investigation Bureau, inmates were let out to the courtyard for exercise and bathing from time to time, on the spur of the moment.

On that morning, Youde was startled to notice a man of small build at one corner of the courtyard — a face he had seen before. The man was exercising in the nude under the still chilly sky of February. His trunk, lean with no body fat, looked firm. His expressionless face suggested unyielding courage.

"Who could he be?"

Youde tried to remember as he and his prison friends circled around the courtyard.

The man, oblivious to his surroundings and expressionless throughout, continued to swing his arms in silence. As hard as he tried, Youde was not able to place the man and since a plainclothes man was standing guard, it was not possible to speak to the man directly. Upon taking a closer look, Youde saw his shackled feet behind a large garden rock. A pretty important criminal for a serious crime, no doubt, Youde figured.

Youde lowered his voice and asked Lin the Bull about the man. Lin replied in a hushed voice, "I think he is Ko Kinan." Then, after circling another lap, Lin added, "he is from Putzu too."

So he was. The man was Huang Chi-nan (Ko Kinan in Japanese), a man Youde knew about but never met. Huang was from the village of Niutiaowan, a short distance from Putzu. Having gone to college, he was regarded as the number one intellectual of the village. Youde had heard that Huang, despite a promising future, had thrown himself into the Taiwan independence movement and ended up in jail.

"He looks familiar, probably because I've seen him around town in Putzu," Youde thought.

Now Huang Chi-nan started to roll his torso to and fro, then right to left. Youde noticed that he had a large, dark purplish bruise in the center of his back, a painful testament to torture.

Youde tried in vain to greet Huang and express his goodwill, but their eyes never met. Huang steadfastly fixed his eyes at one spot in space while he continued to exercise, not paying any heed to Youde and the rest.

Fifteen minutes soon passed. Huang was the first to be ushered inside. "He is probably in a solitary cell," Youde thought. Everybody watched as the shackled man clanked away. Soon, Youde and his fellow inmates were returned to the former crypt of a jail.

Youde asked Lin, "Has Huang been here long?"

"Let me see. He was here during my last stint in this joint. That makes it at least three years. Of course, he could have been to other places in between. I am sure he is from your hometown."

"You are right, but we are not acquainted, since he is about one generation older than me. What's more, he didn't live in town and he had already gone to Japan to study when my friends and I started school. He started the Taiwan independence movement in Japan with Liao Wen-yi, so he did not get anybody from Putzu in trouble. But his name is certainly well known."

When people in Taiwan were still intoxicated with the fine wine of Taiwan's restoration to the motherland, Huang had presciently, ahead of everybody else, given up hope on the KMT government, or rather, on the Chinese, and had advocated Taiwan's independence. In other words, he was the forerunner of the Taiwan independence movement.

Lin again said, "He is known as an eccentric."

"Is that so?"

"Some time ago, he was once thrown into the big room. I heard from his cellmate that he would not eat with the others. When everybody else sat in a circle and shared the foods from their care packages, he would stick to his own corner and eat his own food. They said he wouldn't talk to the others either."

"I wonder why. Might he be a loner?"

"No, he just wanted to draw a line between us and him. You see, he seems to be of the opinion that those of us who joined the Communist Party are bad guys, even though we are all fellow prisoners."

Come to think of it, Youde realized that all the inmates he had come across so far were in for Communism-related charges while none was imprisoned for engaging in the independence movement ... except for Huang. No wonder Huang had a hard time finding anybody to trust in prison.

Lin expressed his own point of view, "In my view, he and I are comrades. After all, we both worked and sacrificed ourselves in order to liberate the Taiwanese people from the corrupt government."

"I guess he is in solitary confinement and has nobody to talk to."

"I think so. Who knows, maybe he himself chose to be in the solitary cell."

Youde had a glimpse of Huang's persevering, uncompromising character, yet wondered if this same characteristic had also made his prison life doubly lonely and miserable.

Remembering the solitary figure that resolutely carried on his one-man exercise, Youde felt a strong pang of what you might call love for one's compatriot or townsfolk toward Huang.

Youde learned later that at this time Huang was already sentenced to death but his execution had been postponed in order to induce Liao Wen-yi, the leader of the Taiwan independence movement, to turn himself in.

81

A Middle-of-the-Night Happening

About a month later, Lin the Bull was finally called in for questioning. The POWs carried on as usual, totally unconcerned.

Ex-assistant chief Ma asked Youde, "Is he really a Communist?"

"I gather he really is. He himself admitted to be one."

"If he carried arms, he is going to get the death sentence."

"He knows that."

"How terrifying," Ma shook his head and shuddered.

Youde asked Ma in return, "Have you ever joined the Communist Party?"

"Absolutely not. If I had, I would have fled to the mainland a long time ago."

Youde thought: Indeed, quite a few mainland students at the Normal University fled fast enough to the mainland on the eve of the mass crackdown, after having recruited energetically and successfully many Taiwanese students into the Party. "Did they receive merit citations over there?" Youde wondered.

"Then why are you here?"

"The bureau chief by the name of Kung snitched on me. He told the authorities that I was in a study group while a middle school student. In fact, I showed up at the study group only once — something I had forgotten myself."

In mainland China, because of the shortage of published materials, all schools had so-called study groups in which people lent and borrowed books from each other or discussed what they read. Because the Communists made good use of study groups as their breeding grounds, the KMT government considered them to be Communist front organizations and censored them.

Conscious of its own failure to get control of the study groups while on the mainland, once in Taiwan, the KMT government ordered all KMT members to come clean with their past involvement with study groups. However, many did not turn themselves in. Some probably forgot; some may not have known for certain that they belonged to one. Still, others may have worried about the impact on future advancement and skipped, thinking nobody was going to know anyway. Ma may well have been among the ones who forgot.

"Did you not get along with Chief Kung?"

"In the beginning we did, both being from the mainland. Some people even said we were like brothers. But then he started to be suspicious of me. He suspected that I kept the monthly red envelopes (bribe money) from the 'special class business' (prostitution) to myself. He was mad, thinking that I was getting all the gravy; and gradually our relationship went sour."

"Didn't he also receive the monthly red envelopes?"

"Of course. It's the custom."

"What custom! We never had such a custom in Taiwan before the Restoration," Youde thought.

"He held a grudge that I did not give him his cut."

"But isn't it also a custom to pay tribute to one's superior?"

"It's not like I didn't pay him his share at all. I had my principle, which was that I would accept the red envelopes that came my way but would not go around myself, nor order my subordinate, to collect them. That's why I had a good reputation among the businesses. That's not a lie. So I did not pay tribute to Kung regularly every month. That's the underlying cause. Then, at a banquet, emboldened by a few drinks, I criticized him to his face. He grinned and listened at the time, but later he immediately started to check into my background to find any fault he could. One month later he told the authorities that I had a 'thought problem.' He made it sound like he had to sacrifice friendship for the sake of greater good. What a dangerous, scheming man he is. You know, he continued to smile at me at work even after he had snitched on me. We northerners could never be as two-faced as those southerners."

"Did they have evidence?"

"No evidence really. But they had a witness, a classmate of mine from middle school, who testified that I was a member of the study group."

"Is that true?"

"I admitted that I did attend the study group, but only once. Well, that was enough to get me thrown in here. I don't know why my case has not been sent to the prosecution yet, since I am done appearing in court for questioning. I am worried that there's going to be more to this."

"No. You don't necessarily get sent to prosecution immediately after court appearance; in fact, it takes about a month usually," Youde tried to ease Ma's mind.

Just as the conversation was coming to a close, Lin returned. He was calm enough but appeared dispirited.

"How did it go?" Youde and Lai showed their concern.

Lin replied quietly, "It was nothing."

Lin did not say much. He relieved himself, promptly returned to his seat, then rolled onto his back and closed his eyes as if he were very tired.

That same day, in the dead of the night, a loud scream, "Ah —," roused Youde and his cellmates from their sleep. It came from Ma.

"What happened?" Lai who slept next to Ma asked.

"Oh boy, I'm glad it was just a dream. I dreamt that I was being executed by a firing squad."

"Is that all?" many muttered.

Youde rolled to his other side and turned his eyes to Lin's bed. Lo and behold, Lin was sitting, leaning against the wall still with his eyes closed, seemingly to have not heard Ma's scream at all. Straining under the dim, naked light bulb, Youde saw traces of tears on his cheeks. And in his hand, Lin was holding unmistakably the picture of his daughter — the picture of the smiling Ah-bi with a pageboy haircut holding a jump rope in her hand. How long had Lin been sitting like that? Obviously, it was since before Ma's scream. It seemed that Lin had gotten up in the middle of the night to stare at his daughter's picture.

82

A Request to Confront the Accuser

At last, Youde was called up for questioning. A guard led Youde up the stairs to a sealed room that was lit dimly by a light bulb in the middle of the day.

Two men in Sun Yat-sen suits entered the room, one in navy and another in khaki. The latter carried a thick stack of documents that looked like investigation folders on Youde.

The two men ordered Youde to sit across from their desk. Going through the documents, the man in navy did the questioning while the man in khaki recorded. Again, they went over the same ground, starting from the beginning. Since there had been no new developments, there were no new questions either. This being his fourth time, Youde answered the questions fluently. The questioning was pro-forma, though tiresome, and Youde was quickly put at ease. Again, the only answer to deviate from his confession was the part about *Mao Wenchi*. Youde denied what was in the confession and insisted that he never had the book at his house. Youde was rather prepared for some sharp follow-up questions, but the man in navy merely drew deeply on his cigarette and said nothing. However, the man in khaki, the recorder, put down his pen and leaned back in his chair.

Youde said to the two men with a determined expression, "Please let me confront the person who said the book was in my house."

The man in navy signaled with his eyes to the man in khaki, who straightened himself up and added something into the record.

The questioning abruptly ended.

When Youde returned to his cell, Lin said to him, "That was short, only about two hours. It must have gone well."

Youde recounted to Lin what had happened in the questioning and told him about the request to confront Yu-kun.

Lin laughed out loud as he said, "Yu-kun has no face to face you. I doubt if he would say that the book was there when it comes to face-to-face confrontation with you. But your request for confrontation could drag this out some more; and if in the meantime the political situation changes, who knows...."

Youde's heart was lightened like a patient after an operation. He was done with all the terrifying, disgusting parts of the ordeal. As the saying goes, "Do all one can and wait for the heavenly edict." From now on, the only thing left was to wait for sentencing.

Lin said, "When I get back to the Military Court Prison, I will tell Yu-kun about you. He'll be happy to hear that you don't hate him at all. But it also looks like his case is coming to a close. I reckon he will be executed as soon as the face-to-face with you takes place. Actually, I don't think they will allow the confrontation."

Then on April 1, April Fool's Day, the time came for Lin to go back to the Military Court Prison. His final struggle appeared to have failed. After shaking each cellmate's hand to say goodbye, Lin squeezed Youde's hand hard and said, "I don't think I'll see you again."

Ignoring the guards' urging and still holding on to Youde's hand, Lin tried to say something but then swallowed it, and finally said only, "Take care."

Obviously, he had wanted to ask Youde to look after his daughter. Youde nodded his head deeply and said, "Yes, I understand. Don't worry about little Ah-bi."

"Thank you."

Lin the Bull dropped his bundle abruptly, took a step forward and crushed Youde in his embrace.

83

Return to the Old Nest

On April 10, following Lin, Youde was transferred back to the Military Court Prison from the Investigation Bureau. Arriving at the prison office about four in the afternoon, he was taken back to the old nest, Cell 7, after a two-month absence.

"Tsai Youde is back."

The message spread ahead of him.

By the time Panchang Teng unlocked the cell door, his cellmates were waiting at the door.

"Welcome back."

Youde had barely kicked off his shoes, when he was half picked up and dragged to the wooden floor. It was apparent at once that the number of people in the cell had decreased. The room felt empty.

"Where's Little Lu?" These were the first words out of Youde's mouth.

There was no Little Lu to be found.

"Oh no." Youde looked toward Liu and Kao.

After a moment of silence, Liu opened his mouth.

"Little Lu was executed about a week ago."

No wonder the air in the cell was leaden.

Ex-policeman Wu said, "This government kills even children without mercy. He was only thirteen when it happened. No law as cruel as this exists anywhere else in the world."

Looking around the cell again, Youde asked, "Chou Shui the woodcutter too?"

Liu replied, "Yes, he was taken soon after you left here."

Wu added, "He walked out of here calmly with a lot of dignity. Really impressive."

Youde recalled the composed Chou Shui standing still like a wax figure.

"Then Chen Shih the man-child too?"

"Yes, he was sentenced to six years. His had the shortest sentence among the people involved in the Luku case."

Wu added the footnote, "It was after Chou Shui was taken out. Chen went out bawling."

"Mori too?"

"Yes. After Chou Shui left, Mori's case was decided. Just like he predicted, he got ten years. He left happily. That's the lightest sentence under Article 4. He was transferred to the military prison in Hsintien. He and Little Lu hugged and cried when he left."

Wu said, "Ten years. He made it just under the wire. Remember how he was going to sign the divorce papers if he got more than ten years? Ten is not more than ten, right?"

Kao said, "He was here for two years and three months. So, subtracting that, ten years is reduced to less than eight years. His wife should be able to wait that long. First of all, she didn't say anything about divorce anyway."

Youde again looked at Liu and Kao, "Was Little Lu's brother taken on the same day?"

"Of course. Ten petacos came that day and took five to the execution yard in one fell swoop."

Youde pained for Little Lu's parents who lost two sons at the same time.

Some say, "In the whole world, pity most the mother of the sweet-potatoes." How true.

Shen the public scribe soon went back to his seat, sat himself down in a Zen position, and started to mumble something — perhaps to pray for Little Lu and Chou Shui's happiness in the netherworld. According to Liu, Shen spent almost all his waking hours in Zen meditation ever since Little Lu's execution.

Youde took out his mug and placed it in its rightful place and hoisted his bundle on the shelf.

Wu said, "This week especially, we were getting lonely, with four fewer people including the ever-talkative Mori. So it's just great to get you back. Of course, I don't mean to imply that you are a chatterbox, ha ha."

Liu described the way Little Lu went out. "When the flush-faced Panchang Teng came to get him, blood did drain from Little Lu's face. But his two eyes were fearless, burned with anger.

"'You, Baldy (nickname of Chiang Kai-shek), so you are going to kill us both. I pity my mother.' He stomped the floor and cried with resentment, then shouted to us, 'Avenge me!' But when we started singing 'We Are Like the Burning Fire of Youth' in unison, he reclaimed his composure and walked out with his head high."

"He was impressive," Wu praised.

"I almost forgot, there's something for you." Liu reached up on the shelf and handed Youde a small package wrapped in paper.

"Little Lu had instructed me to give this to you when the time came for him to go. So when I cleared out his belongings after he was gone, I kept this for you."

Little Lu's vocabulary book fell out of the opened package, the vocabulary book that he had meticulously kept for four years, packed from cover to cover with small handwritten words. "It was all in vain after all," Youde screamed inside. Large drops of tears fell from Youde's eyes.

"He left a parting instruction."

Liu took out an envelope from which he withdrew a piece of paper that he handed to Youde.

It was a parting note to everybody, written in Little Lu's own hand. It contained the unpretentious, childlike anger that was Little Lu.

"Knock down the bronze statue of Baldy in front of my grade school's lobby. Let them worship him if they want. But let the people who want to spit or piss on it, spit and piss on it."

84

Message from the Next Cell

THE best thing about settling back in at the Military Court Prison was to be able to correspond with home again. Youde immediately wrote a letter to his wife the next morning and let her know that he was all right — the first correspondence in two months.

Unaccountably, Youde was distracted by Cell 3, so he asked Wu, "There seems to be fewer people in Cell 3 too."

"You are right. The bucktoothed judge turned informer was taken out by the petacos. That was great. I heard that he did everything to beg for his life to be spared, like writing report after report to exonerate himself, but nothing came of it. Ha ha. I wish I could show you the way that guy went out of here. He bawled like a baby, with a drippy nose yet. Nobody sang any song, as if we had agreed in advance. He killed people like they were dogs, so he was killed like a dog. It's only justice."

Liu said, "I wonder if he would be lauded as a patriot over in the Chinese mainland. What a twisted world this is. He was probably put up in the memorial hall together with the people he had sent to be killed. Do you think his victims will keep quiet? How strange."

"Ha ha," Wu laughed as he said, "If it were me, I would push him out of the memorial hall."

Youde glanced at Cell 3 again. He couldn't see the Bucktooth, but his eyes met those of messenger Sung.

"Hey you," Sung motioned for Youde to come close.

"It's from Lin Jin-so the bull. The message actually came the day before you got here, but I didn't want to bother you last night since the message didn't seem urgent. The message said that a navy Sun Yat-sen suit came to the Military Court Prison and called out Yu-kun for questioning. Lin said to tell you that there's no more need for a face-to-face confrontation with Yu-kun."

No need for a face-to-face would mean Yu-kun had agreed with Youde's side of the story. Yu-kun might have acknowledged that he said he saw *Mao Wenchi* at Youde's house out of faulty memory, or out of jealousy — some plausible reason to refute his own previous statement. Or might he have told them the truth and admitted to his life-extending ploy?

In any case, there was no mistake that Yu-kun had made statements favorable to Youde.

The two months spent at the Investigation Bureau were not a waste after all, and it was not a mistake to persevere and fight for an answer he could accept. If Youde could have just pushed the thought of Little Lu out of his mind, he probably would have broken into happy song.

Sung added some welcome words, "In general, re-education is thought to be for three years. But the law on that is not in black and white. If things go well, your re-education term can be reduced to one year. Though according to the Bucktooth, there hasn't been anyone sentenced to re-education who actually got a reduced term."

As Youde thanked him and was retreating from the front wall, Sung asked, "Do you know a person by the name of Peng Chung-cheng?"

"Peng Chung-cheng? Hmm. Oh, yes. I know him," Youde replied. A name about to fade from Youde's memory, Peng was Dragon-head Peng, a mainlander, at the Taipei Police Battalion.

"He was executed last month for a two-man case. I heard that he was quite a stand-up guy."

"Yes. What's more, he was kind. He did a lot for me. Now that's a genuine Communist patriot."

"He's the one who sent us the message of your arrest back then."

"That makes sense."

Youde told everybody about Peng's affairs and prayed for his happiness in the netherworld.

Time spent with Dragon-head Peng seemed like from the long ago past. Counting on his fingers, Youde figured that it had been six months since parting with Peng.

85

Prison Divorce

The letter from Youde's wife arrived. Surprisingly, nobody else got letters that day. Perhaps writing became infrequent after a few years because one was only allowed to correspond once a month.

A photograph was enclosed with the letter, showing his wife seated and daughter Ah-jing standing beside her. Ah-jing's expression seemed to say "Papa, chi-lin, chi-lin." It tugged at Youde's heart. His wife's pregnancy was apparent now, in the seventh month she said. I guess I will receive the news of the birth in the re-education center. For sure, I can't be by her side when the time comes, Youde thought. He realized and hated the devil's hand that blocked happiness by breaking up a perfectly happy family. Yet his sentence was the lightest among all the inmates and the mark of envy for all. Youde recalled Lin the Bull staring at his daughter's picture in the dead of the night. What did a man faced with certain death feel when he stared at his daughter's picture? Youde sighed.

Youde passed the letter and the picture around for all to see.

Wu examined the picture carefully and said, "Hmm, I think my old lady got a big belly too. Ha ha. Usually when an inmate learned of wife's pregnancy, others are suspicious. Ha ha. Mr. Tsai, you are so fortunate because you know for sure she's carrying your own seed."

"Does your wife still write to you?" Youde asked Wu.

"No, not since last month and probably will never again. Besides, she is not allowed to write to me anymore because she is no longer family. She's become a total stranger since last month."

"So you are divorced."

"Yes. After Mori left, I finally made up my mind. Anyway, I am probably going to get fifteen years, so I thought through a lot from her point of view and signed the divorce papers. It's what you call a prison divorce. I think it's best for the baby about to be born. On my part too, I felt the burden lifted."

"Don't you have a child?"

"Ya. When I left, he was but this little, but he is going to school now. She promised over and over again that she would do a good job bringing up the kid."

Shen the public scribe interjected, "Wu here still carefully keeps all the letters she wrote him, even though he used to get mad every time a letter arrived. Prison divorces just can't be helped." Shen shook his head.

Wu laughed and said, as if discussing somebody else's affairs, "From now on I am relying on that other Wu, the special agent, to love and care for both my wife and son. Ha ha ha."

86

Chou Shui's Mother

One day, Liu said to Youde, "A story about woodcutter Chou Shui's mother and the villagers of Luku is circulating around here."

"I don't know if it's all true, but the story started on the day Chou Shui was executed, so I don't think it's all made up."

With that preface Liu related the story.

"I think it was February 16. Sixteen petacos appeared and took eight out in one fell swoop: all the inmates from Luku, including Chou Shui. The day happened to be a Wednesday, a day to submit care packages. Maybe a little bird told them, but the families from Luku, with bananas in their hands, arrived at the Military Court Prison earlier than usual. As was their custom, they often came in a group despite the arduous journey and despite the fact that they were not allowed to see their loved ones.

I guess it made them feel better just to be near their husbands or their sons. I was told that sometimes some of them would yell the names of their husbands or sons over the high wall.

On that day, the group, consisting of women, old men and children, was stopped at the main gate, because precisely at that moment their very husbands and sons were being read the death sentence in the courtroom. The villagers had no way of knowing that, but somebody spotted two military trucks with the flaps down parked in the middle of the courtyard and sounded an alert. The Luku villagers had gone through a few group executions by this time, so they were tipped off by the trucks right away. Terrified and shaking with fear, and while battling the guards who chased them away, they repeatedly swarmed back to the gate to look inside. The guards called for help and additional guards came. Eventually, the villagers were not able to go near the gate."

Youde could almost hear the snarling voices of the guards.

"But when the military trucks revved up their engines, the villagers broke through the guards' line and ran toward the courtyard. Oblivious to the guards' threats, they fought off hands that grabbed at their arms and legs and ran with desperation."

Youde pictured them dashing, crazed, while crying out the names of their husbands and sons.

"Several of them made it inside the gate. Chou Shui's mother was one of them. They fell to the ground, panting for breath."

Liu's voice choked. He paused before he continued, "Then, when they raised their heads, what they saw was none other than their beloved husbands and sons whom they hadn't seen in several years. And what they heard were the voices calling for their mothers and loved ones 'Ah-bu,'(mother) 'Ah —' And right in front of their very eyes, their sons and husbands, their hands tied to their backs with heavy ropes and a chan-pan stuck in the middle of their backs, were fighting to struggle free from the MP's hold." Liu choked again.

Youde could imagine Chou Shui's mother extending her hands while calling "Ah-tsui, my son!" and Chou Shui calling "Ah-bu!" desperately trying to struggle free of the MP's grasp to approach his mother. Was she able to rise from the ground? Or did she crawl toward her son? How she must have wanted to run up to him and embrace him!

"The guards and MPs working together succeeded in suppressing the villagers and loaded the husbands and sons, one by one, onto the truck, right in front of the flailing and screaming villagers."

Youde thought to himself: The wailing and screaming must have reverberated in the open sky of Chingtao East Road, and the people working in the offices must have stopped their work and watched from the windows. That's why the story spread on that very day.

"The MPs lowered the flaps, cutting off the line of vision connecting the villagers to their loved ones. The trucks passed in front of the villagers, leaving puffs of black smoke. The villagers again pushed away the guards' hands and rose to chase after the trucks. The trucks went through the front gate, turned south on Chingtao East Road and headed toward the Hsintien execution yard.

The villagers chased after the trucks, half-crazed, even after the trucks had disappeared from view."

Youde could imagine how they must have stumbled, then got up to run, run and stumbled again. Their faces and clothes a muddy mess, their arms and legs covered with scratches oozing with blood.

Replaying the scene in each of their minds, nobody so much as even cleared his throat. The room was silent.

"We haven't heard what happened to them after that. But a story circulated about Chou Shui's mother."

"Oh? What is that?"

"When exhausted and collapsed on the roadside, she was helped by a kind passerby. And it was said that despite scratches all over her body and barely conscious, in her hand...."

Liu continued with tears in his eyes, "In her hand, she still clutched the bare, broken banana stems."

87

A Friend of the Bull

ONE morning during the daily outing for bathing and walking, just as Youde squatted in front of the water tank to splash some water over his body, Zong, a fellow inmate of Hakka extraction, came to Youde's side.

"Do you see the guy in blue pants over there?"

Looking up, Youde saw a man standing uneasily cradling his washbasin. Conspicuously, he still had his pants on, unlike everybody else, who had stripped stark naked. He was obviously a newcomer. Youde couldn't help breaking into a grin thinking about his own first few days here.

"He just arrived yesterday. That means he was in the East Penyuan Temple at the same time you were there."

Zong beckoned the man with a hand gesture and the man came over right away. Youde and Zong moved over some to either side to make room between them for the newcomer. The newcomer's name was Kuan. He was a native of Chungli and was also a Hakka. He said that while he was in East Penyuan Temple he was housed in the east wing of the prison, opposite where Youde's cell was. Since the Investigation Bureau followed the practice of housing people involved in the same case in separate wings even more strictly than in the Military Court Prison, inmates from the east and west wings were never to lay eyes on each other, let alone exchange words.

Youde's was a one-man case, so no one in the east wing was connected to him. Youde decided to ask about Lin the Bull's case.

"Were there people implicated by Lin Jin-so living in the east wing?"

"Yes," the newcomer Kuan answered, while shooting side glances at the guard, "a man called Huang Ching-tien in my cell."

Because they only talked when the guard was not watching, the conversation was stop and go.

"What kind of person is he?"

"He is the second in command at the Agricultural Laboratory. He is very mad that Lin has dragged him into this. 'A coward,' he called Lin."

"I see."

To be "dragged in" meant being informed upon. The uncompromising Lin who once said, "That's where I am different from Yu-kun," had informed on some innocent man.

"You mean you roomed with Lin but didn't know about this?" Zong said to Youde incredulously.

One could say that Lin had put his life-extending tactic into practice by falsely accusing his friend Huang Ching-tien of being a Communist, thus betting his life on the time it would take for the authorities to investigate this new wrinkle. This is what he meant by his final struggle, Youde clearly realized. It was a struggle to buy time.

"But Huang Ching-tien was let go within four months, without any charge," Kuan said.

Youde contemplated: There were precious few precedents in which people were let go scot-free after being called in by the Investigation Bureau. Huang's freedom could only come from Lin recanting his previous statement in court. Had Lin had enough of his own life-extending tactic and given it up without reservation?

"Did the two of them face each other in court?" Youde asked.

"Yes, they did. That's when Lin's false accusation was revealed." Kuan obviously took his roommate's side.

Youde remembered Lin coming back from court that day saying curtly, "It was nothing." By that, he probably meant "It didn't turn into a problem."

"You know what they say, 'One feels compassion for a person one meets face to face.' The Bull opened a road to life for him." Zong, who knew something about the way intelligence organizations operated, was not totally unsympathetic to Lin.

"I am glad Huang was able to go home," Youde said.

"But you know what?" Kuan said. "He was worried that this episode would interfere with his future advancement."

"What a pathetic guy," Zong spat out his words.

Huang apparently left here hating Lin and concerned about his own future prosperity.

When the guard pointed a finger at them and warned them not to talk, the three left the water tank, put on their underwear, and switched to walking around the yard.

As they walked, Youde remembered Lin had once said, "I, too, would like to have a friend like you," and understood what the teary glint in Lin's eyes meant.

The whistle sounded, sending everybody back to the cells.

Thoughts about Lin occupied Youde for the rest of the day. Even at night, he lay awake for a long time:

Lin was certainly different from Yu-kun in that he implicated no one, except for Huang Ching-tien, who entered the stage rather late in the game. The dark, purplish bruise attested to Lin's integrity. Nevertheless, he used Huang as a means of his final struggle when the time to face death was near. Naturally, Lin was a coward in Huang's view. Why did he not persevere to the end? Many people would agree with Huang.

But only a person who is not in Lin's shoes can make such an argument, something only the audience of a play can say.

Youde mulled it over in his mind:

The general theater public never truly sees the hero behind the actor. What they usually see is just the actor who plays the role — a beautified human image instead of a real-life person. The person who dies heroically on the stage is not the character himself but rather what the actor impersonates. After the play is over, the actor washes off his makeup and goes home to a cold beer or to contemplate where he will take his daughter the next day. This is why an actor can act out death scenes with such moving beauty. Is it not too much to ask a real flesh-and-blood person to be like the hero in a play?

Youde replayed the scene of Lin staring at his daughter's picture in the dead of the night. It was apparent that Lin decided on the course of his final struggle after he received Ah-bi's picture and learned of her existence. Youde felt for Lin. How long and hard Lin must have stared at little Ah-bi before he was able to make up his mind. Maybe he reneged later, but then looked at the picture again and decided anew to go through with it. Internal struggle probably more aptly describes Lin's final struggle.

In any case, the curtain had come down on Lin's final struggle. What was left was only to wait for execution day. The upheaval in the international situation that Lin had hoped for was unlikely to happen.

88

Lin the Bull, Covered in Blood

One morning, the feared words again arrived: "Two petacos are here."

As usual, the exercise period was suspended. The arrival of two petacos meant somebody involved in a one-man case was to be executed.

Who could that be? Youde felt tense. No one can feel absolutely safe as long as one is in this prison.

"Is it going to be the Bull?" Shen guessed.

Youde rejected Shen's suggestion. "No, Lin's is a three-man case, so all three would be put to death at one time. There would be six petacos for that."

Liu said, "Youde, you may not know it, but the other two in Lin's case have already been executed — about three months ago. As a matter of fact, it was the day after you went to the Investigation Bureau. Only the Bull was separated out into so called 'other case' and subsequently sent to the Investigation Bureau."

That made it precisely ten days after Lin's transfer to the Investigation Bureau when his two comrades were executed. The judge must have anticipated that Lin's "other case" would take some time to resolve, so he singled out Lin from the group and executed the other two as scheduled. So Huang Ching-tien did play a role in extending Lin's life for at least three months. Had Lin bit onto Huang like a crazed dog and not let go, the case could have dragged on a lot longer, just as the judge had predicted. As it happened, it appeared that Lin nevertheless couldn't go through with it. Perhaps facing Huang in court brought forth human sympathy.

On the other hand, the unknowing Huang might have faced Lin with hatred or even berated him to his face, ignorant of the fact that Lin's one word could have changed his destiny. Lin never mentioned a word about Huang Ching-tien to Youde; and Youde, sensing Lin's reluctance, never asked him about it.

At last the intelligence report arrived.

"It's the Bull from the West Area."

"So it is he." Many sighs followed.

"Youde," Wu said as he padded Youde's shoulder, "Do not get too worked up, OK? It's not you."

"My face must be taut with tension," Youde realized. Though having known each other for only two months, Lin was more than a mere friend. Rather, he was someone Youde had shared twenty-four hours a day with and had opened his heart to. To Youde, Lin's execution was not entirely somebody else's affair.

"Bengawan Solo riwajatmu ini," Youde started the song he learned from Lin.

Youde's cellmates quickly joined in. They sang in Indonesian, as Youde had previously taught them the Indonesian verses using Japanese Kana.

Fellow inmates from other cells, also knowing this was Lin's favorite song, started singing it, some in Indonesian, some in Japanese. The singing of "Bengawan Solo" surged ever wider and louder until it reverberated in the entire prison like a torrent.

But the word of Lin leaving his cell was late in coming. Just as everybody began to wonder, the third intelligence report arrived.

"Lin is refusing to leave his cell."

It seemed when the panchang came to order him out for execution, Lin had refused and didn't move an inch.

Youde recalled what Lin had once said to him, something Lin threw in nonchalantly when they were chatting: "Why? Why does everybody allow themselves to be led like lambs to the execution yard?"

Youde thought then that Lin had meant "Why not take the stance of final resistance?" And now he was carrying out his promise. What's going to happen? Nobody knew, as there had been no precedent.

"The guards from our area rushed over there to help," words came from inmates in the cell closest to the entrance.

The singing of "Bengawan Solo" stopped in mid-air.

The unbearable tension spread from the West Area to the East Area, wave by wave.

Youde tried to conjure up Lin engaged in his final resistance: Where in the cell is he standing? The swarm of guards must be all over the corridors on

LIN THE BULL, COVERED IN BLOOD 319

either side of the cell. Is he pacing the room? Or is he standing leaning against the cell partition? Did he block the door with the *matung*? Is he holding any weapon in his hand? What are his cellmates doing? They certainly are not in a position to come to Lin's aid.

Time ticked away minute by minute.

"The guards rushed back to fetch bamboo poles," another report arrived.

"What are they going to do with the bamboo poles?" the inmates discussed among themselves. Are they going to poke the poles into the cell to beat him? Or are they going to constrain his movement by sticking a lot of poles into his cell?

Ex-policeman Wu came up with a likely answer, "They are going to attach a rope to the end of the pole and try to lasso him down, then once his movement is restricted, they will jump into the cell to suppress him."

Of course. That's an ancient trick the Taiwanese used to capture a pig. Youde now pictured Lin fighting on like a beast in a cage.

The fourth intelligence report arrived.

"Lin is covered with blood from head to toe and is not able to keep his eyes open."

Did his head crack open and blood squirt out? He must be glaring and staring down the guards as he wipes away the blood smarting his eyes.

Unexpectedly, the singing of "Bengawan Solo" again surged in the prison building. To cheer him on with his favorite song was all they could do. His prison friends from the West Area, who could only watch and swallow their pain, must also be singing his song, Youde imagined. What irony that a song that serenades the peaceful pastoral scenes is accompanying this incredible life and death struggle. The song seemed out of place yet entirely appropriate.

Two whole hours passed.

At last, the forgone conclusion came from the West Area.

"Lin was suppressed and roped."

From this point on, one after another in quick succession, intelligence reports came from the cell next to the entrance.

"The prison servants from our side rushed over to the West entrance to view the Bull's exit."

Youde could almost hear the guards hollering to stop the servants from crowding the entrance.

"The two guards came back, mouthing "Bastards!" and entered their room to take off the bloodied clothes."

"Lin's blood," Youde thought.

"The two guards are putting iodine on the broken skins of their arms and legs."

"One of the servants came back. He said the Bull looked like a bloodied Chin-kang, the 'Hercules' of Taiwanese folklore."

"Another servant returned and said Lin was bound in ropes and carried out of his cell. Lin is no longer resisting."

"Lin is being shackled, still barefoot."

"Lin is being dragged toward the main gate. He is surrounded by guards and MPs so I can't see him very well."

"A guard is pressing a piece of cloth on Lin's head as he walked alongside Lin."

The blood must still be flowing from the top of his head. Are they going to take him straight to the court like that? They wondered.

Later in the afternoon of the same day, further news about Lin eventually arrived. Lin was first taken to the infirmary, where they washed away the blood and wrapped his head in bandages, then he was taken to the court still wearing his bloodied clothes and was stood in front of the judge while two guards supported him from either side. And when the judge was reading the decision, Lin had, pouring his body and soul into his voice, railed, "Pigs! Pigs!"

Youde's thoughts were filled with Lin that day. But when night fell, his thoughts turned to another friend, Yu-kun.

"That's right, Yu-kun lives next door to Lin, so he watched Lin's saga from the closest vantage point. How does he feel? Come to think of it, my case is about to be concluded. That means Yu-kun does not have many days left to live."

89

Shen's Verdict

Finally, Shen the public scribe was called to receive the court's decision. He came back within an hour bearing his court decision papers.

"I got ten years," Shen said without much expression and showed the papers to everyone.

The essence of the decision said:

> "The accused Shen Shih-kai was previously found to harbor left-leaning, impure thoughts and was sent to the re-education center. While there, he made and displayed a flag of the rebel regime in an attempt to enhance the morale of his Communist comrades. Thereby, we found the accused having engaged in behavior beneficial to the bandit Party and he shall be sentenced to a prison term of ten years."

"This for merely patching up a cracked plate glass window with paper stars!" Youde thought indignantly. "One would think this a monstrous, ridiculous joke, if it were not for the fact that Shen was standing in front of everyone with the decision in his hand.

To imagine the mustached Shen, a man looked to be cautiousness personified, cutting out star shaped papers is to bring smiles to everyone's face. What rebellious intention!

Back in the re-education center when someone pointed out that the patched window resembled a five-star flag, Shen should have smashed the plate glass to smithereens; then there would be no photograph to stand as evidence against him.

Still holding the decision paper, Shen's expression was ominous.

"Congratulations!" Liu slapped Shen on the shoulder suddenly and said.

"It's good. This puts an end to it," Kao said, half trying to comfort Shen, half feeling envious. "Take away the time you've spent during the investigation and the time in the Military Court Prison awaiting decision, ten years becomes less than eight. Mr. Shen, you get to go home in eight years! I am rather envious. As you know, I am one of the permanently unsentenced."

Wu chimed in, "These permanently unsentenced, like Liu and Kao, even though convinced of their innocence, are still terrified every time the petacos show up. They would gladly take ten-year terms, as they said themselves. Mr. Shen, don't you think you can be happy about the decision?"

Suddenly, Shen slammed the decision paper on the floorboard and said, "Damn it! This is an absurdity. How can I be happy about that!"

His face twisted in anger, Shen turned and fixed his eyes in a spot in space.

Having studied Zen, Shen ordinarily appeared wise and dispassionate. But once misfortune fell on him personally, he proved to be unable to contain his anger after all.

The next morning, Shen said goodbyes and left Cell 7, which had been his home for the past sixteen months. Thus, the Military Court Prison on Chingtao East Road had one less inmate, while the Military Prison of Ankang of Hsintien added one.

Kao said, "I had a nightmare last night."

"What about? You were moaning about something," Wu asked.

"I dreamt that this place was deserted. You were not here, neither was Mr. Tsai. The cells on either side were empty too. And there was no panchang, no guards, no servants. The two of us — I mean Liu and I — were left in this terrifyingly silent space. When I hollered 'Hey!' only echoes of 'Hey!' 'Hey!' bounced back, and still nobody came. Liu and I ran around and around the cell and continued to cry for help, 'Hey, help!' Then I was awakened by my own voice. Boy, was I relieved."

"Hmm," Wu nodded, "something like that may actually happen. Of course, it won't be just the two of you. Still, just the people in your case will be left here."

Liu said, "Should we say 'be forgotten,' rather than 'be left?'"

Now that only four people were left to occupy the cell, the room appeared spacious and empty. After supper they kept to the routine and walked around and around the room for exercise; but loneliness dogged them. Singing, half-hearted at best, did not help either; it merely amplified the emptiness.

Youde noticed that every cell had lost about half its inmates compared to when he first came. Were the authorities executing the political prisoners with more dispatch in order to get back at the Chinese Communists for the rising tension in the international situation? Or was it because the new addition to the Hsintien prison had been completed? Or was it because a new prison administrator had sharply increased efficiency? Nobody knew the reason.

Nevertheless, the fact that there were more people going out than coming in clearly indicated that the government's political terrorism had succeeded in drastically reducing the ranks of dissidents, who turned cautious in their speech as well as actions.

90

An Old Taiwanese Communist

As if taking Shen's place, a balding man in his fifties came to Youde's cell. Instead of a cloth-wrapped bundle, he had a rolled-up blanket slung over his shoulder that contained his toiletries. His calm demeanor betrayed the air of an old-timer and his seemingly gentle, narrow eyes shone with sharpness.

With no forethought, Wu instinctively addressed him as *senpai*, a respectful Japanese term for someone who is one's senior in school, on a job, or in the same profession.

He was clearly the oldest in terms of age.

"Ojisan, this way please." Liu tried to turn over the dragonhead seat to the newcomer, but the newcomer declined.

After putting down his blanket roll in the last available seat, he introduced himself.

"I am Chang Chao-chih, a native of the Tataocheng district of Taipei. How do you do?"

Tataocheng was a well-known, old neighborhood of Taipei.

But it was rather rare to find a Taipei native among the political prisoners, as most people of this capital city busied themselves with making money during the day and seeking fun at night and were largely apathetic to politics. Mr. Chang was the first Taipei native among the numerous political prisoners Youde had met so far.

Liu introduced the inmates of Cell 7 to Chang, and one by one Chang shook their hands.

"I can see you are all here without just cause," Chang said and continued to introduce himself. "I am what you would call an 'old Taiwanese Communist.'

You see, I joined the Japanese Communist Party as a young man. Though I did not go to college and was not a learned man, I sure was active running around in various localities as a Taiwan local operative for the Party. Once, I even got to meet Tokkyu, short for Tokuda Kyuichi. I worked my heart out. In fact, I was quite prepared to sacrifice my life for the sake of the proletariat. I was young then and idealistic. I didn't think it was particularly hard work either."

"What did you do after the Taiwan Restoration?" Liu asked.

"When the Restoration took place, we too rejoiced. At the time, we Taiwanese Communists had to fight oppression on two fronts. First, there was the oppression of the colonial Taiwanese by Imperial Japan. Then there was the oppression of the proletariat by the capitalists. With the Restoration, we were glad that we were at least liberated from one of the oppressions. But at the same time, since our nationality changed we were severed from the Japanese Communist Party. Of course the Japanese Party by then could hardly take care of themselves in the aftermath of Japan's defeat and had totally forgotten about us.

"Still, I say the Japanese Communists were far luckier than we because they were able to openly engage in political activities. You know a Communist by the name of Katayama even became the prime minister later on.

"On the other hand, look at us. We were called the Old Taiwanese Communists and were avoided by everybody, as if we were relics from the past. Not a few people called us fools even."

"Oh, no. I want to thank you for all your troubles," Liu said, as if he represented everybody.

"After the war, I, as well as many other Old Taiwanese Communists withdrew from politics entirely and led a quiet life.

"You may say that we turned into onlookers as far as politics were concerned. 'Hermits' might even be more apropos."

"Then why did you get thrown in here?" Youde asked.

"Well, when one is minding one's own business, disaster can still fall like rainwater from a leaky roof. I was splashed by the eruption of the February 28 Incident. At the time, I ran a magazine stand in the portico of a store owned by an old friend of mine. The business did well enough to sustain my livelihood. Besides, my life was quite interesting from watching the passersby and the changing worlds reflected in them. That was the least eventful period in my life. On the day of February 28 and the turbulent days that followed, I stuck to my resolve to be an onlooker and just tended to my business and observed the event's development from the sidelines.

"As a Taiwanese, I was all for a mass movement to resist a corrupt regime. But I told myself 'your act is over' and was able to keep calm.

"Then midway through March, Hou Kan, an Old Taiwanese Communist comrade, showed up at my magazine stand. He pretended to be a customer, flipping through this magazine and that one, and advised me to flee as soon as possible. According to him, the government had started to blame the Communists for inciting and planning the February 28 riot and had already arrested several Old Taiwanese Communists as sacrificial lambs.

"The KMT government wanted to shift the blame to the Chinese Communists for an incident whose root cause was their own profound corruption and incompetence. It would be an especially convenient scapegoat if Big Daddy United States, which had seen a rising anti-Communist sentiment domestically, and other free nations could be convinced of it.

"However, the fact of the matter was that the Chinese Communists had their hands full fighting the civil war and were not able to reach their hands over to Taiwan at the time. Moreover, only a handful of Communists had infiltrated Taiwan before the February 28 Incident — not enough to plan and incite a riot. That's why the government started to arrest the Old Taiwanese Communists to come up with a decent number of schemers."

"So did you evade the headwind?" Wu asked.

To evade the headwind meant to go into hiding until the storm blows over.

"No, I rejected the idea without a second thought. I hadn't done anything that required me to flee; and I figured I had many witnesses, since I stand all day in a busy thoroughfare. Nevertheless, I was arrested just as Hou had predicted. A special agent came to my magazine stand and, whether I liked it or not, forced me into a car and took me to the Garrison Command Headquarters."

"And you have been in jail ever since?" Somebody asked.

"Oh, no. That's not the case. I was released after about a week."

"How so?"

"You see, on February 28 I saved the life of a mainlander. An ashen-faced man in a Sun Yat-sen suit passed by my business. I stopped him and told him that he would be beaten senseless were he recognized as a mainlander. And I made him take off his Sun Yat-sen suit and put on my windbreaker instead. The man quickly grasped the seriousness of the situation, thanked me, and hurried off. Somehow the man learned of my arrest and showed up at the Garrison Command Headquarters as my witness. He turned out to be a man of high position in the government and knew somebody in the Garrison Command. The man signed on as my guarantor and I was released."

Numerous similar incidents happened during the February 28 Incident. Youde, too, had personally warned a mainlander who passed him by on the street to take off a shirt that bore the characteristic hand-woven stripes from the mainland. The fact was most Taiwanese couldn't bear to see mainlanders churned up in the waves of Taiwanese anger toward corrupt officials and beaten up merely because they were from the mainland.

Chang took a sip from the mug of tea Wu had handed him and continued, "But on December 8 last year I was again arrested, and I've been in ever since. It's getting to be five months. I gather that still makes me the least veteran among you. Well, I sure didn't expect to be thrown in jail again at my age."

"Were you imprisoned when you were young?" Kao asked.

"Oh, sure. We were in and out of jail all the time. In my personal experience, the sentences from the Japanese government were only one, two, or three months at the most each time. Sure, I was severely beaten by Japanese MPs; but I never had to worry about a death sentence."

Chang looked at the four faces around him, one by one, and said, "It's great to be able to talk face to face with you all. This is the first time in five months."

"What?"

"I've been in solitary confinement in the Secret Protection Bureau, so I've been living a lonely existence all by myself."

"Is that so!"

"The cell was less than six feet square, with solid walls on all sides. The door had an opening like a mail drop and the guard passed me food and water through that. And even the opening had a cover. Sometimes the guard would lift the cover of the opening and peek inside. And we sometimes were able to push up the cover from inside and exchange a word or two with people next door. That's about the extent of communication we got, let alone seeing each other's faces. Compared to that, this place is easy street."

Chang smiled.

The Secret Protection Bureau was reputed to be the most terrifying among the intelligence organizations, Youde had heard.

"What are you in for this time?" Liu asked.

"I'll tell you the whole story later."

Chang extended his hand once more and firmly seized everybody's hand one by one.

"It's been a long time since I grasped human hands this way."

And he smiled again as he spoke.

91

Implicated by a Big Fish

After dinner Chang talked about the reason for his arrest. The person who brought the disaster upon him was none other than Hou Kan, the man who showed up at Chang's magazine stand right after the February 28 Incident. Hou had since fled successfully to Hong Kong then, subsequently, into mainland China. It was soon after the establishment of the People's Republic, and its people were full of hope and the nation full of energy. Despite the fact that Hou hadn't been politically active since the end of the war, he received a hero's welcome based on his past achievements as a Communist in Taiwan. For the next several years, he worked on China's Taiwan policy under various august titles. An old Taiwanese Communist was thus turned into a new Chinese Communist, you might say. Then, last December, he brazenly snuck back into Taiwan with a new mission: he was appointed the supreme director of Taiwanese Communists.

"But," Chang continued, "he was captured within the first twenty-four hours after landing."

"I wonder why he was caught so easily." Liu was miffed.

Youde thought it strange too, so he said, "The Secret Protection Bureau didn't have to arrest him in such a hurry. After all, he was as good as a bagged turtle. They could arrest him any time they chose. I wonder why they didn't let him roam free so they could observe him and choose a good time to bag his associates too. Even with a small fry like myself, they observed me for one month after I returned home. Could it be that the agency was eager to get the credit for bagging a big fish?"

"I got it!" Wu said loudly. "Nothing to it. I think Hou Kan himself was betrayed by the Chinese Communists. After all, they are Chinese too — what's betraying a comrade? Hou must have done something to tick off the Chinese authorities; but they couldn't very well arrest and execute a so recently celebrated hero. So they appointed him the high honor of the supreme director of the Taiwanese Communist Party and sent him to his death, taking care to leak the intelligence in advance to this side. This is what's called 'to kill by borrowed knife,' an ancient tactic in China. That is why Hou found upon landing not Communist connections but KMT special agents waiting for him." Wu laid out his theory with full confidence.

"In any case," Chang continued, "Hou told them about me after his arrest. He told them that he showed up at my magazine stand and that I had given him money. As this all happened six or seven years ago, I don't remember how much money I gave him. But it couldn't be more than a day's take and that wasn't much. Hou told them that he applied the money I gave him to finance his escape."

"What a coward. For a so-called big fish to mention something like that," Wu lamented.

"I was taken to the Secret Protection Bureau right away for questioning. I admitted frankly that I gave him money. Also, I couldn't very well deny that I knew his identity and his past. So the charge of Article 4 against me was quickly established."

"But," Liu cocked his head as he asked, "the Hou Kan you knew was Hou of the Japanese Communist Party. I would think his Communist identity was no longer in effect after the Restoration, and since he was not yet a Chinese Communist when he came to see you, I should think the Law on Sedition would not be applicable."

"I argued the very same point also, of course. But it didn't do any good."

"Was Hou Kan sent over here with you?" Liu asked.

"No. One other person came here with me. Hou Kan stayed behind in the Secret Protection Bureau."

"What this Old Taiwanese Communist brain of mine can't figure out is that Hou was constantly drinking and having call girls with the special agents."

"Is that so!" Everyone was impressed.

To be able to have call girls and to be able to drink in the prison! Nothing can beat that.

Liu asked again, "Was the other man who came here with you also connected to Hou Kan?"

"Of course. He was in the cell next to mine, so for two months we exchanged simple words several times a day. But I only saw his face for the first time today — tall and cultivated looking. I really feel for this man. All he did was help Hou Kan."

Chang paused briefly as if taking the man's plight into his heart, then continued, "After the February 28 Incident, the man initially went into hiding and later fled to Hong Kong, where he waited until the dust had almost completely settled before returning to Taiwan and turning himself in. He said he was freed under the Self-Renewal Policy and was able to live two peaceful years. If Hou Kan had not returned, he would still be continuing his peaceful existence. But after Hou's arrest, just like me, he was called into the Secret Protection Bureau and was accused of aiding Hou Kan's escape to Hong Kong. You see, in his Self-Renewal confession, he had confessed all about his activities related to the February 28 Incident, except for his dealings with Hou Kan. Hou was by then safely in Hong Kong and was not expected to dance back on the stage and blab about him. You could say the man was bitten by his own dog. For this omission, his pardon under the Self-Renewal Policy was withdrawn and he was charged with Article 4. Seeing that the authorities have Hou Kan's testimony, I think the man's life probably can't be saved."

As Youde listened to Chang's story about the man, he had a sudden hunch. "What's the man's name?"

To an anxious Youde, Chang answered, "His name is Wang Tien."

"Eh? Is he from Putzu?"

"Yes. He is a man from Putzu. Are you too?"

"Ah!" Youde cried in a loud voice even before Chang was finished. It was such an unusually loud uttering for Youde that everybody turned their eyes on him.

Youde said broken-hearted, "Wang Tien is my cousin."

92

Cousin Tien

THE first thing that came to Youde's mind after learning of cousin Wang Tien's arrest was his mother, Youde's auntie San-yi.

Auntie San-yi was a younger sister of Youde's mother by five years. But because cousin Tien was the oldest of his siblings and Youde the youngest among his, Tien was ten years older than Youde. Auntie San-yi was of tiny build with a sickly constitution. As a matter of fact, Youde often thought of Auntie San-yi and the medicine cabinet in the same breath.

Cousin Tien was born a multitalented man. He was adept at musical instruments of all kinds and in *go* too reached the level of Shodan. It was still during the Japanese era, when he was recognized for his ability and was appointed an officer in the town's credit union. Consequently, when the February 28 Incident erupted, he was promptly elected to the town's Aftermath Management Committee. Fortunate as he might have been to escape the subsequent wholesale massacre of the committee members by the KMT government, he became a fugitive after that. "The hardships of a life on the lam are beyond words," Cousin Tien had once told Youde. At long last, he escaped to Hong Kong — a fortunate turn of events, one would think. Except cousin Tien took along Hou Kan in the same small boat. They had become acquainted during hiding. Cousin Tien couldn't have known even in his dreams that the helping hand he extended was to cost him his life.

After living in Hong Kong for five years as a fugitive, Cousin Tien learned about the Self-Renewal Policy and returned to Taiwan to turn himself in. That was a year prior to Youde's sojourn in America. It was plain that cousin Tien had put the consideration of his mother's health above his own safety.

He confessed to every involvement he had with regard to the February 28 Incident. Given that five years had passed since the Incident, and also because the authorities had begun to reflect on their own initial wanton killings, cousin Tien was set free without much difficulty. But cousin Tien did not broach the subject of Hou Kan because Hou was then already safely ensconced as a revolutionary hero in the Chinese mainland.

How Youde remembered auntie San-yi's extraordinary joy when cousin Tien was home as a free man. She rose from her sickbed and visited one and every Buddhist temple, even Christian churches, to offer her thanks to gods of all ilk. She kept that up every day without a break. During the two years she spent with cousin Tien, she was joyous and happy, oblivious to her ailments.

But fewer than two months after Youde's arrest, cousin Tien was also arrested, thanks to Hou Kan's confession. In the final analysis, cousin Tien was taken in by the Self-Renewal Policy when he should have remained in Hong Kong. The special agents barged into his house, handcuffed him, and took him away in front of a surprised Auntie San-yi. Youde could picture San-yi crumbling to the floor, begging the special agents for mercy.

Youde's thoughts went to his Auntie San-Yi: By now San-yi is probably again clinging to her sickbed, praying daily for her son's release instead of her own health. Sadly, the gods are about to abandon her. Cousin Tien's death sentence and his subsequent execution were a fait accompli. Auntie San-yi had endured the pain of her son's arrest, but how was she going to survive her son's execution?

Chang said, "Wang Tien is resigned to his death. He said he can go in peace because he did not implicate a single person."

There must have been many helping hands extended to him during his five years of hiding. Among them, especially the person who provided the boat for Tien's escape, some could face a death sentence. That cousin Tien did not bring trouble to anyone was indeed to be commended.

"Wang Tien also said that, if possible, he would rather his mother die peacefully than to hear about his execution," Chang added.

93

A Common-Law Wife

The first letter arrived for Chang. It was from his common-law wife. She was his only kin, as they had no children.

The first page of her letter was passed around. It mainly said that her livelihood was not a problem so he should not worry. The writing was fluent and refined.

"Great penmanship and wonderful writing too," Youde praised her letter.

Chang smiled and said, "My wife has more schooling than me. I only had a sixth-grade education, but she is a graduate of Taipei's No. 3 Girls High School."

High schools for girls of that age were the preserve of only highly intelligent girls from wealthy families.

"How come she married you?" Wu was blunt, to say the least.

"We never officially married. I can't say that I blame them, but my wife's family was violently opposed. I was then but a hapless worker in the refinery and an underground Communist to boot. Besides, not only was I hated by the local police, I actually had been to prison. Her mother supposedly fainted when she learned of her daughter's intention to marry me. You see how there's no way we could have had a wedding and all that. Actually, because the police were constantly watching and harassing us, we Old Taiwanese Communists all pretty much stayed away from marrying openly."

"You must have been handsome or something," Wu was not one to beat around the bush.

"No, no. Not for my good looks, rather, I think she fell for my devotion to social activism. I will tell you the whole story sometime."

"No way, senpai. Such a good story, you've got to tell us now!" Wu was insistent.

Chang started to tell his story, rather relishing the opportunity.

"Our story began over twenty years ago at a bonsai and ikebana exhibition at Lung-shan Temple at a time when the newspaper headlines were screaming about Japan entering the Extraordinary Period. I was about to leave after viewing only the bonsai displays because I held the opinion then that ikebana was but masturbation for women of the bourgeois class. But for some reason I changed my mind and went over to the ikebana section. As I glanced through the exhibition absent-mindedly, I noticed a flower arrangement entitled 'Double Oppression.' 'Double oppression,' being a term we used among the Taiwan Communist circles, naturally, it was with great interest that I went to the office to find out about the entry. And there in the office, I ran into her, the artist. It turned out her 'Double Oppression' was somewhat different from ours. The first one referred to the same oppression of colonial Taiwan by Imperial Japan. However, her other oppression meant the oppression of women by men, she being also a feminist. As we talked we found that we were of the same mind, and I fell for her like a ton of bricks. Hmm, I'd better stop here, because what followed was plain mush. We designated the day we met as our wedding anniversary. She enriched my life and made my life worth living."

Kao asked tentatively, "The flower arrangement, 'Double Oppression,' what was it like?"

"Well, I don't understand it very well either, but I remember a pathetic pink flower covered by some bamboo leaves, which in turn were sat upon by even larger leaves."

Chang was not very good at describing the art object.

For a person with only a grade school education, Chang seemed to be well read. The Old Taiwanese Communists were known for reading many difficult books. Perhaps that explained why Chang chose to be a book vendor for his livelihood.

"Hey!" Wu suddenly yelled after starting on the second page of the letter, which he snatched from Chang's hand.

Liu and Kao encircled Wu from either side and peeked at the letter.

"What a tear-jerker love story this is," Wu said with obvious lament and handed the letter to Youde.

The gist was that, belated as it was, she would like to make their marriage legal.

Chang muttered, "And at a time like this."

"No," Wu approached Chang who was ignorant of Wu's divorce and embraced him by the shoulders. "Senpai, I am envious of you. Your situation is exactly the opposite of mine."

94

Two Documents

On May 10, a man with the title of secretarial officer appeared outside Cell 7 and handed Youde two documents. Immediately after making Youde put his thumbprint on the receipt, he left.

The first document was a petition, namely the prosecutor's indictment to send Youde to re-education. The second document was the judicial decision in response to the petition.

Youde had thought all along that he would be required to appear in court to receive the decision. The fact that his case was being disposed of with such casualness made him feel somewhat deflated.

He read the petition first:

Security Protection Headquarters Petition (44) — #1478
Accused: Tsai Youde, male, age 31
Occupation: teacher (in detention)

Having investigated the accused in relation to a case of sedition, we conclude that the accused needs to be sent to re-education for the following reasons:

The accused Tsai Youde had frequently associated in the past with rebels Li Shui-ching and Chang Yu-kun, had organized the Student Friendship Association and the Blue Cloud Drama Club in his hometown of Putzu, in which rebel Cheng Wen-bang and others participated. The accused admitted during investigation to having read the Japanese edition of

Materialism, The Treatise on Art, Fundamental Questions in Philosophy, and other reactionary literature such as Lu Hsun's novels. The above were found to be facts based on the investigation conducted by the Chiayi Police Bureau. According to the accused himself, he had never joined any rebel organizations, and the plays he produced had not been pro-rebel nor had they benefited the rebels' propaganda. The accused further stated that he was unaware of the Communist identities of Li Shui-ching, Chang Yu-kun, Cheng Wen-bang, and others. Nevertheless, the fact that the accused closely associated with rebels and had read reactionary literature indicated that the accused, more than likely, harbored pro-rebel sympathies. Thereby, we petition the court to decide in accordance with Item 1.2 of Article 8 of the Statutes for the Denunciation and Punishment of Bandit Spies During Emergency Period.

Addressed to: Department 2 of Military Court
Dated: April 11, 1955
Signed by: Fan Chueh-fei, Military Court Prosecutor
Verified by: Sung Ya-ting, Secretarial Officer

The prefix (44) in the document number indicated the year was the forty-fourth of the Republic of China, while #1478 meant there had been 1,477 people sent to re-education for brainwashing. After reading the petition, Youde's cellmates were unanimous about it being an unbelievably generous indictment.

Next, Youde read the second document, the judicial decision:

Security Protection Headquarters Decision (44)-#54
Accused: Tsai Youde, male, age 31
Occupation: teacher (in detention)

Re: the prosecutor's petition to send the accused to re-education, in accordance with the Statutes for the Denunciation and Punishment of Bandit Spies, the decision is as follows:

The court decided that Tsai Youde be sent to re-education for a duration to be determined by a separate order.
Reasons:

The accused, Tsai Youde, closely associated with convicted rebels Li Shui-ching, Chang Yu-kun and others around 1949 and had read the Japanese edition of *Materialism, The Fundamental Questions of Philosophy*, the *Kuang-ming Daily*, and Lu Hsun's novels. The prosecutor, having judged the accused to harbor pro-Communist thoughts, had petitioned the court to send the accused to re-education. Having reviewed the case and found no deviation, the court thereby grants the petition.

Dated: April 23, 1955
Signed by: Fan Ming, judge, Military Court
Verified by: Wu Chun-sheng, secretarial officer

The document #54 meant Youde was the fifty-fourth person to be sent to re-education this year.

After finishing reading both documents, the first thing to strike Youde was that *Mao Wenchi*, which the investigators so tenaciously pursued, was nowhere to be found. Of course, the disappearance of *Mao Wenchi* was more than Youde dared to wish for.

"Yu-kun must have recanted his own testimony about *Mao Wenchi* during the final witness interrogation," Wu spoke what everybody was thinking.

"Well," Liu said, "It's not so easy to recant what one once said. Take our case, no matter how much we tried to retract our own statements, they would not take us up on it. It has gone well for you, Mr. Tsai. That was great."

"Congratulations!" Kao said.

"But," Chang spoke in a measured way, "even under the colonial rule of Imperial Japan, the fact that one has a few Communist friends or having read those books was never reason enough to be convicted of a crime. They didn't have anything called re-education either. You may have been forced to retire from a government job and that would be the extent of it."

Wu started to laugh, "This goes to show you that this country of ours is advanced in the anti-Communist stance."

In any case the decision had come down, and Youde sensed the matter had come to a close. If one stopped to think about it, it had been a long ordeal. Yet Youde's troubles couldn't begin to compare with the hardship and misfortune of other prison friends, for he received the lightest of the sentences.

Youde put away the documents and started to write a letter to his wife.

95

The Decision on Ex-policeman Wu

Youde expected to be sent to the re-education center at Panchiao right away, but the order didn't arrive. One day after another he waited. Eventually, twenty days passed and it was June.

As he had already said his goodbyes to his cellmates and neighbors, Youde felt somewhat awkward about staying put. But his cellmates seemed more than happy about not losing a companion.

The deliberate pace of business, even when it concerned a person's freedom, could only be characterized as "mainland style," Youde fumed.

Sung, the communicator in the next cell, had an explanation.

"The new re-education center in Panchiao filled up the day it opened. They are going to make you wait here until a slot opens in Panchiao," he said. "But it is better to be here," he added. "Here, we can talk to each other without fear and suspicion. I heard that Panchiao has a great facility but it also houses all kinds of people. They said you have to lie or play dumb and be suspicious of everybody. Some say days there are like sitting on needles."

"There are some good things over there though," Wu chimed in. "They have guest houses, where I heard you can have conjugal visit. Hey, you are going to enjoy being with your wife again. I am green with envy."

Halfway through June, good tidings arrived from Youde's wife: she had given birth to a boy. She added that the mother and baby are both doing fine. This was the best news yet since his imprisonment. The news soon traveled from cell to cell and was known throughout the prison. Everybody was happy for him, almost extraordinarily so. While it had been only eight months since Youde lost his freedom, most people here had been separated from their families for more than a year, and nobody had yet heard about a birth. In Taiwan, the birth of a baby boy was believed to bring good luck.

"I would love to share some of the good luck," Wu said with an uncustomarily serious face.

Then, the very next day, Wu was called out for the first time in five months.

Panchang Teng came to fetch Wu. The squad leader's face was sober. "Court appearance," he said.

But after Wu left, the intelligence bulletin arrived that six petacos were seen in the guards' office. The cell was instantly dead silent. Is Wu, the ex-policeman, to become a man of no return after all? Tears glistened in Liu and Kao's eyes.

Believing there were no petacos, Wu had left rather happily. He must have been greatly startled and disappointed when he spotted the petacos in the guards' office. Did the petacos cease to show themselves after Lin's resistance?

Liu recounted to Chang about Wu's case of "Failure to Report." Silently, Chang shook his head from side to side.

"I thought he would get fifteen years if lucky and life at the worst. But death! I guess he was given the additional penalty because he was a policeman," Kao said with vehemence.

"Oh," Liu stood up abruptly and took down a package from the shelf, then extracted an envelope containing Wu's parting notes.

Liu's hand hesitated as he was about to open the envelope and he asked, "What shall we do?"

"Why don't we wait a little longer," Kao suggested.

"All right." Liu replaced the envelope in the package.

Liu said, "The day he put his thumbprint on the divorce papers, he ripped up his parting notes to his wife. So the envelope should contain only his letter to his son."

Time passed oppressively. Here and there singing of "Horse-Drawn Wagon" sounded like funeral music. Youde and his cellmates, only four remaining, started to circle the room while singing "Wishing Your Early Return," a Taiwanese song Wu loved.

Every day, I think of only you
Yet we have no way to meet

Like swans we followed each other
Never expected ever to separate....

In short order, the song was picked up by others and reverberated throughout the prison walls.

Between verses, Liu said in a voice thick with tears, "I don't have to open his notes to know what it says. I had the opportunity to glance it over."

"Is that so?" Youde awaited Liu's next words, more with sympathy than with curiosity.

"I was impressed most with one sentence in it."

"What was that?"

"Wu told his son, 'When you grow up, you must be good and do your best for your mother, because this is your father's most fervent wish.'"

Liu's eyes glistened with tears again.

Everyone was moved.

The true person of Wu, who had constantly bad-mouthed his wife, was now unmasked.

Then in the middle of a fitful nap after a late lunch, a commotion started by the prison entrance. The clamor mixed with shouts, and sounds of hands clapping quickly surged like an angry wave and reached Cell 7.

To the startled eyes of Youde and his cellmates, here was Wu grasping the hands and greeting the inmates in other cells. Wu had come back safe and sound.

The panchang opened the lock, and Wu stooped to pass through the door. Three cellmates pulled him up to the wooden floor.

Youde hugged Wu with all his strength.

"Four were called out, but I alone was refused entry by Yen-lo, the gatekeeper of Hell," Wu said and showed his court decision document to all.

It had: "accordingly, sentenced to life."

Two lines were drawn through the word "life;" and "fifteen years" was written alongside instead.

When the commotion finally died down, Wu slapped Youde by the shoulder and said, "Hey, it could really be due to the good luck from the birth of your son."

"No, no," Youde waved his hand and stopped Wu's words, saying with conviction, "It is because your son's prayer has reached heaven."

Instantly, Wu's smiling face froze and his eyes flooded with tears.

96

Loo Spoke of Mosula

A few days later, Wu was sent to the Military Prison and Cell 7 was left with four.

Despite the loneliness, there was an advantage to having fewer people: mixing with inmates from other cells during the bathing and walking period.

Among the new bathing companions was the clownish Flimflam Loo. While Youde was glad to see a hometown fellow at such a place, Loo, too, repeatedly said how glad he was to be together with Youde. Learning Loo had yet to receive a care package, Youde gave him a towel and a bar of soap, for which Loo thanked Youde every time they met.

Loo had many special skills, ventriloquism being one of them. So during bathing, Loo would station himself next to Youde and tell Youde all sorts of things right in front of guard's eyes. It was ironic that Youde never spoke with Loo while they both lived in Putzu, but they talked like old friends now.

Loo spoke of his own case, the cases of his cellmates in Cell 12, about people implicated by Yu-kun; his topics were abundant. Loo pointed out to Youde two inmates among the bathers who were also implicated by Yu-kun.

It turned out that both men were named Li and they were villagers of Hsiachitzu, where Yu-kun hid during his first escape. One knew at a glance that they were honest-looking peasants. As time passed, they both started to exchange words with Youde whenever possible. Youde found out that they were both charged with Article 4 for hiding Yu-kun and had been incarcerated for a year and five months.

"Can't do good deeds," they spoke sardonically and with regret. Simple words. Yet they made Youde shudder, for they embodied a serious prophecy about Taiwanese society: Almost all who were charged with Article 4 helped somebody out of kindness and now must face incarceration or even the death penalty for their actions. No wonder we see a drastic reduction in the number of people willing to help others. The civility of society deteriorates no end, Youde lamented.

One day, Loo brought up Mosula.

"Mosula missed you coming in and was sent away right before you came back. You and Mosula just passed each other by."

Mosula was the nickname of Youde's grade school classmate Yeh Chin-kuei. During Chiayi's interrogation, Youde was questioned tenaciously about his relationship with Mosula. A superb student, Mosula passed the notoriously difficult entrance examination to Tainan Normal School on his first try. He was recruited into the Communist Party by Li Shui-ching while teaching at a grade school. Arrested soon after Li's capture, Mosula had already been sentenced to a twelve-year term, which he was serving in the military prison on Green Island.

Mosula had a stubborn streak about him that earned him a reputation for being an intransigent underling. In prison he must have been viewed as incorrigible as well, because he was said to have sustained injuries all over his body from repeated punishments. And by surviving the ordeal, he earned himself the nicknames of "death-defying Yeh" and "Mosula, the Amazing Beast." This time he was sent back from the island not to be tried for sedition but for staging some kind of disobedience.

Mosula arrived at the Military Court prison when Youde was routed to the Investigation Bureau. By the time Youde returned, Mosula had been taken somewhere else.

Youde asked Loo, "Where was Mosula taken?"

"I don't know."

"Do you think he was sent back to the island?"

"Back to the island? If so, he is sure to die there this time."

"How was he physically?"

"He sustained injuries inside and out. Not a single organ was unharmed."

"……"

"He was strung up and beaten. They tied his hands to his back, then strung him up by a rope over a building beam, then took turns beating him with clubs."

"……"

"I heard that more than the pain from the clubbing, what happens to one's shoulders is the most excruciating. When a man is strung up all night, his arms that are tied to the back gradually get stretched out by his own body weight and eventually they were above his head pointing backward, like a person shouting *banzai*. They said Mosula was unconscious when they cut him down the next morning."

"How cruel."

"Cruel guys, these pigs."

"Any idea why he was treated so harshly?"

"It seemed that he rebelled against the counselor."

Youde recalled a young Chin-kuei, ever unyielding despite his small and delicate physique. But for him to resist to such a degree there must have been something that really sat wrong with him.

"Did he suffer aftereffects from the beating? Is there something still wrong with him?" Youde asked.

"His shoulders did not mend completely, and his head still hurts from time to time. But he moved in good stride during the walking period."

"Well, he is Mosula, 'the Amazing Beast,' after all."

The next day, prodded by Youde for more about Mosula, Loo told about the lockers on the Green Island.

"Mosula was once put in the locker for a week, which was but a concrete underground bunker. He was confined for a week inside with his own bodily waste. The ground inside was flooded with water so he couldn't lie down, and the only source of light came from the gun windows. His meals were passed to him through the gun windows too; meals consisting of brown rice and salt in little matchboxes. But do you know what was most intolerable? Guess."

Youde shook his head.

"It was the mosquitoes. There were a million mosquitoes in there. They fed on Mosula non-stop for a week! Anybody else would have died."

How could such inhumane treatment still exist today! Youde was indignant.

"When he was carried out from the bunker after the week was over, his body was rotting and he was just a breath away from death."

The thought of the hellish sufferings of his childhood friend filled Youde with anger. Many wakeful nights followed.

97

Leaving the Military Court Prison

It was now July. Still no word about a move to Panchiao for Youde. For the next three months, the same condition persisted as if the whole matter had been forgotten.

"Why don't you write a report?" Liu suggested.

But Sung the neighbor was of the opinion that there was no reason to hurry.

Sung said, "There is no clear, pre-set curriculum in re-education. The term is usually three years; but the rules don't require that it be served in a re-education center. Unlike schools, it doesn't give a graduation exam either. I know some people who spent two of the three years as prison servants.

"The counselor gives you points solely by his subjective judgment anyway, and you are done when you accumulate enough points.

"I heard that the scoring goes like this: One point for completing the day's lesson, two points for notable good behavior, etc. Show gratitude to Baldy (Chiang Kai-shek) and pile on tearful praises of his contributions and you get three points for sure. You are supposed to accumulate three thousand points in three years. But points can also be taken away. So, Mr. Tsai, you must be extremely careful about what you say when you go over there. Just utter the word 'Baldy,' and if somebody informs on you, it's going to cost you one hundred points!"

Liu interjected, "And I guess the informer gets additional points, right?"

"Exactly. That's why I say it's rather safer to be here than being over there and having points subtracted for doing something stupid. Well, don't worry about it too much and enjoy your life here."

Following Sung's advice, Youde lived day by day pleasantly, paying little attention to the matter. Then, just past the middle of July, he received a notice informing him of the transfer to the re-education center the next day.

Youde again bid farewell to his friends.

Sung offered his final advice, "Bribe the counselors. You will get out sooner."

To ask the family already deprived of its breadwinner to send money for bribery was absolutely reprehensible. Youde knew Sung was only half kidding, nevertheless, and said flatly, "Never. My pride would not allow it."

Sung laughed out loud and added another piece of advice.

"One more. And this is not a joke. Don't open your heart to anybody. You know the saying *Silence is golden*? Well, that's the truth in the re-education center. You must swallow and keep mum even if you are itching to say something."

Sung's expression was dead serious.

The next morning during bathing, Youde told Loo of his impending departure. Loo was sentimental. He said, "I would be so happy if I could see you again on the outside. As you know, I don't have a permanent address, but I know where your house is. May I visit you?"

"Of course. I'll be very happy too."

Loo said, disheartened, "But that will be at least eight years from now."

Youde presented Loo with an undershirt — Loo's hole-dotted undershirt had pained Youde for some time — which Loo received with such exaggerated thanks that he attracted the guard's attention. The guard came over with his gun pointing and examined the undershirt. Fortunately, the present was passed to Loo without incident.

Around ten o'clock, the panchang arrived. Hugging Liu, Kao, and Chang, Youde said goodbye yet another time then stepped out of the cell. No handcuffs. Youde, carrying his bundle under his arm, waved goodbye with his free hand. The panchang followed from behind. Prison friends from other cells waved goodbye. Youde and the panchang walked past the open yard and entered the guard's station by the gate. Once again, Youde passed through the iron gate to enter the prison office — by now a familiar route. After paperwork, he was made to wait standing. A short time later, a man with a full beard was brought in from the West Area. The man's name was Yang, Youde learned when the clerk addressed him.

Finally, two guards in different kinds of uniforms arrived to receive Youde and Yang. They took out the handcuffs and linked the two prisoners together. Yang whispered, "Are you going to the re-ed? Me too." Youde nodded.

The guards took the two out and seated them in the front seats of a waiting jeep. They themselves guarded from the backseats. One of the guards said, "Listen, we are taking you to a nice place from where you'll soon go home. So don't try anything funny, OK?"

Out of the gate of the Military Court Building, the jeep entered Chingtao East Road. The outside world that greeted Youde anew had turned into mid-summer. But this time, Youde's heart was light. Yang must have been of the same frame of mind because, spontaneously, their eyes met and they exchanged smiles. The jeep headed east then south. After a short while, Youde became aware that the jeep was not heading toward Panchiao, where the re-education center was located. Several times he wanted to ask the guard about it but refrained.

The jeep passed the front of the National Taiwan University and kept on going toward the southeast. At last, the direction became clear to Youde. We are heading toward Ankang of Hsintien — the Ankang of the Military Prison, the Ankang with the execution yard — and this is the identical road traveled by the executed Lin the Bull, Chou Shui, Little Lu, and countless others. The difference was their trucks had the heavy canvas flap to keep them from seeing the outside.

Youde decided to ask the guard.

"Aren't we going to the re-education center?"

No answer. Youde repeated his question. One guard answered impatiently, "Yes, we are. Shut up."

The jeep passed through the crowded main street of Hsintien, crossed the suspension bridge, and entered a mountain path.

At last the notorious Ankang Military Prison came into view, enclosed by a fear-inspiring high concrete wall that snaked as far as the eye could see. The jeep came to a halt in front of the stately gate. A guard with a gun came out to check the papers and gave Youde and Yang a once-over.

The jeep entered the gate and this time stopped in front of a brand-new building. Youde and Yang, linked by handcuffs, were again made to wait like a couple pieces of luggage.

98

Beginning Re-education

After having the handcuffs removed and finishing the admitting procedures in the front office, Youde and Yang were taken by a guard in a khaki-colored uniform to a room identified by two separate plaques: "Consultation Room" and "Counselor's Room." It turned out that the room was partitioned by a plywood wall; the room on the right was the Consultation Room, and the one on the left was the Counselor's Room.

Youde and Yang were taken into the Consultation Room, which had a set of rattan furniture in the center and a small table by the wall with a tea set on it. The large wall clock, an object of nostalgia, was pointing to twelve. The room was filled with sunlight, bright and airy. Youde couldn't help but remember with pity the last prison cell he occupied where a light bulb strived to illumine the mid-day.

When a man in an olive-green T-shirt came out of the Counselor's Room, the guard shouted "Salute!" Youde and Yang quickly complied. The counselor ordered them to sit down. He leisurely opened and browsed the file, all the while inquiring about their personal data. Youde thought the counselor cracked a small smile at one point as he was going through Youde's file. Youde was relieved to find the counselor not a devil incarnate as they were reputed to be.

As if to answer Youde's unspoken question, the counselor said, "This is the temporary branch of the Panchiao Re-education Center. I am responsible for everything here. This place is not as well equipped as Panchiao, and that causes various inconveniences. On the other hand, we have a bit more freedom here. I'm not fond of nitpicking."

The counselor grinned.

"But you must do your daily lessons and not be sloppy about them either. In the morning you write a study report; and in the afternoon you will express your opinions in study sessions to learn from one another. Remember not to get into fights no matter what. If you find something intolerable, write it up in a report to me."

The counselor turned to the guard and said, "Call Comrade Cheng in here."

A moment later a half-bald, middle-aged man entered. He was wearing a navy-blue uniform.

"This is Comrade Cheng," the counselor said. "He will look after you. Listen and follow his words as my orders."

Youde and Yang bowed slightly to Cheng and said, "Thank you in advance for looking after me."

After following the counselor to the next room, Cheng soon returned with some books and handed four books each to Youde and Yang. They were Sun Yat-sen's *Three People's Principles*, *Writings of Sun Yat-sen*, Chiang Kai-shek's *The Fundamentals of Overturning Communism and Opposing Russia*, and *The Biography of President Chiang* by Tung Hsien-kuang.

As he led them out of the room, Cheng lowered his voice and said, "I am also in re-education. I was once appointed a section leader but my Mandarin Chinese is too poor to do the job. Now I work as prison servant. I am allowed to smoke on the job."

Soon they reached the sentried iron gate which opened to a half-round, rather spacious hall. In the center of the space sat a cluster of about ten desks and a few guard-like men in khaki-colored uniforms who were taking their lunches. Here and there men who looked like prison servants — in navy-blue uniforms like Comrade Cheng — were sitting around smoking and chatting. They barely glanced at the two newcomers before resuming their chats. Various items — a score of large kettles, mops, hemp sacks, paper cartons — lay around haphazardly, giving the place a market-like appearance.

From the hall, five arcade-like buildings fanned out and extended in different directions. Voices from these buildings, voices from caged human beings, could be heard in the hall. Each building had a rather wide corridor in the middle and was lined on each side by a row of wood-floored, cage-like rooms, fronted by iron bars. Each row extended for about one hundred meters, affording the building a capacity of one thousand.

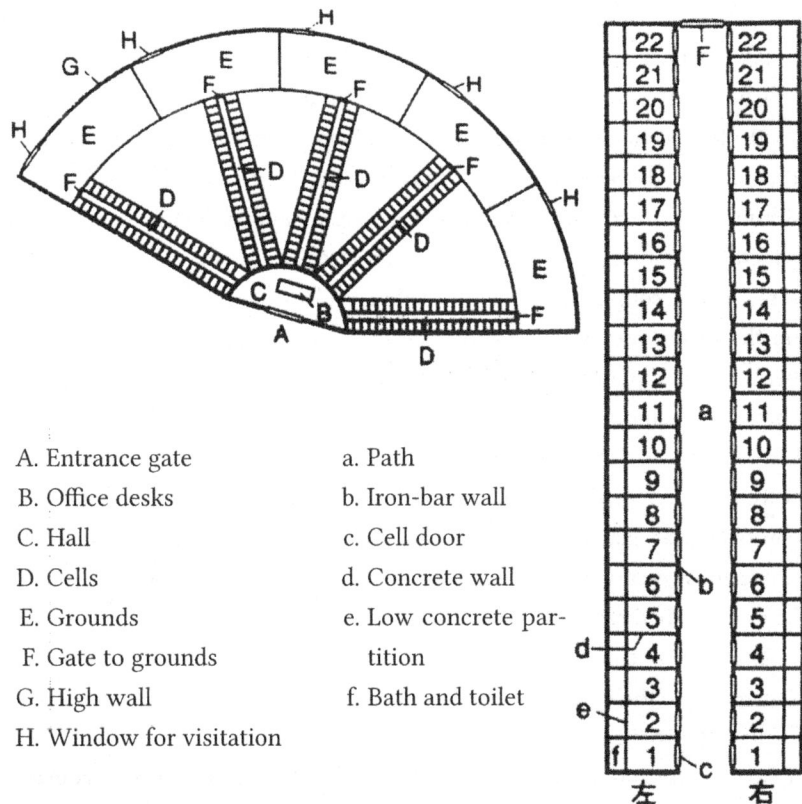

A. Entrance gate
B. Office desks
C. Hall
D. Cells
E. Grounds
F. Gate to grounds
G. High wall
H. Window for visitation

a. Path
b. Iron-bar wall
c. Cell door
d. Concrete wall
e. Low concrete partition
f. Bath and toilet

左　右

A different guard with the keys joined the party. The party of four walked into the middle building and stopped at the nearby Room 2R — the second room on the right side. Youde noticed the door to Room 1 was left open. "Perhaps it's the servants' room," he thought.

They stepped into Room 2R to find about ten people there — some were taking lunch and some, having finished eating, were picking their teeth; all were in underpants, some wearing sleeveless T-shirts for tops. Others were bare-chested.

All gave the two newcomers a once-over but none came to greet them. What a difference from the welcome at the Military Court Prison, where Youde had been greeted with "Mr. Tsai, glad to see you" and been pulled up to the room by his cellmates. No matter, some did smile and show friendliness.

Cheng called over two men who occupied the seats on either side of the entrance and made the introductions.

"Here is Tsai Youde of Section One, and here is Yang Chi-min of Section Two."

To Youde and Yang, Cheng said, "Comrade Chen here is the section leader of Section One, and here is Section Two's leader, Comrade Hsiung."

Cheng left as soon as he finished the introductions.

The two section leaders were both mainlanders. Section Leader Chen made them approach the wall next to his own seat. On the wall was the roster of Section One, from which one name had been scratched. Section Leader Chen added Youde's name to the bottom of the list. "I came to fill the hole of the scratched person," Youde thought. Section Leader Chen, pointing to the names on the roster one by one, introduced his comrades to Youde. Each person being introduced nodded and returned immediately to what they were doing, showing no sign of getting up to shake hands. Next, section Leader Hsiung introduced those in his section. All together, including the newcomers, there were twenty, exactly half of them mainlanders. Addressing each other as "comrade" was exactly like what Communists do. Youde found it ironic that Communist manners were employed in a place where people were sent to be brainwashed clean of Communism.

The section leaders took the two newcomers to the back of the room and showed them their spaces, a first in Youde's experience to have a space in the back of the room offered to a bottom-rung newcomer. The fact that a bath area and a flush toilet were on the other side of a half-meter high, concrete fence at the end of the room might explain why. Youde untied his bundle and put his stuff on the shelf.

Comrade Cheng kindly brought lunches in for them. Youde was not hungry but could not very well refuse, so he hurriedly took a few mouthfuls and dumped the leftovers into a bucket. Naptime was from lunch till two. Youde sat down on his own seat.

He took a rough measure of the room: four meters wide and eight meters deep. The floor was mopped to a shine. The room was bright even without any light bulbs, thankfully. Despite twenty people being crowded in the room, one could not detect body odor or any sweaty smells, perhaps because the room was new and spacious, and also because the building was situated in the mountain village of Ankang.

Toe to toe, they lay down in two lines to take naps. Between lines of toes, a space of about sixty centimeters was left open as a path.

Youde examined his new prison friends — rather, his comrades.

"There are all kinds of people over there." Youde recalled vividly what Sung had said.

This place has its own way of life. It was said that if one were to utter the word "baldy" or to hum a Communist or even a Japanese song, one could be promptly informed on. Can I adjust quickly to this kind of life? Youde was somewhat worried.

99

A Rain Shower

"It's raining!" Somebody gave a small yell. Several people sat up from their nap to listen. Sure enough, raindrops were falling on the roof tiles.

"Wow! It's raining!"

Cheers arose. Everybody was elated like a bunch of children.

"Why are you so happy about rain?"

Wearing a big grin, a smallish man by the name of Wang who slept next to Youde explained, "The study session will be canceled. That's why."

The study sessions were to be conducted outdoors every day from two to four, right after the midday nap.

Wang became Youde's first talking friend. He was addressed as Little Wang for there was another Wang in the room. Little Wang was a native of Kuanmiao and was a vendor in the town market. He was in the habit of criticizing the government; but the trouble started when he was overheard by a customer, a mainlander housewife, and got into an argument with her. It had been six months since he had been detained for questioning and one month since arriving here.

Little Wang added, "Almost everyone here got into trouble because of their mouths. Somebody — a superior, a spy-colleague, or a neighbor — informed on them to the authorities for criticizing the government."

"That's exactly what happened to me," Yang abruptly joined the conversation.

Yang was a native of Changhua and worked as a technician at the Telegraph Bureau.

"At work, I observed day after day the corruption of my superiors and had often mouthed criticisms in private. But one day, at a wedding banquet of a guy who worked for me, I had a few too many and loudly denounced the pigs."

"Shh," Little Wang placed his index finger across his lips and gestured Yang to stop. Yang quickly rolled his tongue and closed his mouth. Yang seemed to realize only just now that half the members in the room were mainlanders.

Little Wang asked Youde, "Let me guess, Comrade Tsai, I think you are here for reading forbidden books."

"How do you know?"

"You look like one of those. I have a good feel about people, an inborn ability."

"I see. But I read the books before they were banned. What was I to do?"

"I'm sure that's the case. Because you wouldn't be here if you had read them after they had been banned. Instead, you would have gotten three years in prison followed by re-education at Panchiao. As it is, people sent here all received the verdict of 'not guilty, need re-education;' therefore, only very few are here for reading banned books. Yu over there is the only one."

Comrade Yu glanced at Youde, then said to Wang, "Hey, Little Wang. Don't spread anything funny about me. I read newspapers, not books."

"What's the difference?"

"Oh, no. I did not read banned books. It was only the widely available *Kuangming Daily*."

Yu came over to join the small cluster around Youde. Youde wondered if the duration of re-education depended on whether one read newspapers or books. Judging from his accent, Yu was apparently from the Fukien Province, China. The *Kuangming Daily* was well known and widely available. It was mentioned in Youde's decision document as well.

Yu said, "At the time, the *Kuangming Daily* often showed up at people's mailboxes in the morning. One time when I was down south on business for a few weeks — it's part of my job with the Monopoly Bureau — my maid took the newspapers inside and kept them in a stack for my return, she being illiterate you know."

"Lucky break for her. Otherwise she would be here too," Little Wang chimed in.

"It was partly my fault because I didn't burn the papers as soon as I got home." Then, Yu added, "I had always been a staunch anti-Communist."

Section Leader Chen, a native of Shanghai, stopped by on his way to the toilet. He said, "The so-called maid, though, was doing wifely duties night after night, right?"

Yu shot back, "I see you are speaking from experience."

As Yu was making his way back to his seat, the man next to Little Wang by the name of Chou pointed to Yu and said, "The man's brother is a big shot, supposedly a supreme court justice."

Chou continued in a whisper, "That's why you can't take what Yu says at face value. Who knows? Maybe he was involved in something far more serious, something a 'sweet potato' nobody would have gotten ten years for, but with his brother's influence he was slapped with re-education."

"After all, it was only the *Kuangming Daily*, they would normally ignore it." Little Wang also lowered his voice.

Servant Comrade Cheng came in and made a formal announcement, "The study session is canceled due to rain," then started to collect purchase orders from everybody. Youde hurriedly acquired an order form and ordered a few stationary items.

"Look at Comrade Cheng," Little Wang said, "he is but an errand boy here, but he used to be a distinguished councilman of Tainan prefecture. A very nice man, a native of Tachia. He criticized Chiang Kai-shek in the council meeting by a slip of the tongue."

"Hey, Little Wang, you won't be going home in three years judging from your progress," Chou teased. "What you are supposed to say is, 'Comrade Cheng is here to study because he failed to appreciate the many benevolent policies of the great President Chiang and made improper criticisms.' Got it?"

Little Wang in turn pointed to Chou and said, "This guy, too, was informed on for criticizing Chiang Kai-shek."

Chou shook his head slowly, a bitter smile on his face. Youde too broke into a grin.

"Comrade Tsai, you are a lucky man. If you had gone to the other side you wouldn't be laughing like this at all."

"The other side? Where?"

"Room 2L, across the hallway where Section Three and Section Four are housed. They seem to have squabbles all the time, sometimes even fistfights. And their servant, Chu, was convicted of false incrimination, hardly a person we can call 'comrade.' It's not of much concern to us; but we do mix with them during study sessions, so we do need to be wary."

Youde strained to look into the room on the other side. He found, behind bars, twenty other men of similar fates conducting their lives in a similar manner.

That's the extent of the Ankang Branch of the Re-education Center. Without a building of its own, it operated out of two borrowed rooms of the military prison.

The afternoon shower soon passed and the room cooled off somewhat.

"It would be great if it rains every day," Little Wang muttered.

100

Two Section Leaders

With the study session canceled, the next event to wait for was bath time. Youde went over to the front of the room and studied the daily schedule pasted next to the roster.

- 5:00 Rise
- 5:30 Breakfast
- 6:00 Room cleaning
- 7:00 Study, outdoor exercise, individual counseling
- 12:00 Lunch
- 12:30 Nap
- 2:00 Study session
- 4:00 Bath
- 5:30 Supper
- 6:00 Lecture, free activities
- 9:00 Lights out

Youde asked Section Leader Chen, "Do we have lectures every evening?"

"By regulation, we are supposed to have two lectures a week. But in reality, we make it about once a week."

The 6 a.m. room cleaning involved picking up and cleaning the floor, polishing it being the major chore.

Section Leader Chen explained the activities listed under 7 a.m. to noon: "Think of it as a time for self-directed study and taking walks. We in Building 3 take walks outdoors in five shifts for a duration of about forty minutes.

This week our room goes out at ten. You can use the rest of the morning to write your study report or your re-education progress report. Sometimes, the counselor might call you for an individual counseling session. That's when you can tell them whatever opinions you might have. Lucky for us, our counselor Fu is not very demanding. As far as I know, nobody has had his re-education report turned down for being too short or for it being a copy of somebody else's."

Section Leader Chen was friendly and considerate. Youde felt kindly toward him.

"The water is running!" somebody shouted.

Water, available only for a limited time daily, started to drip from the faucets in the bath area. In groups of four, they took turns to bathe under the four faucets. Youde was in the last group.

Section Leader Chen, being the first to finish, politely inquired about Youde's story. Youde knew that he need not hide anything; yet knowing Chen's obligation to write a daily report to the counselor, he should exercise caution and never utter a hint of dissatisfaction.

When Youde finished telling his story, he asked Chen, "May I know why you are here?"

"On account of radios. I listened to the radio broadcast from the mainland. You may say that my misfortune sprang from the ears. Many people here belong to this category." Chen pointed to Comrade Hsiung and three others in Section Two who had just come back from bathing.

"These four people were school teachers on Quemoy Island, and they used to gather at night to listen to broadcasts from the mainland. They got together naturally because there were only a few radios, not because they were forming an organization or a secret society, nor were they in contact with the Communists or anything like that. If to be faulted, they were just more curious than others. But being firm believers of the Three People's Principles to start with, their records here are great, way above the rest."

Drying his hair with a towel, Hsiung said with a smile, "Well, I think being here gives me time to get down to real studying and will actually be beneficial for my future. Good and bad fortunes are entwined together sometimes."

"Oh, Comrade Tsai," Section Leader Chen turned to Youde as if just reminded of something, "Did either Counselor Fu or Comrade Cheng tell you about family visits?"

"What? Family visits? No, I haven't heard anything about it. So I will be allowed visits?"

"Yes, on the second and fourth Sunday of each month. You had better let your wife know right away."

The thought of seeing his wife and children in person stirred Youde with excitement.

But when Youde recovered from his excitement, Section Leader Hsiung had switched the topic and was expounding on his view on Taiwan.

"Taiwan is nice. I had only seen it from a car; but I can tell that the stores are large and are lined with all kinds of things. And people of Taiwan dress well, on par with Shanghai if you ask me. Taiwan has good roads that lead in all directions, and there are many cars too. It has many modern buildings. On top of that, with abundant rain, rice crops must grow well. From where I came from, this place is really a treasure island."

Then Hsiung added, all seriously, "Taiwan really lives up to the name of 'The model province of the Three People's Principles.'"

For some reason Comrade Hsiung failed to mention "Taiwan has lots of modern prisons too."

101

Unexpected Reunion

The next morning, after room cleaning, the morning study session began. The group sat leaning against the wall with their knees drawn, a piece of plywood across their laps for placing a book or for writing. Some people used a rolled-up blanket as a desktop instead.

Youde took out the four books given to him the day before. *The Three People's Principles* and *Essays by Sun Yat-sen* were familiar ground, as they were required reading for all college freshmen. *The Fundamentals of Fighting Communism and Resisting Russia* was a pamphlet of a mere seventy pages, an easy one-day's read if one put his mind to it. And there was nothing new in the fourth book, the biography of Chiang Kai-shek, since the main events of Chiang's life had been widely circulated in newspapers and magazines, usually accompanied by illustrations or photographs. Nonetheless, the Chinese way of studying required rote memorization of entire books, and the thought of a daily regime of studying and rote recall of such books for the next three years filled Youde with dismay. Youde stifled a sigh, a sure reason to have points subtracted if seen.

Counselor Fu came up to the entrance to inspect the study session.

"Comrade Fu, how are you?" all said in unison.

Counselor Fu nodded with satisfaction, smiled and moved on to Room 2L across the corridor.

Around ten in the morning, the guard opened the door; it was time for the outdoor walk. All headed out at once, some wearing shoes, some barefoot. The wide corridor leading outside was instantly crowded by the two hundred people let out from ten rooms; the regular prisoners and the "re-eds" mixed together in one surging horde. After passing Room 25 at the end of the long corridor, they entered the open clay yard surrounded by a high wall. The morning sun was shining brightly, casting the shadow of the high wall and the prison building into part of the yard.

Following the guard's orders, the two hundred men formed into four columns and started to walk around and around the yard. In no time at all, some people took off their shirts to get some sun. This was the most enjoyable part of the day and also the only time a prisoner was able to communicate with people other than his own roommates. Despite the fact that there were no prison rules that prohibited them from speaking to people in other rooms — since all of them had already been tried and sentenced — the brick room partitions and wide corridors made it impossible in practical terms.

A man walking ahead of Youde in the next column turned his head and asked with a smile, "Mr. Tsai, do you remember me?"

Youde drew a blank.

"I don't blame you, Mr. Tsai, because you never got a good look at me really."

The voice. That's right! It's Fu-lin, the fellow who followed me into the Chiayi jail.

"The name was Fu-lin!" Youde shouted.

It was merely ten months ago, but Youde recalled with fondness the several days they spent together as if a lifetime had passed. Back in Chiayi's jail, Youde was only able to look at Fu-lin across the hallway through the prison bars. No wonder he couldn't recognize Fu-lin. And Fu-lin, he only had one opportunity to have a good look at Youde too — on the night Youde was sent to Taipei. What a good memory for faces! Youde was amazed.

The man directly in front of Youde kindly switched places with Youde, so he was able to walk side by side with Fu-lin.

"I remember you were with another man called Po-sung," Youde asked.

"Yes. As you predicted, both of us got ten years. Po-sung is here too, in a different building, so I don't get to see him."

"How about Mr. Chuang. Did he as expected...?"

"Yes. He was sent to Taipei the same time as us. Soon after, he was executed. Well, he was our leader after all. It's been six months already since we've been here."

"Is that so? In that case, you have seniority over me."

Fu-lin laughed. "You were nice to us back in Chiayi, a couple of know-nothings we were. We must have come across as real immature to you."

The fearful Fu-lin of yesterday was nowhere in sight. He had turned into a different person, strong and impressive.

"Mr. Tsai, are you here for re-education?"

"Yes."

"You may be able to go home pretty soon," Fu-lin said with a decisiveness that suggested more than an attempt to console.

"Is that so? I thought one term is three years, isn't it?"

"It was, but right now the home campus at Panchiao is filled to capacity and so is this one. I know for fact a fellow was released directly from here, and he was here for only a year."

"He must have compiled a superb record," Youde said. Yet momentarily a new ray of hope reared its head. "It's not a piece of bad news in any case," Youde surmised.

But the man on the other side of Fu-lin cut in, "The fellow was sent away to an intelligence organization to be a spy, he being fluent in both Japanese and English. They need people like him badly."

This was not a joking matter, Youde was alarmed. "I can't possibly become their lackey and push fellow Taiwanese into hellish misfortunes for their so-called crimes. Yet to refuse is also to endanger oneself." His newborn hope quickly turned into terror. "I would much rather stay here than become a spy," he thought.

The man in front of Youde turned his head from time to time and opined, "In a nutshell, the length of your thought-reform is already decided at the time of the court decision. Depending on the degree of your Communist poisoning, you are either in the 'heavy,' 'medium,' or 'light' class. For a guy in the 'heavy' class, no matter how hard he works or how great a record he compiles, it's no use. And you know there are the 'extreme heavy' among the 'heavy' class who, in essence, are no different from people with life terms. That's why I say there's no reason to work too hard. Just wait for your destiny, ha ha."

Fu-lin asked, "You seem to know a lot. You are not making things up, are you?"

The man looked back again and said, "No, an ex-judge told me about it before he was executed."

Turning to Youde, Fu-lin said, "If they have 'extreme heavy,' they may have 'extreme light' as well. The man who went home could be one of them. I pray that you are one of the 'extreme light,' Mr. Tsai."

Fu-lin seemed determined to hold out bright hope for Youde.

Suddenly, the guard yelled in a high-pitched voice, "T-u-r-n around!"

The two hundred prisoners in four-column formation turned on their heels and started in the opposite direction, some flinging their arms high, some rotating their necks as they walked.

As walking was about to draw to a close, Fu-lin asked, "Do you know Mosula?"

"Yes, I know him well."

"He is also in Building 3. You will run into him one of these days during walking."

The man next to Youde kindly added, "Mosula is in Room 15. You might want to look in on him on the way back."

Youde never addressed his childhood classmate Yeh Chin-kuei as Mosula, a nickname he acquired after surviving horrendous tortures. As Youde's image of Yeh did not quite match that of "Mosula, the Amazing Beast," he did not wish to call his friend Mosula, yet that was the name he was known by around here. How unexpected it was to see him here! Youde was elated. On his way back to his room, Youde carefully counted the rooms he passed by and stopped right in front of Room 15.

Mosula, né Yeh Chin-kuei, was expecting Youde by the front of his room. And the moment he saw Youde he stuck both his hands through the iron bars and anxiously sought Youde's hands.

Youde ran to the iron bars and firmly grasped Mosula's hands. Their eyes glistened with tears as they locked their eyes and called each other by their childhood names.

Mosula was as thin as ever, but his face and his physique appeared firm and solid. His rough hands, however, told the story of a life full of hardship. Youde recalled at once Loo's stories about Mosula's ordeals. To think that the Chin-kuei he had played catch with in the school yard had miraculously survived and is now the celebrated "Mosula, the Amazing Beast!" Youde squeezed the hands in his grasp with extra force.

Two classmates who used to vie for number one in grade school, now again are fellow prison friends under the harsh, foreign regime. Who would have foreseen the meeting of these two men, grasping each other's hands in a prison? Youde's heart was full with lament.

102

Study Session

THE study session started at 2 p.m. A guard came to open the door and everybody, carrying books and notepads, stepped out. They then put on their shoes, which were lined up outside the room, as bare feet were not permitted. From the room across the corridor, people of Sections 3 and 4 also straggled out. They proceeded to the large hall, where each picked up a canvas folding stool and lined up in a neat formation.

With the section heads leading the way, they walked toward the open yard via the long corridor. The comrades, who were attired mostly in tanks and boxer shorts, could hardly have been taken as anything but a bunch of prison inmates.

"Again!" Some people in rooms along the corridor stared from behind the bars, not a few with abject contempt. With good reason too, Youde thought. Because the marching column was about to attend a gathering to sing the praises of the very dictator who had wasted these inmates' lives. As they passed in front of Room 15, Youde instinctively turned to look and met Mosula's eyes head on. Mosula gave a small nod.

The re-ed counselees, forty in all, entered the open yard and settled in a shaded corner. Counselor Fu sat down by the wall. The counselees opened their folding stools and sat in front of and around him. Section Leader Hsiung quickly took the place to the right of Fu. While Youde was still trying to make up his mind — thinking maybe he should stay far away from the counselor — and was still wandering about carrying his stool, Counselor Fu called him by name. Yang was called upon too. The two newcomers ended up sitting next to Fu and became the focus of everybody's attention.

Section Leader Hsiung was to conduct today's proceedings. He stood up and commanded briskly and in succession: "Stand up!" "Bow to Counselor Fu!" "Take your seats!" "The superior officer will speak!"

Counselor Fu stood up and introduced Youde and Yang, then raised his voice as he started to talk. He first commented that the work of re-education was progressing smoothly with everybody's cooperation and that all made good achievements in their studies, a fact the headquarters also recognized. Then he admonished the group to carry on the good work and not to slacken. That concluded his customary introductory remarks. Next, he gave a "report," which was a rundown of news events on the outside. Everybody listened with great interest. Newspaper reading was not permitted in here. Starved of outside news, the inmates were thankful for the "report." Youde thought with irritation: But why can't they permit newspaper readings to the already-sentenced, especially since the newspapers are heavily censored to start with?

After the news report, Fu gave the following sermon:

> "The world situation is developing in our favor. President Chiang had given us clear and accurate directives: Prepare in the first year; attack in the second year; root out the enemies in the third; and achieve the victory in the fifth year.
>
> "The moment of victory is approaching. You must correct your past mistakes as soon as you can and, as our fellow comrades, work toward the construction of the true, new China of the Three People's Principles. Our government has been humane and generous toward you. Suppose tables were turned and you were arrested by the Communists for being pro-KMT? You know, without exception, you would all have been shot. You must be thankful for our great leader, President Chiang, and pledge your allegiance to him!"

A familiar sermon no doubt, because the group sometimes smiled and sometimes nodded. Nodding was not a problem, but it was not so easy to smile properly, lest it be taken for a sneer. Youde noticed that Section Leader Hsiung was maintaining a Mona Lisa-like smile in suspension. Youde thought of Mosula's horrendous abuse by a counselor. Could it have started from not being able to sustain such a smile?

Following Counselor Fu, Section Leader Hsiung stood up and announced, "Today's topic of discussion is 'The immediate goal and the ultimate ideal of nationalism.'"

Hsiung called on Comrade Ting, his fellow teacher from Quemoy, to speak first.

Comrade Ting stood up and started to speak from a prepared draft: "The immediate goal is to overturn the Manchu regime in order to construct a nation of the Chinese people. Then, to abolish all the unequal treaties that China had signed under duress with the strong nations of the world, so as to pull China out of the status of sub-colonialism. The ultimate ideal of nationalism is to help all weak and helpless peoples of the world and to realize the Confucian ideal of a peaceful One World."

These were Sun Yat-sen's enlightened views, except the Manchus had collapsed some fifty years ago and the unequal treaties had also been abolished way back when. What was the sense of rehashing this stuff? Youde brooded.

After Comrade Ting spoke, Section Leader Hsiung asked the rest of the group to express their opinions. Two or three raised their hands and quickly read their mostly formulaic opinions. When no more raised hands were to be found, Section Leader Hsiung went down the row, one by one, and asked for their opinions. Waiting for one's turn to speak was tiresome at best. Yet it continued on and on, compelling all to wish for the afternoon shower.

Little Wang, who was sitting across from Youde, hurriedly covered his mouth to stifle an unguarded yawn. Then, as if satisfied with a successful cover-up, he smiled.

The time was up when there were still a few people ahead of Youde to be called on.

Counselor Fu stood up, assigned the person to conduct the next session, gave the next day's topic and disbanded the study session.

For Youde, the very first two hours of brainwashing was finally over.

103

Visitation

At last, the fourth Sunday of June arrived. It was the day for family visits. Youde's wife had written to say she would surmount all difficulties to make the visit.

The visiting hours for Building 3 were set for 1 to 5 p.m. Youde waited impatiently all morning long. This was the first time in ten months he would see his wife since his arrest on October 2 of the past year.

Youde's name was announced soon after one o'clock. Together with Yang and two others, Youde left the room. He saw a few others coming out of other rooms, among them Fu-lin. The group passed through the iron gate at the end of the large hall and was taken to the side of a tall fence. This modern, brand-new prison facility apparently had no visiting room.

There were five eye-level openings on the fence, each spaced a few feet apart. The openings were covered with shutters that had large numerals in white paint on them. The visits were to take place through the openings, with the fence in between.

Youde's name was called. He stood in front of the number 1 opening, which was the size of a large roof tile. The guard gestured for Youde to open the shutter himself.

Youde pushed the shutter to the side.

Three feet in front of him was his wife's face in close-up.

"Oh, Panto!" Youde blurted.

"Honey," Panto called. No more words were possible.

Tears flooded their eyes, choked words gurgled in the back of their throats — a teary scene that Youde had not expected.

"Mama, why are you crying?" came a child's voice from the other side of the fence.

Finally his wife's voice formed into words: "I brought Ah-jing with me."

Youde could hear the sound of Panto stepping off a platform. The opening was apparently higher than eye-level from the outside.

No sooner had he wiped the tears from his eyes than he saw his daughter Ah-jing's face, hoisted up by Panto. Ah-jing had just turned two and half and was reputedly a good talker.

"Papa!" Ah-jing called in a loud voice and stared at Youde with interest.

"Good girl, Ah-jing!" Youde choked again.

"Papa, look at my new dress," Ah-jing tried to show her dress to Youde.

Panto raised Ah-jing up higher. It was a white dress with red polka dots, a makeover from Panto's own dress, Youde immediately realized.

"It's a pretty dress," Youde stuck his hand through the opening to reach Ah-jing's face. The reach was short by a tad.

"Hey!" a guard yelled. Youde withdrew his hand in a hurry. Right away a guard approached to examine Youde's hand, suspecting a sharp object might have been received.

Ah-jing, pointing with her finger, asked, "Mama, is it America over there?"

Her innocent words brought up tears afresh.

His wife's face switched back.

"I've been telling her that you are in America."

"I see. Not a bad idea."

"She's been praying for your early return."

"How is mother?"

"She's in very good health. You don't have anything to worry about. Baby Liang is doing fine too."

"I am glad it's a boy."

"I would love to show him to you soon. Everybody says he's a dead ringer for you. Maybe I should bring him next time."

"Better not try to do too much. Where is he today?"

"Mother's taking care of him. That's why I have to go back home by today's train."

"You look a bit tired."

"Really? It's probably from lack of sleep. I didn't sleep well last night. You look like you have lost a little weight. I am sorry that I couldn't manage to send more care packages. But today I did bring a lot of stuff, mother's homemade *bafu* (seasoned dried pork) too. I had to turn them in at the Service Office."

"I don't need care packages anymore, really. The food here is the regular military fare and is not bad. Please don't bother about care packages. I would rather you folks at home eat good nutritious food and stay healthy."

Panto chuckled as she said, "You seem kinder and gentler."

"I've always been kind and gentle."

"You also seem to be more manly."

"I guess so. I've been through a few things."

"I read the court decision. It did not seem like much."

"It was nothing to start with. Anyway, it's a not-guilty verdict."

"Then why don't they release you? It's a not-guilty verdict, isn't it? When can you come home?"

"I have no idea," Youde couldn't quite bring himself to say it was going to be three years from now. It was a matter not so easily explained to somebody who has no knowledge of how re-education works.

"Maybe another three months?" his wife was concerned about the amount of time left to serve.

To live day by day without thinking about the passage of time is the way of the prison. Instead, Youde said, "Ya, it would be nice. How are you getting along money-wise? You probably had to go to some trouble to come up with the travel expenses for this trip, did you not?"

"It will be all right. Travel expenses are nothing. Don't you worry about it. Not too long ago I sold the gold cigarette case you got in Mexico. I'm sorry for doing so without asking. You know, I sold it for two thousand yuan. The money will last awhile."

The gold cigarette case fetched a sum equivalent to two and half months' salary. Youde was quite grateful for the unexpected windfall, except the cigarette case had been the only valuable they owned.

"I see, that's great. Sell anything you like — the fan, the record player, the records. We can acquire them again later."

"I can't. I can't sell the things that you took so much pains to bring home. How can I?" Tears filled her eyes anew.

"The fact is," she said after catching her breath, "I have applied to Chiayi prefecture's Department of Education to return to teaching. I may get the good news sometime next month. You see, I wasn't going to tell you until then.... But, well, it's out now."

"What are you going to do with the children when you go back to work?"

"We can hire a nanny. Besides, mother is there, so I don't have to worry. Mother, too, likes the idea very much of me getting back to work."

"I see. But it's probably better not to put too much stock in getting your job back. I wonder if they will allow a thought-criminal's wife to teach."

"Sure. There is already one who's a wife of a thought-criminal. Chen Ching-tu's wife is teaching at Ta-tung Elementary."

"In her case, her husband was arrested while she was still on the job. They can't very well fire her for her husband's arrest."

"What's the difference? Besides, you got a not-guilty verdict."

His wife was strong willed and rather optimistic. "Does she know that once branded a thought-criminal one would come under all sorts of restrictions?" Youde wondered.

"One way or another, I will know something about it come next month," his wife said with confidence.

Teachers' contracts usually come out before the beginning of the new school year in August.

"Next month is only three days away."

"There are cases where people did not receive their contracts until the latter half of August. As long as it's in time for school opening in September."

The guard blew the whistle.

Ten minutes of visiting time had evaporated.

"Do look after yourself." Panto once again hoisted Ah-jing up to the opening.

"Papa, goodbye!" Ah-jing said spiritedly as she waved to Youde.

Pshiit! The shutter of the opening slid shut with indifference.

104

America Amid the Bitter Sea

Youde stepped back from the fence into the shade. Fu-lin, having just finished his visitation, came over to talk to Youde.

"Did your wife come to see you?"

"Yes. My daughter too. Did you see your wife too?"

"No, my wife was just here not too long ago. Today, Mrs. Chuang came to see me, all the way from Hengchun. She really didn't have to."

Hengchun is the southernmost town of Taiwan.

"Is that so? I'm surprised." Youde was impressed.

Fu-lin said, "Chuang left a note before he was executed. How foolish of me, of course, it's before ... ha ha...," Fu-lin laughed at his own linguistic bungling. "In it, supposedly, he told his wife that he had done us wrong and asked her to do whatever she could to help us for his atonement. This is the second time Mrs. Chuang has come here. She brings a large care package when she comes. I told her not to bother anymore, but she still comes. I would imagine it's not easy supporting a family by herself."

"I see, what an unusual story. But do you hate Mr. Chuang?"

"Not at all, not anymore. Actually, I feel so sorry for him. I talked about Mr. Chuang with hatred back in the Chiayi jail, didn't I?"

"Not that I remember."

"Yes, I hated him then. But the hatred has long since gone, because I came to understand Mr. Chuang's predicament after witnessing and hearing so many different stories since then. On the contrary, if I had the chance, I would have told him not to blame himself to such an extent."

"Does his wife still run the charcoal business?"

"Yes, she does. Just today, she said the business is doing well. But it must be quite a job to have to toil covered from head to toe in black powder. I can see traces of black on the tip of her nose, on her earlobes, as if the black powder has penetrated into her skin."

"She apologized too, saying the blackness doesn't come off even after repeated washings."

"It hasn't been a year since Mr. Chuang's passing. I guess she still doesn't feel like putting on makeup."

"When we get out, Po-sung and me, we will do something for the Chuangs in return for their kindness."

"To return the kindness" seemed to be another linguistic misrepresentation in this case. Youde chuckled to himself. Nevertheless, Fu-lin's sense of loyalty was evident.

When all ten people gathered again, the guard led them back to their rooms. On the way, Youde told Yang and Fu-lin about what his daughter had said. At "Mama, is it America over there?" Yang, Fu-lin, and others in the group all burst out laughing. Even the guard, who did not seem to be paying attention, smiled and asked, "How old is she?"

Returning to the room, Yang immediately told of what Ah-jing had said.

The room bubbled with light-hearted laughter. Even the ever-serious Section Leader Hsiung laughed out loud. That people would get such a kick out of it was totally unexpected to Youde.

Little Wang, fanning a paper fan, his shoulders and pelvis gyrating, strutted across the room like a merry Pierrot the clown while sing-songing, "We are in America, in America. Ha ha ha."

The reason for the laughter came to Youde as he watched Little Wang's antic. Postwar America was indeed the symbol of wealth and freedom. To think that these people who live in the bottomless pits devoid of freedom are really in America, heaven on earth, was hilarious indeed.

Youde joined Little Wang in the sing-song, "It's America. We are in America."

They laughed until they cried.

105

Walk with Mosula

Soon after August, Youde and Mosula got together in their walks. While the group was walking in the four-column formation, by switching with people walking in front of him one row at a time, Mosula managed to get close to Youde. In no time, they were walking side by side. Youde noticed immediately the peculiar gait of Mosula's and wasted no time asking, "I heard you were tortured severely."

Mosula chuckled and said, "It's a wonder that I didn't die."

Youde was concerned about the way he walked, so he asked, "Is your hip hurting?"

"My hip doesn't hurt anymore, but I no longer can walk in strides like I used to."

"Your legs seem fine."

"Not really. I had a lot of trouble there. They beat me at the shins, where it hurts the most, and broke both my shinbones, causing my legs to swell to twice their normal size."

Youde instinctively looked down at Mosula's legs.

"For three months, I was not able to walk at all. To go to the toilet, I had to either crawl or have somebody help me. It took a good six months before I could truly walk. But you know the saying, 'The ground hardens with rain; the bones strengthen with breakage' is really true. My legs are stronger than ever."

Youde looked again at Mosula's bare legs beneath his short pants. Here and there, atop of his shins, were gumball-sized lumps, something Youde did not notice at first.

"I see some lumps...."

"Yes. My shinbones not only broke but also sustained numerous cracks. Gradually, calcium congealed over the cracks and turned into growth-like things. I have at least ten of those on either shin. You see, I was clubbed by huge men wielding hoe handles."

Youde imagined the unimaginable beatings. The conversation ceased for a while.

"From whom did you hear about my torture?"

"When I was in the Military Court Prison, I heard it from Loo. But he didn't mention anything about your legs."

"That clown, Loo! What did he say?"

"He said that you were strung up with your hands tied to your back, beaten, and left strung up all night."

"Exactly."

"He said that at the end, pulled down by your own body weight, your arms were stretched out of joint, still tied backward."

"That's correct too."

"Finally, you had your arms raised over your head as if shouting *banzai*.... He was pretty irate about the inhumane treatment."

"Saying *banzai* with arms raised backward, I see.... Loo is pretty good at describing, isn't he? But that wasn't all. The counselor climbed on my back as I was hanging. My shoulder joints, already about to be pulled out of their sockets, had to support the additional weight of a big man!"

"Can a human body really endure such strain?"

"Hard to believe, but it was true. My joints were completely ruined. It's been almost three years, but I can just raise my arms to eye-level — in front of course, ha ha ha."

Mosula smiled a lonely smile.

Again, silence took over — silence in which the abused shoulder joints loomed large.

"But more than my shoulder joints, this is the worst," Mosula stuck out his wrists to show Youde. People walking in front of them also turned their heads to look. What Youde took to be rings of thick, black rubber bands on his wrists turned out to be dead tissue left from being strung up.

Running his fingers over Mosula's painful looking wounds, Youde asked, "And this is more painful than the shoulder joints?"

People all around stopped talking in order to listen to Mosula's reply.

"Exactly. They handcuffed me from the back, then passed a rope through the handcuffs to string me up."

"I always pictured them using a hemp rope...."

"The germ-covered handcuff cut into right here, breaking the skin first, then cutting into the flesh, then reaching the bone."

"The kind of things they do!" Somebody's irate words could be heard.

Not even in the movies had Youde ever seen such inhumane practices.

"Overnight, my two wrists were infected and festered, covered with blood and discharge. That's how I got my five-centimeter rings of hurt."

Silence again. How did he survive that?

"What's interesting," Mosula said unexpectedly — Youde said to himself, what's so interesting, nothing but inhumaneness! — "is that the human sense of pain seems to converge on the most painful spot. Like the pain from beating slackened and ceased when the shoulder joints started to hurt. Likewise, the pain in my shoulders was taken over by pain in my wrists. At that point, I didn't feel any other pain. Then I lost consciousness."

"It's really something that your body endured," Youde said with appreciation.

"Truly a Mosula," somebody was heard saying.

"When I came to the next morning, lying in the middle of the room, my body was on fire. Not until I saw the worried faces of my prison friends did I know I had survived."

"It's a miracle your wrists did not develop tetanus," Youde said.

"Fortunately, a prison friend had a magic potion for injuries like that. I used up all he had, and it worked."

The person in front turned to ask a question, "There's an infirmary even on the island, isn't there?"

"It's in name only. They gave me some bandages. Other than that, they didn't do anything."

Changing the subject, Youde asked, "I heard you were put into a locker?"

"Ah, the concrete bunker. Did Loo tell you this too?"

"Ya. According to Loo...." Youde verified what he heard from Loo with Mosula himself.

"Yes, you've got it right, by and large. The only thing different was that later on we got pickles with rice instead of just salt."

"And you survived that miraculously too."

"Yep. Somebody did die right in the bunker, a very able man, a member of the Self Governing Committee at Taiwan University. They recorded it as a suicide."

"Were you in the same bunker?"

"No. These bunkers were constructed by the Japanese military during the war, and there are many of them all along the coastline. They used these bunkers as solitary rooms, one per bunker."

"I heard that the mosquitoes were horrendous," Youde said.

"Ya. Not an inch of skin left unbitten."

"I'll bet. But it was fortunate there were none carrying malaria."

"As it happened, about a week after I came out of the bunker, my father came to the island to visit me without any prior notice."

"How were you able to meet with him?"

Mosula chuckled again. "My father said he dreamt of me dying, so he went to the temples to pray to Goddess Matsu, whereupon he received a revelation — he must go to the island to save his son's life. After seeking desperately in Taitung and Taipei, he finally was able to secure a visitation permit in Taipei. But when he arrived at the island, he was refused the visitation. Not one to give up, for three days and three nights, he settled down in the front lobby of the prison office and persevered.

Finally, he was permitted a ten-minute meeting with me."

Youde conjured up Mosula's father in his mind — a doting father without parallel. He remembered well the happy father's crumbling face and broken smile when Mosula was accepted by the Tainan Normal School.

Preoccupied, Youde missed the guard's order to turn to the right and bumped right into the person in front. The group continued on in a different direction while again listening to Mosula's story.

"However, there was a condition. The counselor called me in and warned me not to breathe a word about being strung up or being in the bunker. And there were to be two guards supervising the visit between the father and the son.

"They made me put on long pants and a long-sleeved shirt, a black shirt with sleeves long enough to cover my palms. They even made me put on a hat that covered my brow. Even then, because there were still wounds that were not concealed, they chose for the visitation to take place at dusk, in a dim room without any lighting.

"As I entered the room, and as soon as he saw me, my father immediately embraced me and wept out loud."

Mosula's voice faltered somewhat, then continued, "My father took off my hat and caressed the scars. He rolled up my sleeves and examined wounds on my arms and wrists. The injuries on my wrists were still raw with discharge, a year after the torture. Tracing the wounds with his fingers, one by one, he berated, 'Damn you, damn you' and cried. Furthermore, my father rolled up my pants legs and despite the guard's objection caressed the lumps on my shins and again cursed 'Damn you, damn you.' Then he finally noticed, in the dim light, the red dots all over my body and my face. Alarmed, he asked, 'Is it a contagious disease?' When I answered, 'No, don't worry. It's not a contagious disease. It's from the mosquito bites,' he was beside himself with fury. He slammed his fists on the table and jumped up. Now my father was always fearless when he got angry. He shouted, 'I will sue you!' And the visit ended there."

Youde could remember that Mosula's father was the talk of the town for fighting with a Japanese policeman during the Japanese colonial occupation. Like father like son.

"During the visit, I said almost nothing, so the counselor couldn't exactly punish me. Perhaps because they were intimidated by my father's outburst, they became quite restrained toward me from that point on. It's been a year and ten months since."

"Has your father been back here to see you?"

"He came this past second Sunday. He has turned into an unsteady old man, though he is barely fifty years old."

"Your father, did he actually sue?" somebody asked.

"You must be kidding. Where is he going to sue? There isn't such a place," another person answered for Mosula.

Youde said, "But your father's courage is really something else. Maybe your father did save your life."

Mosula nodded. "Because I haven't been tortured since. But though we can't legally sue, there's a way to send in a plea. My father sent in a plea letter to the Military Court. A year later, right after you, Youde, were sent to the East Penyuan Temple, I was called back to the Military Court, where they ascertained my wounds. By the time you were sent back to the Military Court, I was already here. I don't imagine I will be sent to the island again."

The walk was about to end. Youde eagerly asked, "But why were you singled out for such abuse?"

"I was not alone by any means. Quite a few people were strung up like me, and there was always somebody in the bunkers. But judging from me being nicknamed Mosula, maybe I did get the roughest treatment. You know how I could never beg for mercy?"

"But there must be some reason."

"The ostensible reason they gave was that I was involved in a POW rebellion at Nanjih Island. But they know perfectly well that it was not possible. In the end, it was my stubbornness that got their goat, I think. They used me to set an example for the other prisoners, but also to satisfy their sadistic needs. They were laughing all the time they were beating me."

"But you were not at all stubborn as a child. I know it well."

"Ya. Maybe it started after I entered Tainan Normal School and began studying side by side with the Japanese. Then you start to notice all the discrimination. I was already a known eccentric while at Tainan Normal. Looking back, the six years of grade school were the happiest."

"That is truly so."

Youde and Mosula walked side by side accompanied by happy childhood memories.

The whistle sounded. The walk was over.

"Next time, you must tell me about your story," Mosula slapped Youde's shoulder.

The four-column formation noisily kicked off the dirt from their shoes at the building's entrance and returned to their rooms.

As they reached Room 15, Mosula stopped and said, "Let's see. It's been two or three months since you received your verdict, hasn't it?"

"It's been more than three months."

"In that case, Yu-kun will probably be executed pretty soon."

They parted with a wave.

106

A Parting Note

It was a short time after the start of the afternoon nap and the building had quieted down. Youde was about to lie down when Yang, who was waiting for servant Comrade Cheng at the front of the room, gestured for Youde to come over. Youde rose right away and went over. Looking through the iron bars, he saw four men approaching slowly, each shouldering a large blanket roll.

Yang called to one of them in a hushed voice, "Hey, Li!"

The person was startled. He looked toward the room. Then, recognizing Yang, he smiled and waved back. He also greeted Youde with a nod. To his surprise, the person behind Li waved at Youde. Upon closer examination, the man turned out to be no other than Li Chiang, whom Youde knew through Loo during bathing time back in the Military Court Prison. Now properly attired, he looked like a different person from the half-naked man Youde used to know.

Youde realized that the four had just arrived at the facility after receiving their verdicts. He also remembered that Li's case was part and parcel with Yu-kun's case.

Yang muttered, "The man I greeted is Li Teng-ke. He lived next door to me when I was in the West Area. His case was also related to Chang Yu-kun's."

That these four people, who should have been charged with Article 4 for hiding Yu-kun, were here signified to Youde that Yu-kun's case had been decided and Yu-kun was no longer of this world. For a moment, Youde mistook the silent, blanket-carrying figures for messengers of death.

Yu-kun is at last executed. The place of execution must be no other than the Ankang execution yard of this very facility. But the sound of gunshots cannot reach here. Youde realized.

"When?" "Together with whom?" Youde's mind raced with questions, even wondering unnecessarily about who would come to fetch Yu-kun's body.

The four men passed by and disappeared. Youde laid down again but stayed awake until two o'clock, the time for the study session.

Youde searched for the four men as he passed by the rooms to head toward the open yard. He knew that it was unlikely that the four would be placed in the same room. Rather, they most likely would be split among two or three rooms. Halfway there, Youde spotted Li Chiang watching the passersby from behind the bars. Li waved to Youde and acted like he had something to say. But with the counselor following close behind, Youde was not able to break away from his group, so he gave a small nod and walked by. Li looked visibly disappointed.

The day's discussion topic was "Communist atrocities." The topics of the study sessions usually fell into three, large categories: one, Sun Yat-sen and the Three People's Principles; two, Chiang Kai-shek's achievements and his virtuousness; and three, Communist atrocities.

Youde thought indignantly: By all reasoning, instead of studying Communist atrocities, we should engage in a critique of Communism itself. How else can we be brainwashed? Yet we are not allowed to read any books on Communist ideology, so a critique of Communism is out. That leaves nothing but Communist atrocities to take up where Communism is concerned. But how absurd to ask native Taiwanese, who lived the daily reality of KMT atrocities, to discuss Communist atrocities of which they have no firsthand experience — except for a few people who fell victim to the spy judge? How about KMT atrocities? There are five thousand victims here at Ankang alone at this very moment, each with his own story of heartbreaking misfortune. And if we were to gather all the victims since the February 28 Incident, there would be enough to fill a large compendium. Or do they not think the tortures that Mosula endured an atrocity? Can they possibly say to the parents of the executed that executions are not atrocities?

As it is, how effective can this kind of propaganda be unless they point out that Communist atrocities are far worse than KMT atrocities?

Factual or not, the collection of Communist atrocities presented in the study sessions were voluminous. Each person was required to present cases of Communist atrocities, as speaker after speaker droned on with hearsay cases; the listeners head the same stale stories over and over.

A PARTING NOTE

It came Youde's turn to speak. Having used a case from the book on a previous occasion, today he related from memory what Big Shantung had told him during his stay in the Chiayi's prison. But Yu-kun's execution hung heavily on his mind. To Youde, the atrocities at hand were a lot closer and more real than those committed by the other side.

On his journey back to his room, Youde pointedly stayed in the back of the pack. Li Chiang lives in Room 13, Youde's mental note said. Conveniently, Counselor Fu had overtaken the team and was walking briskly ahead of them as if in a hurry to take care of some business.

When he got to Room 13, Youde casually approached it. As Youde expected, Li was waiting at the iron bars. He quickly handed Youde a small piece of folded paper and said, "Yu-kun's parting note to you. My uncle asked me to give it to you."

Passing notes was quite common among prisoners. But a re-ed counselee could not do it quite as openly, lest somebody should inform on him.

Holding Yu-kun's folded parting note in his palm, Youde remembered that Li's uncle had been imprisoned in the West Area and surmised that the uncle was among the four new arrivals whom Yang greeted the other day and the one to whom Yu-kun had entrusted his parting note to Youde.

As soon as he got back to his room, Youde hid the folded paper between pages of a notebook. He was pulled strongly by the impulse to open it right away, yet on the other hand, he also wanted to just let it lie. Not so much out of fear of informers but because the piece of paper was the last communication from a now-deceased friend, and he wanted to read it without intrusion, savoring it word by word. Youde knew it meant little to get to it sooner.

Youde decided to patiently wait until bedtime to open the note.

107

A Phantom

Lights out was at nine o'clock, but the hallway lights were left on so the guards could observe the inmates' movements. A nightlight was also left atop the partition between the bathing area and the toilet. As a result, since his space was right next to the toilet, Youde was able to make out the words by the nightlight.

Youde leaned against the wall and took out the folded piece of paper from the notebook. The folded object, half the size of a calling card, was made of crude paper and turned out to be glued on the sides and ends to form an envelope.

As Youde cut open the envelope and spread it open, a thin, white piece of paper fell onto his lap. Youde unfolded the white paper and read it under the dim light. It had only three lines; it was not addressed to anyone in particular and was unsigned — no doubt a precautionary measure. But the handwriting was unmistakably that of Yu-kun.

Youde focused on the first line and made out the characters one by one.

"I am sorry. I wept, moved by your friendship."

The second line and the third line said, "I am ashamed that the blood of the Chinese Han people runs in my body."

Words were few. But they shot through Youde like a bolt of electric current, for these were cries of shame — shame for one's country, for one's people, and of oneself. How could Yu-kun, who used to regard himself a Han Chinese and once sang the praises of the Han people, write such words? What drove him to this?

Youde found more writings on the wrapper also, written in such tiny characters that they called to mind a cheat sheet in school exams. They were hard to decipher. Youde curled up his fingers into a tube and made out the characters through it, one character at a time. The hand tube acted like a magnifying lens making the characters readable — a trick Youde learned as a boy scout together with Mosula.

"Case of Yeh Cheng-sung and Chang Yu-kun."

The names of the two leaders were on the top of the page. It continued:

6	death sentence
2	life term

Little Wang, squinting, was observing Youde with curiosity, "A harmless fellow," Youde decided and ignored Little Wang. He read on:

6	ten years
5	seven years
2	five years
1	one year
3	not guilty

In all, twenty-two people were convicted in this one case. Six death sentences out of one single case was on the high end. The names of the four other men after excluding Yeh Cheng-sung and Chang Yu-kun were not recorded, but no doubt they were the ones who had sought cover at Yeh's place at one time or another.

Who were the sixteen others? Prison lore has it that Cheng-sung did not implicate anybody. That means all sixteen were implicated by Yu-kun, among them the Li family, who hid him, and Loo the clown, who gave him money.

Through Wen-bang, Youde was also acquainted with the other leader of the case, Yeh Cheng-sung, the pampered son of a wealthy doctor in Chiayi. Wen-bang and Yeh were two peas in a pod, sharing similar family backgrounds, of like personality and contemporaries at the College of Law and Commerce by way of Chiayi Middle School. Youde remembered Yeh as a handsome standout whom Yu-kun used to call Tsuruta Koichi (Number one Tsuruta), insinuating that Yeh was more handsome than the famous heart-throb Tsuruta Koji. In life, Yeh was gentle, intelligent and fair minded — a fine young man no one could find fault with. He was elected president of the student government at the college, as well as the president of the Collegiate Friendship Association.

Then, as a matter of course, he went into hiding after the April 6 student crackdown. Now again, as a matter of course, he was executed by a firing squad. For this was the plot of the destiny that God had written for the Taiwanese elite.

Suppressing his angry tears, Youde put away the paper and lay down. As he did so, Yu-kun appeared in the back of his closed eyelids.

The phantom spoke to Youde, "I am sorry, to make you suffer so."

"It's OK. Too bad I wasn't any help to you."

Tears ran down from the corners of Youde's eyes. Little Wang rolled himself over with a thud, perhaps for fear of seeing what he shouldn't have.

The phantom talked again, "I really wept, moved by your friendship. By God's arrangement, I was able to see you on the day you went to court, but I didn't have the face to meet you. Yet I couldn't bear not to call your name because I knew intuitively that it was our last chance. But I was not able to say anything when you turned around and shouted, 'I don't hate you.' Even now, I can still hear those words clearly. I wept that evening. Not only that evening, I wept every time I thought of what you said. Those words were most precious to me. Thank you."

The phantom continued, "I heard quite a few things about you from the Bull. He also said to me, 'I wish I, too, had a friend like Tsai Youde.'"

When he opened his eyes once more, Youde found Little Wang had rolled back to face this side again and was stealing a glance at him.

Little Wang hurriedly closed his eyes.

Youde wiped off the traces of tears, gently tapped Little Wang on the stomach and said with a smile, "It's nothing. It's all in the past. Let's sleep."

Little Wang grinned and rolled onto his other side. Soon Youde could hear Little Wang's easy breathing.

108

On the Train

Youde lay awake silently mouthing the last two lines from Yu-kun's parting note: "I am ashamed that the blood of the Chinese Han people runs in my body."

The words brought back to Youde a vivid, contrary memory. The event took place after Taiwan's Restoration, soon after Youde and Yu-kun had entered college.

College students from Putzu, some ten plus, customarily arranged to go home together by train during school recess. The railroad was operating then, albeit with shabby, unrepaired cars that had escaped direct hits during the war. The third-class train that the students rode — the only one to give a student discount — used to take anywhere from six to ten hours to travel the two hundred kilometers between Taipei and Chiayi. From there, they switched to the narrow-gauge light rail to travel for another hour to the white train station of Putzu.

But the long journey was not at all a hardship to the home-bound students. They swapped news about campus life. They sang. They talked about girls, books, studies, about their dreams for the future — and they laughed. The time passed joyously.

On one of these trips, a group of fellow passengers on the train began to openly criticize the government. From the government incompetence to the craven corruptions of the bureaucrats, they cited example after example, their voices growing ever more agitated; and they cursed the mainlanders as "pigs" at every turn.

Criticisms like this were already commonplace barely six months after the Restoration, which the Taiwanese had welcomed with enthusiasm. Martial law was not yet in place; therefore, one did not risk immediate arrest for criticizing the government then.

Now the group's conversation was about the army. The loud voice of a man who was wearing only a tank top on that winter day said, "Look at that Chink army. Isn't it exactly like what's in the Japanese cartoons? I didn't believe it back then, but it turned out to be true. Can you believe they actually march carrying paper umbrellas on their backs?"

Another voice said, "I wonder what they do with the umbrellas when attacking."

"What opportunity did they have for attacking? They retreated all the way!"

"The soldiers are mostly illiterate too."

"It turned out to be true, too, that they made pairs of soldiers shoulder a bamboo pole with kettles and pots and pans dangling from each end."

"And what do you think of the way they do their leg garters? They don't know to fold it back in the middle!"

"At first, some people said they wrap lead plates in the garters for training purposes, for extra weight you know, and that accounted for the clumsy look. Supposedly, they would take out the lead plates in battle so the soldiers would be able to soar with a lightened load. I thought it was pretty clever."

"Don't be stupid!"

Suddenly, Yu-kun stood up and approached the group of bantering passengers.

"Hey, brothers, I am a Taiwanese too; but I frankly think your views are wrong."

All eyes on the train turned to Yu-kun.

"China is different from Japan. It is not a militaristic nation. In Japan, the military was given every advantage. People could be starving, but the military had plenty. People could be in rags, but the military was always in sharp uniforms. The Japanese military was able to allocate resources at will. But our country, China, is different. It is not militaristic. That is why the military had to endure inadequate supplies. In my view, the errant party is really the people of China who sent them into battle without sufficient equipment. Yet with their pitiful equipment they did battle with the Japanese for eight years. An achievement if you ask me. Despite victorious assault after assault by the

Japanese, the Chinese fought back and persevered and finally brought the Japanese army to their knees so that Japan surrendered. Isn't that so? Which one, tell me which one do you think is greater? The well-equipped Japanese army or the Chinese army, who fought carrying their pots and pans?"

The car was at once silent. One person started to clap, then many followed with loud hands.

"We the Han people," Yu-kun was on a roll, "are one of the most superior peoples in the world, no less so than the Yamatos, the Anglo-Saxons, the Germans. We have five thousand years of glorious history and culture. At a time when our ancestors were already enjoying a highly developed civilization, the ancestors of today's self-appointed 'cultured' people were still mired in barbarism. No natural calamities nor external invasions were able to vanquish the Han people. It has survived and grown in strength. One quarter of the world's population is Han. Just wait and see. The twenty-first century will be the century of the Han people. And think! In our bodies pulses the blood of the Han people. We must never forget and should always be proud of it."

Again, applause.

Yu-kun returned to his seat. Youde and his friends greeted him with applause too.

This was eight years before his execution.

109

To Repay Enmity with Virtue

After two days hiatus due to rain, the topic of the study session that followed was "President Chiang's spirit of brotherly love."

Books about Chiang's great accomplishments were ubiquitous, yet stories about his "spirit of brotherly love" were rarely seen for some reason. One could hardly make a speech out of Chiang visiting a remote village with Madame Chiang in tow and patting the school children on their heads. Consequently, the talk that day centered on his policy toward postwar Japan: To repay enmity with virtue.

During the eight years of the Sino-Japanese war, the Japanese military spread the war to all corners of China, costing China tens of thousands of lives and imposing untold sufferings on the entire people. They also committed numerous deliberate atrocities. Nevertheless, at the war's conclusion, President Chiang raised high the banner of Confucian teachings — to repay enmity with virtue — and admonished the Chinese people from taking revenge on the Japanese military or other Japanese. Furthermore, he transported the one million Japanese army members ahead of others back to Japan. Compared to the constant American refrain of "Remember Pearl Harbor," and America's vengeful actions during the Tokyo war tribunal, Chiang's actions were indeed an expression of his spirit of brotherly love, deserving of praise and being remembered in perpetuity. In fact, the Japanese, too, are grateful for this benevolence, as evidenced by the yearly visit to Taiwan by their parliamentary representatives to pay respect to President Chiang.

The day's study session turned into a series of speeches on "To repay enmity with virtue," all of such similar content that they could be more aptly termed recitals. When it was Youde's turn to speak, he stood up and repeated the familiar refrains but then added a personal anecdote. It was about what a Japanese business executive had said to him as they shared the smoking area on the propeller plane traveling from Tokyo's Haneda airport to Taipei on Youde's trip home from America. The Japanese executive, who claimed to count many members of the parliaments of both Japan and Taiwan among his friends, had said he thought President Chiang was a rare, great leader of modern history and that he was deeply grateful for the generous treatment of the Japanese after the war. He also said that the people who owed their early repatriation to Chiang had contributed greatly to Japan's postwar construction. Unlike the Japanese, who were detained by the Soviet Union, he thought the Japanese soldiers in China were fortunate indeed. He said he would never forget Chiang's charity. Youde added that he believed the man's words were sincere and his feelings of gratitude genuine and evident.

The anecdote pleased Counselor Fu evidently, because he clapped when Youde was finished.

Nevertheless, Youde sat down with a heavy heart. Yu-kun's and Yeh Cheng-sung's executions clung to his mind. Just several days ago, this very President Chiang had signed the orders for their execution. The slogan "to repay enmity with virtue" had disappeared to nowhere. In its stead was Chiang's personal directive that said "Do not let one guilty escape even if a hundred are mistakenly killed." Why?

Letting pass the praises his comrades were piling on Chiang's spirit of brotherly love, Youde reasoned:

The soldiers of the foreign army did not pose any threat to his regime. On the contrary, it was probably more dangerous to let them stay around. Hence, Chiang was able to carry out the policy of "to repay enmity with virtue." However, to his fellow compatriots who could pose real threats to his power, he showed no mercy.

As far as the Taiwanese were concerned, what Chiang did was exactly the opposite of "to repay enmity with virtue." Rather, it was a case of "To repay favor with retribution."

Youde recalled the day when Chiang first visited Taiwan soon after the war was over. On that day, Yu-kun had clung to a tree branch and over and over, in his already hoarse voice, shouted "Long live President Chiang!" It was on that occasion that Youde met Yeh Cheng-sung through Wen-bang's introduction. Yeh and Wen-bang, both astride the same tree branch, were shouting "Long live President Chiang!" at the top of their lungs. One by one, Chiang had sent these patriots to the execution yard, these young men who had once admired him and welcomed him with such fervor. And for what? For actions that no other democratic country would consider crimes! The explanation could only be that Chiang was taking revenge on Taiwan for his loss on the mainland.

Youde also remembered a photo-story in a *Life* magazine he picked up immediately prior to his return. The reporter, who inexplicably was allowed a visit to Green Island, had taken a few photographs of the prisoners on the island. The caption read: By American criteria, not one of these people needs to be incarcerated.

Suddenly, the class conductor announced the conclusion of the day's session. The counselees stood up, folded their stools, and straggled back to one of the buildings in this prison.

Youde mused: Suppose the *Life* magazine reporter were to come here, he would probably report this: By American standards, not one of these five thousand prisoners needs to be here.

After all, the five thousand here are supposed to be less guilty than the ones on Green Island.

Youde further contemplated: I have no doubt an American president would release them all. Does one really need to drag in the Confucian teaching of "to repay enmity with virtue?" Isn't the constitution of the Republic of China a sufficient basis for freedom? After all, it is fundamentally a democratic constitution, based as it is on Sun Yat-sen's Three People's Principles, which in turn originated from Lincoln's "The government of the people, by the people, and for the people."

However, similar constitutions in practice resulted in two governments as different as heaven and earth. Taiwan's government shelved the constitution and secured a dictatorship with myriads of special laws in order to carry out its rule of terror.

Be that as it may, the evaluation of Chiang's merits and demerits can only await the research of future historians. Surprisingly enough, the Little Lu of fourth grade education might have bluntly provided a most democratic conclusion: "Let those who want to worship him worship him. Let the ones who want to spit on him or urinate on him, spit and urinate on him."

110

A Father's Heartbreak

It was a rare occasion that four people from the same hometown of Putzu were able to walk side by side in a row: Youde, Mosula, Li Chiang, and Li's uncle. As Youde had guessed, Li's uncle was the person who greeted Yang upon arriving. The uncle's name was Li Teng-ke.

Youde assumed this was their first encounter; but it turned out that Li's uncle already knew Youde and Youde's wife, Panto, too, because he was the mayor of the village where Panto taught school before marrying. The uncle said he had even attended Youde's wedding reception as a guest on the bride's side and had sized up the bridegroom then. Youde and Li shook hands like old friends.

"I never thought I would see you here," Mayor Li said with a sigh. He went on to praise Panto's teaching, recalling how he had made sure that his own daughter was assigned to Panto's class.

But such idle conversation had to take a backseat today, for who knew when they would be together again like this. The guard usually picked ten rooms arbitrarily out of fifty to let out at a time. Youde told Mayor Li that he and Panto had two children now and that she had come to visit him just the other day, then quickly switched to ask about Yu-kun.

"How did you feel when Yu-kun was taken out for execution?"

"Nothing in particular." Mayor Li was obviously reluctant to talk about Yu-kun. But he spoke of Yeh Cheng-sung at great length. After heaping praises on Yeh he added, "In the West Area, the person everybody feels for the most is Yeh's father."

"Is that right?"

"His father must be crushed. He must be sobbing day and night."

Many parents of the executed collapsed in their sorrow. Why did Yeh's father merit special mention? Youde waited for Mayor Li to continue.

"You see, it's his father who got him out of hiding."

"What! Oh no."

"Cheng-sung and Yu-kun were hiding in the safe house in the mountains, or to be accurate, I should say Yu-kun moved in on Cheng-sung after leaving my place. There were five of them, all executed now, sharing that house, with the expenses all paid for by Yeh's father, who as you know, is a wealthy doctor and a landowner. The safe house was almost perfect. If they had lived there quietly I bet nothing would have happened. But, because of Yu-kun, it began to unravel. One day, Yu-kun went into Chiayi and did not return. So the rest of the fugitives took precautions and scattered to other hiding places. Sure enough, the secret agents soon ambushed the safe house based on Yu-kun's confession."

"Why did Yu-kun go to Chiayi?" Youde asked.

"To gather intelligence or, should we say, to find out what was going on in the world. From time to time, he would come out to the city to read the newspapers."

"Didn't they have a radio?"

"Supposedly they did. But it was on the fritz that day. Like they say, when you are out of luck bad things pile on top of each other to make a tragedy. Of course, even after getting the news from the radio, they still wanted to read the papers. So they used to go into town in peasant disguises and buy an ordinary item, then wrap the item with the newspapers to avoid suspicion."

Youde appreciated the fugitives' desire for news.

"Some people say Yu-kun didn't go out there to gather information that day, but rather, because he craved the food. Wasn't he captured while eating noodles at the city's Eastside Market? Some say even worse things about him."

Mayor Li grinned.

"What else do they say?"

"Some say he went out for women."

Other people in the group laughed.

It was no wonder, since sex happened to also be the most urgent problem among the listeners. But Youde thought the rap on Yu-kun was most likely slanderous.

Mayor Li went on, "Anyway, Cheng-sung escaped to his second hiding place by himself while the secret agents searched for him in vain. That's when they used Cheng-sung's father. The secret agents promised the father if he persuaded his son to give himself up, the son would evade the death penalty and be sentenced to less than ten years. Otherwise, they warned, the son would sooner or later face the firing squad and he, the father, could get ten years under Article 4 for aiding a bandit. After repeated assurances, the father agreed to contact Cheng-sung. The way they went about it was kind of theatrical though. Since going straight to his son would be like admitting to the crime of either 'Aiding the Bandit' or 'Failure to Report the Whereabouts of a Known Fugitive,' the secret agents had the father feign ignorance and went around with a megaphone calling 'Ah-Sung, come on out. The authorities have promised to reduce your sentence!' Sometimes, the father shouted the message atop the agent's jeep, sometimes on foot by himself. Eventually, Cheng-sung gave himself up in the Security Defense Headquarters, accompanied by his father. I heard that the father was completely fooled by the agents' promises, right up to the time he received the words of his son's execution. If you ask me, Cheng-sung's father, a product of the Japanese educational system, was no match for the special agents when it came to acting. We felt so sorry for the father. I imagine he probably fainted when he received the news of his son's execution."

A moment of silence prevailed. One imagined an old, white-haired doctor howling with heartbreak.

After the marching formation turned right, Youde again asked Mayor Li, "But did you receive a ten-year sentence?"

"Yes, he did too," he said, pointing to his nephew Li Chiang.

"The two of us got ten years. The other two who arrived here with us the other day got seven and five respectively. Fortunately, my father got 'not guilty,' so he was able to go home recently."

"So your father too was arrested."

"Yes, imagine a man over seventy thrown in jail without mercy. Not guilty though his verdict was, he was in jail for a whole year. His health is OK now, but I heard that many old people become ill as soon as they get home, so I am kind of worried about him. It was for hiding the bastard Yu-kun that my entire family suffered this calamity. Do you see why I felt like punching him in the nose?"

Li Chiang cut in, "My uncle ran into Yu-kun a lot at bath time."

"Then you must also know Lin Jin-so, the Bull?" Youde asked.

"Of course I do. I often ran into him during baths too. The day he was taken out for execution, it was terrific, wasn't it? Oh, ya, Lin always used to praise you, saying you were a hopelessly nice guy. He said to give you his regards when I saw you."

Youde came close to tears thinking of Lin the Bull.

"Thank you for everything," Youde bowed his head and thanked the mayor. It was meant for relaying Lin's sentiments, but more for passing Yu-kun's parting note. Given the location, both men knew better than openly discuss the passing of the note.

"For that thing, thank you," Youde said once more realizing it was nice of the mayor to do the detested Yu-kun a favor at all.

"That?" Mayor Li smiled a wicked smile and put his mouth to Youde's ear. "I didn't do it for that fellow's sake. I just wanted to do a favor for the nice-guy bridegroom of that wedding day."

111
Individual Conversation

Days passed in quick succession in more or less the same routine. Soon it was October 2, exactly a year to the day Youde lost his freedom.

In the one year he spent in America, Youde traveled widely at an almost frantic pace: first going from Seattle to Washington, D.C., and New York, then touring the states of Tennessee, North Carolina, and Florida, and from there to Mexico. Doubling back to Virginia, he was off to Michigan, Indiana, and Canada, back again to New York then on to Los Angeles and San Francisco before returning to Taiwan via Tokyo. His was a life of wide-open horizons and wide-ranging new friendships. The year was easily the equivalent of five years of normal living.

In contrast, Youde spent the past year in a cramped, closed world of small prison cells. And this year too felt like five years. He had met and got to know many people, and the experience of this small world was by no means less interesting than the year abroad, notwithstanding the two worlds were diametrically opposed — one of freedom and one of terror.

After breakfast, when Youde was indulging in mournful melancholy, Servant Cheng called on Youde, "Tsai Youde, get ready for individual conversation."

Youde got up and got himself ready.

The guard opened the door. Youde followed Cheng out.

"There appears to be good news," Servant Cheng whispered.

Cheng led Youde toward the counselor's office instead of the Conversation Room.

Counselor Fu was at his desk, scanning through some documents. When Youde bowed, Fu smiled agreeably and ordered Youde to sit in the chair opposite the desk.

Cheng set a cup of cold tea in front of Youde.

It had been a long, long time since he was served tea by someone. "I am being treated like a human being," Youde realized and thanked Cheng profusely.

To Youde's further surprise, Fu extended a pack of cigarettes in his hand and offered him one. Cigarettes were without a doubt a sign of favorable treatment. Youde hesitated a moment but firmly declined Fu's favor. That's because back in the Chiayi police station, Youde had sworn to never taste tobacco again until he regained his freedom. A strange pledge maybe, but Youde had considered it a test of his resolve.

Counselor Fu said while browsing through Youde's file, "Your record is not bad. But where is the photograph you presented as counter-evidence? Do you have it with you?"

Youde thought he detected a chuckle from Fu, whose smiles were always fleeting at best.

"Yes, I have it right here." Youde took out the photograph from his shirt pocket and handed it to Fu. Youde had dropped the photograph in the pocket hoping to find just such a chance during his face-to-face with Fu.

"I see, you are well prepared," Counselor Fu laughed, "Where was it taken?"

"In America."

"I can see that. Where in America?"

"It was taken during the International Folk Fair, on the campus of the University of Michigan, in front of the Chinese booth."

The picture showed Youde giving a speech in front of a blue-sky/white-sun flag of the Republic of China.

"I was hoping that you would see that I was pro-KMT and anti-Communist."

Fu again grinned imperceptibly.

Youde thought to himself:

Maybe he is thinking, "It's transparent what you are trying to do!" For sure, the picture was a pose, but it was also true that I had refused to join in picture-taking under the five-star flags raised high by the pro-mainland students. And although the investigators had refused to believe me, it was also a fact that I never once expressed sympathy for Communism in spite of counting numerous Communists among my friends. At the same time, however, it was also true that I had wished from the bottom of my heart for the early demise of this corrupt regime and that it would disappear forever from the face of the earth.

Some people might argue that if that was how you felt, you should work for its betterment within the system. Alas, it's an assertion only people ignorant of the White Terror under the dictatorship could make. They don't know that a mere call for reform could promptly invite the fate of first having a "red cap" or a "black cap" placed on your head and subsequently being eliminated — like the Taiwanese elite who died in the aftermath of the February 28 Incident. They spoke neither of Communism nor of Taiwan's independence, they merely spoke of reforms.

Those who can openly speak of reforms to their government should realize how fortunate they are to be living in such a country and thank God for it.

"Can I have this?" Fu asked.

"Yes," Youde made his answer terse.

Fu put the photograph away in Youde's folder and shifted his position in the chair. Then in a businesslike tone of voice he started to ask questions:

"What are the superior points of the Three People's Principles?"

"Why does Communism not fit China's circumstances?"

"Do you think the retaking of the mainland will be successful?"

"Why is President Chiang revered as the savior of the Chinese people?"

Youde was able to answer all of them, although some answers were patently embarrassing to say the least.

Fu asked, looking somewhat amused, "Would you swear that what you just said was truthful?"

The only possible answer was yes.

"Yes, I do."

"Then, stand up and swear to it."

Youde stood up, facing the twin portraits of Chiang Kai-shek and Sun Yat-sen on the wall, raised his right hand, and swore that his earlier answers were all from the bottom of his heart.

Fu made Youde write the pledge: "I, Tsai Youde, swear to believe in the Three People's Principles, to support President Chiang, and, to the best of my ability, to work for the sacred war against Communism and Russia."

After putting away the pledge in the file, Fu again opened his mouth.

"The truth is we may select a few comrades with superior records and let them go home. I can't guarantee that you will meet the conditions. And I also don't know when that's going to be. But I thought it would be good to take care of the procedures first."

Youde doubted his ears. This sudden good news, his heart raced.

"In that eventuality, you need a guarantor, do you have anybody in mind? It's best to find somebody in Taipei."

"Yes, would my brother do?"

Fu nodded and made Youde write down his brother's name, occupation, job history, and address.

Fu warned Youde in all seriousness, "You must not tell anybody about this, because we sure don't need to stir up any unnecessary disturbance. Besides, it's not like it's been decided. We'll let you know when things are decided, so I would like you to go on as before until that time."

"Yes, I understand. Please do what you can for me."

Youde rose and bowed deeply.

"One more thing, it's about after leaving here. You must not tell people about what you've heard or seen in here. Let me assure you that there are a hundred harms and not a single benefit in telling others. Actually, it's equivalent to engaging in behavior beneficial to the enemy, punishable according to Article 7 of the Law of Sedition. Can you promise me not to talk about it?"

"Yes."

"And I want you to keep in close touch and help us."

Asking me to be a spy! Youde's happy heart was overcast with dark shadows.

"How about it?" Fu asked again.

"Yes."

"All right. I wish you good luck."

Counselor Fu stood up, extended his hand and shook hands with Youde. The "individual conversation" was over.

On the way back to the room, Servant Cheng kindly whispered to Youde, "Really, don't tell anybody, not your cellmates, not your walking companions. If they know that you are about to get out, they will ask you to relay a lot of stuff they can't put in their letters, and that can become troublesome. Don't forget, there's an inspection of your belongings at exit time."

After thanking Cheng, Youde stood still for a bit and rubbed his face vigorously with both his hands before approaching Room 2 to join the group with an innocent face.

112

Parting with Mosula

Many days continued during which Youde had to hide his feelings. Each day, one or two comrades would return from their individual conversations, none showed any unusual expressions except Yu. Yu had his conversation with Fu immediately ahead of Youde and had since seemed fidgety. He sometimes even broke into grins unknowingly.

Youde felt most terrible during walking because he wanted to, or rather he knew he must, let at least Mosula know about the possible, pending release. Yet Servant Cheng's admonition was never far from his thoughts either. Youde walked with Li Chiang many more times but never ran into Mayor Li again.

One day Mosula again brought up the matter of Yu-kun and his cohorts. The regular prisoners, unlike the re-ed counselees, tended to have better access to prison intelligence, though the information was not always accurate. Like the time when the prison was briefly thrown into turmoil by news of the impending landing of the Chinese army.

"Do you know which song they sang to see Yu-kun and his friends off to be executed?" Mosula asked.

"I don't know."

"I heard it was 'Moon's Desert.' Supposedly, Yeh Cheng-sung learned this song from his father when he was a child. It was sung over and over."

"Toward the remote, moon's desert, the camel trudged...."

Mosula and Youde gently mouthed the song as they walked.

Some moments later, Youde asked, "I wonder if they sang Yu-kun's favorite song?"

"Which song was that?"

"In the moonlight, longing for your image, I walk and walk." Youde sang the last half of the song.

"No, I don't think they sang Yu-kun's song because, of the two, Cheng-sung was far more popular. He did not implicate a single person."

"Well, how about if we belatedly sing one for Yu-kun?"

The two of them softly sang as they walked, deeply immersed in their reveries.

A few days later in their walk, when Youde was still unable to break the news of his own possible probation to Mosula, Mosula relayed a piece of intelligence.

"This re-education center may be dismantled."

"......"

"I heard they are making preparations to dismantle it. I guess it will mean our parting."

"Do you know if they let people go home from here?"

"It's possible. That's entirely possible because Panchiao is super over-capacity. Just wait and keep hoping. You were always a lucky guy."

Others walking close by seemed to have perked up their ears. Youde changed the subject.

"I was told that my birthday fell on Taoism's Heaven Amnesty Day, a most propitious day that comes only once in several years. It is said that people born on that day are forgiven by God even if they have committed wanton wrongs."

"Ha ha ha. That's why you are so lucky!"

"But I am here, am I not? It might not be working after all."

"Don't be greedy. Look at Cheng-sung, Yu-kun, Chou Shen-yuan, Wen-bang, and others. You could have —"

Mosula stopped. Maybe he thought he had gone a bit too far. Then, moments later, he dropped his voice and went on, "When Yu-kun was captured, it was February, I remember. You were so fortunate to be in America. Otherwise, you would have been arrested along with the Li family. And in your case, I doubt if you could have escaped torture. You see, six months before, because of several deaths due to torture one after another, they changed the policy to allow no torture unless there was solid evidence. Only after then did you saunter back to Taiwan. Of course, the fact that you did return knowing full well of Yu-kun's capture played in your favor, else I don't think you would be let go with just re-education. And you really did well, to be the only high school teacher picked to go to America! It just seems that everything went well for you."

"I also had a photograph as counter-evidence," Youde confided to Mosula about the picture.

"I guess it wasn't a waste of time to show that piece of counterevidence in court. I am glad you don't have to be saddled with the false accusations in silence. In any case, the time to part seems to have arrived."

"I am so happy to have run into you here and we have been pretty lucky to be able to walk together often."

"I will be lonely though after you are gone," Mosula uttered, a fainthearted sentiment totally unbefitting his nickname Mosula.

"Whenever I am able to walk with you, I always get this calm and peaceful feeling that carries me through the day. It's like we have been on a school trip. Do you remember the time we went to Tainan at the semester's end? We stayed in an inn called Honest House, and a bunch of us slept on the floor of a large room? I think of those days. And as long as you are here, I can go back to those days. It's strange, isn't it?"

Shoulder to shoulder, they walked in silence. Youde screwed up his resolve and asked, "Do you have any words you would like me to give to your father?"

"No, nothing. Don't worry about something like that. Thank you anyway."

The walk ended. As they parted to return to their rooms, Youde and Mosula clasped each others' hands with more strength than ever before.

For some reason, the walking schedule changed after that day and they never saw each other again.

113

Release from Prison

It was on Wednesday, November 2, when the afternoon naptime was about to begin, that the guard showed up suddenly at Room 2 and called for Yu and Youde.

"Gather your belongings and come out here," the guard ordered.

Youde's belongings had expanded beyond the large square scarf: clothing, bedding, books, notebooks, toiletries, and the multipurpose mug. But as Youde had already gone through them, it took only two minutes for him to gather them all up and sling the blanket roll over his shoulder.

Other comrades from the room, taken by surprise, seemed lost for words. Only Little Wang leaned forward to look at Youde in the face and asked, "Are you going home?"

"I don't know," Youde could only answer.

Hurried on by the guard, Youde left the room without shaking hands or saying goodbye to anyone.

"Ah," somebody uttered, half envy, half self-pity.

Room 2 became boisterous as soon as the two men left. Voices from the room followed the two as they walked down the corridor. The room across started to stir as well when its inmates noticed the two men walking by lugging their belongings.

Servant Cheng accompanied them to the iron gate.

"Thank you for your troubles," Youde shook Cheng's hand, whose eyes showed obvious envy.

At the front office, Youde opened up his blanket roll to have the contents inspected. The inspection turned out to be less stringent than he expected. No matter, Youde had taken special care of Yu-kun's parting note ahead of time.

Unspent money in the account was returned to Youde. It totaled about three hundred New Taiwan dollars. That made Youde's expenses for the year less than two hundred New Taiwan dollars. A very frugal year indeed, Youde mused.

Two plainclothesmen — it was obvious that they were military personnel by their carriage — approached and took charge of Yu and Youde.

"You are going home!" one said with a smile.

The civilian clothes fit uneasily on them. Youde thought they were probably panchang (squad leaders) from the Military Court.

When they got out of the front gate, they found two pedicabs waiting. Yu and Youde, each paired with a plainclothesman, stepped onto separate pedicabs. The pedicab drivers looked at them with curiosity. These pedicabs were probably hired from Taipei for the round trip, Youde observed.

Slowly leaving behind the military prison, the pedicabs crossed the suspension bridge and entered the town of Hsintien. This was the first time since the arrest for Youde to be entering a town without handcuffs. Youde was elated as if on a sightseeing tour.

"How long has it been?" the plain-clothed panchang asked. He also took out a pack of cigarettes and offered them to Youde as he himself took one.

"A year and one month," Youde replied but held tight his tempted hand. I've waited for over a year, another few hours isn't going to hurt me now. But admittedly, the cigarette offer was the greatest temptation ever.

"Not bad, not bad," the panchang nodded with understanding. He then added, "I've rarely heard anybody let out after only a year and one month of re-education."

The duration of one year and one month included the whole length of time since he was first summoned for investigation. The actual time spent at Ankang Re-education Branch was three months, and the time served since the verdict was six months. Youde did not see any need to correct it for the panchang.

A long while later the panchang said, "A man who says he is your brother has been waiting in front of the office since we left to pick you up."

Youde asked him where they were going. They were headed for the Military Court on Chingtao East Road, of course.

As they approached Taipei, the traffic got busier and the pedicabs moved with maddening deliberateness.

People on the outside world busied themselves in the hustle bustle and paid no attention to this small procession. "Are they as unconcerned about the executed ones or the ones still in prison," Youde wondered.

At long last the pedicabs arrived at the Military Court Building.

For Youde, this was the third time to enter this front gate.

Yu's and Youde's brothers were waiting in front of the office. They must have waited like that for a few hours, for they were conversing with ease. As Youde had expected, Yu's brother, wearing a Sun Yat-sen suit, looked like a government bureaucrat.

Youde's brother walked over and lent his hand as Youde got off the pedicab. He asked the driver for the fare, took out his wallet and paid it despite the squad leader's empty gesture to stop him. The panchang piled on friendly smiles and told them to step inside for the release processing.

Youde's brother said, "In any case, it ended well. I got the notice only last night."

Counselor Fu was there as they stepped into the office. Fu asked Youde's brother to sign and place his thumbprint on some documents, then asked Youde to do the same. He then led Yu and Youde into a room in the back to meet a man who appeared to be his superior — a sharp-looking man in military uniform. The man looked at Yu and Youde through the top of his lenses and said, "You must become good citizens and never enter here again."

He then asked Fu, "Have you told them?"

"Yes," Fu answered, standing ram-rod straight.

"All right then."

Yu and Youde copied Fu's action, bowed to the man, then left the room. Whereupon Fu immediately said to them, "Don't forget what I told you in our individual conversations."

"Yes."

"If you do something untoward, I'll be in trouble too."

He meant that they should never tell anybody about what they've heard or seen during their imprisonment.

They thanked Counselor Fu at the door as they shook hands and parted. More than ever, Youde felt lucky to have Fu as his re-education counselor.

Walking out of the gate, they found the same pedicab drivers still waiting. Once more Youde climbed into the pedicab, this time sharing it with his brother.

They waved goodbye to the Yu brothers, though Youde was never able to get close to Yu while inside.

The pedicab rolled toward his brother's home on Hsuchow Road. Youde's brother reached over and took Youde's hands from his knees.

"You've been through a lot. But let's be thankful that you returned home whole and healthy."

"Thank you. Is mother in good health?"

"Yes. She's lost some weight but is in good spirits. I phoned her last night to let her know right away."

There was no phone at Youde's house, so the telephone messages were relayed through his uncle.

Soon they arrived at his brother's Japanese-style house.

Youde's sister-in-law scrambled out of the house. Upon seeing Youde's prisoner-like appearance, her eyes brimmed with tears. Obeying mother's instructions to the letter, the sister-in-law burned some silver-paper (a money offering to God) at the doorway, then lit some incense and handed them to Youde and made him offer thanks. Next, she sat Youde down by the hallway facing the garden and made him eat a bowl of plain noodle soup. This was another ancient custom.

Stepping up to the tatami room, Youde's eyes went straight to the wall clock. It was half past four. His sister-in-law prepared a bath for him right away and laid out a new set of underwear. On the kitchen counter, he saw an assortment of dinner dishes awaiting him. Youde was grateful for his sister-in-law's trouble.

Oh, the joy of soaking in hot water again after thirteen months! It was beyond words. As soon as he got out of the bath, the sister-in-law urged him to go get a haircut. In the old days people getting out of prison were required to shave their heads. Nowadays a cut and a shampoo would do.

Youde got on a bicycle to head for the barbershop. The ride was more than a bit rusty.

It was dusk when he came out of the barbershop.

His sister-in-law's hearty dinner was waiting.

Youde's family traditionally rarely touched alcohol, maybe an occasional beer just to be a good sport. In this, the Confucian admonition against drinking might have something to do with it, but more likely it was because the family was never upper crust. Just the same, Confucius never said a word about smoking; for whatever reason, the men in the family were all heavy smokers. Now Youde sat across from his brother, lit a cigarette, and took a long, long draw, for the first time in thirteen months.

Youde's brother said, "Panto's attempt to go back to work seems to have failed, but you will get your job back for sure. I looked into it and was assured that people with not guilty re-education verdicts can get their jobs back. First of all, you have yet to fulfill the teaching obligations for being sent abroad to study."

Teachers who studied in America on government scholarships were obligated to work at their original posts for three years upon their return, in Youde's case in Putzu High School. If it weren't for Yu-kun, Youde would have been working at the school, promoting democracy and, if advancing smoothly, would have been heading for a brilliant future in education. But now, for one thing, the government was not likely to put a person with a "Red" label in an important position. On Youde's part too, he had not a scintilla of desire to rise to a high position under this government. From this point on, all he wanted was to treasure the happiness of living peacefully with his mother, his wife, and his children.

After the cigarette, they sat down to dinner. Youde's eyes moistened at the sight of the bowl of white rice. "My prison friends are probably walking around the room after eating their dinner." Youde picked up the chopsticks, barely containing his tears. Every dish was delicious. Youde felt it was almost too wasteful to eat them all in one meal. The conversation at the dinner table ranged from talk about family members to talk about prison life and international developments. It continued long after the dinner and into the dead of the night.

114

Going Home

At daybreak the following morning, Youde bade goodbye to his brother and sister-in-law and got on the first express train from Taipei to Chiayi. This time he carried with him not the bundle tied in the floral scarf but a smart, American-bought suitcase that his wife had sent to Taipei just for this occasion. The suitcase that had once been jam-packed with novel gifts from the land of America — even Santa Claus would have looked upon it with envy — was now filled with only dirty laundry and items in need of sanitization, not a single item to please little Ah-jing. Yet he looked forward to this reunion with more yearning than any before.

The train was not crowded. Nevertheless, it was noisy with chatter. People talked about trivial things in exaggerated manners. But Youde, sitting by himself in a corner seat by the window, was not at all annoyed. Rather, he enjoyed the fast tempo of human conversation that he had been long deprived of. "There's no need to hush and I can talk to any man or woman as I wish. I am free now," Youde realized with ever-greater appreciation.

The train sped south.

The scenery outside the train window soothed his ravaged heart. The fields of Taiwan's late autumn in November were still abundantly green, a rich brocade woven from the blackness of harvested fields, golden rice stalks awaiting harvest and the brilliant emerald leaves of the sugarcane.

The nearby hills and mountains were a whole cloth of green from the dense evergreens, only a few red leaves poking through here and there. And faraway, the dark-green mountain range meandered, drawn sharply against the blue sky. The landscape was peaceful itself. No matter how you looked at it, it was not a landscape that could cultivate violent personalities, Youde thought.

The train entered the tunnel. The passengers hurriedly lowered the windows.

Youde recalled the ride a year ago when he was sent to Taipei. Unlike that trip, this time he saw in the window's reflection not the pitiful Huang Sheng-san in the drama he once played but rather a well-groomed, fine-looking young man, one with all the appearances of a man heading for home to hug his wife and children! A smile came to his face. And for no reason, he remembered how he had spurned the offer of cigarettes from the kind police officer who accompanied him last time. Youde reached into his breast pocket, pulled out a cigarette and lit it. "I am free now."

The train stopped at a station. The food vendors swarmed to the window.

Youde stood up and bought a can of candy drops, a humble present for Ah-jing. The image of the Bull's daughter, little Ah-bi, quickly doubled up with that of Ah-jing's.

The express arrived at Chiayi ahead of schedule. Youde walked the length of the overpass toward the light rail station where the train to Putzu originated. This small train had always meant the smell of home to Youde. A train of only two or three cars, it was the only suitable transportation for people lugging a load and Youde took many a trip home on it during his student days. He remembered how lots of people would greet the students at the platform and vie to carry their luggage.

It was also by this train that Youde returned from America roughly a year ago, with three suitcases no less. At that homecoming, many friends and co-workers also came to the station, not to mention the special agents who coldly looked on from the station master's window.

"Will my wife be there to greet me? I informed her last night that I'd be arriving by this train."

The train traveled west along the Tropic of Cancer, cutting across the golden rice paddies and brimming, green fields of sugarcane.

The ride, with its comforting swaying, had always induced sweet dozing. But today Youde was not able to get any shut-eye, too worked up by the approaching reunion with his family. Instead, on the back of his closed eyes, first the images of his mother, his wife, his daughter, and the son he had yet to meet went by like a slide show. They were soon replaced by the images of his fallen friends: Yu-kun, Wen-bang, and others. He could see them vividly and down to the last detail, now talking, now gesturing. They will never again ride this train and step off at the platform of that white train station.

The train whistled, a loud one for a light rail.

Youde poked his head out of the window to look ahead. The white building at the edge of the huge expanse of green field came into view. As it got close, he spotted a figure on the platform, a lone figure holding a child's hand. That's got to be Panto. She is here after all!

Youde took out his handkerchief and waved widely.

The figure loomed larger and larger till Youde was able to make out it was Panto. When he got even closer, he could see that she was holding a baby in the other arm — the baby he had yet to see. Youde imagined the small cluster of mother and children waiting patiently for the train to appear on the horizon.

The small train whistled once more, then glided into the platform. Youde jumped off the train before it barely stopped.

Suddenly a plume of white steam spewed out from under the engine with a puff and streamed onto the platform, temporarily obscuring Youde's vision.

"Papa!"

Breaking the wafting white steam, Ah-jing was running toward him dressed in her red polka-dot dress. And on her heels was Panto racing over with the baby in her arms.

A river of tears, no longer stoppable, streaked Youde's cheeks.

He dropped the suitcase and picked up Ah-jing in his arms, his tears wetting her cheeks.

"Honey, welcome home...." Youde's wife, choking back her tears, reached out and grabbed tightly onto his arm. A husband who had returned from a place worse than hell. When Youde put Ah-jing down, Panto unabashedly slipped herself into his arms. Youde found the four-and-a-half-month-old baby smiling innocently in her arm.

"I caused you a lot of suffering," Youde said, squeezing Panto tighter.

Panto simply said, "I'm glad it's over," and let the tears freely run down her cheeks.

The baby in her arms was livelier than his snapshot suggested, a robust little fellow. Looking down at the baby, Youde broke into a smile: No wonder everybody said he looked like his father.

The baby laughed when Youde put his face close and poked at the baby's cheek.

The author and his family at home after his release in November 1955

"We had better hurry. Mother's waiting at home."

"Then let's go."

Youde picked up Ah-jing again and carried his suitcase with his other hand.

They walked the length of the deserted platform and exited the station from the narrow ticket-taker's gate.

The large clock in the waiting room was pointing at half past twelve.

Outside the white station building, the mid-day sun was brilliant, flooding the road that led to Youde's home with white light, as if making a lie of his nightmare of the past thirteen months.

Postscript

Youde was fortunate to be able to go home at that time, but the elegy of sweet potatoes did not end there.

The White Terror pressed on. After the death of Chiang Kai-shek (April 1975) there followed waves of tireless struggles and much sacrifice by many who advocated democratic reform and Taiwan independence. As a result, martial law was dissolved in July 1987. But the notorious Law of Sedition — the law that sucked the blood of many innocent Taiwanese — remained in effect until May 1991, three years after the death of Chiang Kai-shek's son, Chiang Ching-kuo. That is seven months and thirty-seven years after Youde's release. The martial law period of Taiwan spanned eight months and thirty-seven years, the longest in the history of the world.

Due to the abolition of both martial law and the Law on Sedition, it was finally safe to speak about Taiwan's gulag. Youde belatedly decided to take up his pen.

But by then Youde had turned into a sixty-six-year-old grandfather with five grandchildren.

Historical Chronology

Events related to characters in this book are marked with an asterisk (*).

1544
- Portuguese sailors exclaim "Ilha Formosa" upon sighting the island, thus recording Taiwan in Western writing.

1624
- Holland occupies Taiwan and establishes its capital city in Tainan.

1626
- Spain occupies what is now the port city of Keelung.

1628
- Spain occupies Tamsui.

1642
- Holland chases Spain out of northern Taiwan.

1661
- Koxinga (patriot of Ming China) wrests Taiwan from Holland.

1683
- Shih Lang of Ch'ing China invades Taiwan. Koxinga regime collapses.

1684
- Taiwan incorporated under Ch'ing jurisdiction as Taiwan Fu of Fukien Province.

1874
- Japanese military land on Hengchun Peninsula. The Ch'ing accede to Japanese military action as a justified protective act and pay 500,000 taels of gold in reparation.

1885
- Taiwan becomes a province of Ch'ing China. Liu Ming-chuan appointed its first governor.

1894
- The capital of Taiwan is moved from Tainan to Taipei.
- Sino-Japanese war erupts.

1895
- Sino-Japanese Shimonoseki Treaty signed (April 17), ceding Taiwan to Japan.
- Republic of Taiwan proclaimed by a group of patriots (May 23).
- Japanese military lands at Auti (May 29).
- General Liu Yung-fu of the Republic of Taiwan escapes. Republic of Taiwan collapses.
- The first Japanese governor, Kabayama, reports successful pacification of the entire island (November 18).

1898
- Governor Kodama Gentaro and Civilian Affairs official Goto Shimpei takes office (March 28).
- Criminal Codes for Bandits takes effect.

1904
- Russo-Japanese war erupts (February 10).
- Governor Kodama Gentaro appointed the chief of staff in Manchuria.

1919
- First civilian governor, Hata Kenjiro, arrives in Taiwan (November 24).

1921
- Taiwan Cultural Association formed.
- Crown Prince Hirohito undertakes inspection tour of Taiwan.

1928
- Taiwan branch of Japanese Communist Party formed (April 15).

1937
- Onset of Sino-Japanese war (July 7).

1939
- *Huang K'un, Li Chin-min, Huang Chia-tsung imprisoned for anti-Japanese activities (May) and sentenced to prison terms of fifteen and twelve years.

1941
- Imperial Subject Service Society formed to promote Japanization.
- Japan attacks Pearl Harbor. Onset of World War II.

1942
- First Taiwanese volunteer army instated.

1944
- Military draft instituted in Taiwan (September 1).

1945
- Japan surrenders (August 15). End of World War II.
- Governor Ando transfers administrative powers of Taiwan to the Executive Governor Chen Yi of Taiwan Province.
- October 25 is henceforth called Taiwan Restoration Memorial Day.
- *Huang K'un et al. return home from prison and receive tumultuous welcome.

1946
- Chiang Kai-shek and wife visit Taiwan from Nanking to attend the first anniversary ceremony of Taiwan's Restoration.

- Inflation worsens.
- Tsai Youde enters Normal University (September).
- *Chang Yu-kun, Cheng Wen-bang enter Taiwan University.

1947
- February 28 Incident erupts (February 28).
- Nationalist army reinforcements begin to land on Taiwan (March 8).
- Massacre of Taiwanese begins. Tsai Youde's class of fifty reduced by ten.

1948
- Temporary Provisions during Mobilization to Suppress Rebellion take effect (May 10) — beginning of the White Terror.
- Chiang Kai-shek inaugurated as first president of the Republic of China (May 20).
- Nationalist government publishes martial law (December 10).

1949
- April 6 student incident — mass arrest of students and intellectuals.
- Martial law takes effect (May 20).
- Statutes on Sedition published.
- 40,000 Taiwan Yuan exchange for one New Taiwan Yuan (June 15).
- U.S. State Department issues White Paper on China (August 5), castigating Nationalist government for its corruption and its ineffectualness.
- Nationalist government moves its capital from Nanking to Taipei.
- *Tsai Youde's class dwindles to nineteen.
- *Chou Shen-yuan, the president of Student Self-Government at Normal University, escapes arrest.

1950
- Onset of Korean War (June 25).
- President Truman proclaims neutrality of Taiwan Strait (June 27).
- Self-Renewal Policy published.
- *Li Shui-ching case concluded. Li Shui-ching, Cheng Wen-bang, Huang Shih-lien, Yeh Sheng-chi, et al., eleven in all, executed by

firing squad. Yeh Chin-kuei (aka Mosula), Chen Ching-tu, and others, thirty-two in all, sentenced to long prison terms.
- *Chang Yu-kun and Yeh Cheng-sung, from the same case, evade arrest and become fugitives.
- (Although Yeh Sheng-chi does not appear in this book, he is the hero of the book *Tragedy of a Taiwanese Intellectual*, published by Iwanami Shoten of Tokyo.)
- *Tsai Youde graduates from Normal University and starts teaching.

1951
- U.S.-Taiwan Mutual Defense Treaty signed.
- *Tsai Youde marries Panto.

1952
- Sino-Japanese Peace Treaty signed (April 28).
- Chiang Ching-kuo (son of Chiang Kai-shek) creates Chinese Anti-Communist Youth Corps (October 31).
- Taiwan government prohibits use of Japanese and Taiwanese languages in school.
- *Huang Lieh-tang executed (March).
- *Wu Che-fu, Tu Ping-lang arrested (February).
- *Chou Shen-yuan killed by special agents after a shootout.

1953
- Land reform program "Land to the Tiller" goes into effect (January 26).
- *Tsai Youde begins study tour of United States (September).
- *Mass arrest of villagers of Luku.
- *Chang Yu-kun, Yeh Cheng-sung captured (Feb).
- *Li Teng-ke, Li Chiang, Lu arrested subsequently.

1954
- Chiang Kai-shek inaugurated into second term as president (March 22).
- *Tsai Youde returns to Taiwan (Sept).
- *Tsai Youde arrested (Oct).

1955
- Sun Li-jen incident occurs. Chiang Ching-kuo consolidates military powers.
- *Chuang Shui-ch'ing, Lin Ching-shou executed (March). Chou Shui and twenty others from Luku executed.
- *Lu Min-jen (alias Little Lu), Lu Kuo-jen, and others executed.
- *Wang Tien, Chang Chao-chih executed (July).
- *Tsai Youde released from prison (November).

1956
- Liao Wen-yi forms Provisional Government of the Republic of Taiwan in Tokyo (February 28).

1960
- *Taiwan Youth*, a magazine advocating Taiwan independence, publishes its first volume in Tokyo (April 10).
- Chiang Kai-shek inaugurated for third term (May 20).
- *Free China* magazine shut down, its publisher Lei Chen arrested.

1965
- Chiang Ching-kuo appointed defense minister.
- Liao Wen-yi negotiates surrender and returns to Taiwan (May 14).
- *Huang Chi-nan released.

1966
- Chiang Kai-shek inaugurated to fourth term (March 21).

1970
- Peng Ming-min escapes from Taiwan.
- World United Formosans for Independence formed (January 15). Its members attempt to assassinate Chiang Ching-kuo during his visit to New York (April 24).

1972
- Chiang Kai-shek inaugurated for his fifth term.
- Chiang Ching-kuo takes office as premier (June 1).

- Japan normalizes relations with China. Sino-Japanese Peace Treaty abrogated. Taiwan terminates diplomatic relations with Japan (September 29).

1973
- Ten Great Constructions project initiated.

1975
- Chiang Kai-shek dies (April 5). Vice President Yen Chia-kan becomes president.

1978
- Chiang Ching-kuo inaugurated as the sixth president of the Republic of China (March 21).

1979
- United States normalizes relations with China (January 1). Taiwan-U.S. diplomatic relations cease.
- U.S. Congress passes Taiwan Relations Act (April 10).
- A celebration of Human Rights Day in Kaohsiung (December 10) develops into the so-called *Formosa* Magazine Incident (*Meilitao* Incident). Mass arrest of dissidents ensues.

1980
- Provincial assemblyman Lin Yi-hsiung's family massacred on February 28, while Lin was detained in connection with the *Formosa* Magazine Incident.

1981
- U.S. professor Chen Wen-cheng (of Carnegie Mellon), while visiting his family on Taiwan, found to have fallen to his death on the campus of National Taiwan University after answering a summons for an interview with special agents (July 3).

1984
- The biographer of Chiang Ching-kuo, Henry Liu, murdered in the United States.

1986
- Democratic Progressive Party formed.

1987
- Martial law abolished. National Security Law goes into effect (July 15).

1988
- Chiang Ching-kuo dies. Vice President Lee Teng-hui becomes president (January 13).

1990
- Lee Teng-hui inaugurated as the eighth president. Democratization and Taiwanization make strides.

1991
- Temporary Provisions abolished (May 1). Period of Mobilization for the Suppression of Rebellion ended.
- Tsai Youde begins writing *Elegy of Sweet Potatoes*.